# COMMUNICATION
# IN EVERYDAY LIFE

## Blaine Goss

University of Oklahoma

Wadsworth Publishing Company
Belmont, California
A Division of Wadsworth, Inc.

Communication Editor: Kristine M. Clerkin
Production Editor: Toni Haskell
Designer: MaryEllen Podgorski
Cover Design by Dare Porter
Copy Editor: Anne Draus
Illustrators: Joan Carol, Nanette Biers
Photo Researcher: Lindsay Kefauver
Signing Representative: Henry Staat

Printed in the United States of America

1 2 3 4 5 6 7 8 9 10—87 86 85 84 83

**Library of Congress Cataloging in Publication Data**

Goss, Blaine.
    Communication in everyday life.

    Includes bibliographies and index.
    1. Communication.   I. Title.
P90.G58            1982            001.51            82-8667
ISBN 0-534-01215-9                                  AACR2

■

Dedicated to my parents, Lou and Ruth

■

# CONTENTS

■

# PREFACE

This book is about communication in everyday life—at school, home, work, church, the gas station, the doctor's office, anywhere. In essence, it is about your daily communication skills and how you can improve them.

This is a college textbook, but I am not assuming that the reader is somehow tucked away on campus, unaffected by the outside world. Rather, I am assuming that the reader is a person who may be found not only in classrooms, but in banks, grocery stores, and shopping centers. Thus, the book is written for all people who have normal communication experiences.

*Communication in Everyday Life* takes a realistic approach to everyday communication, combining both theory and practice. Each of the important areas of communication is covered in several chapters. More specifically, there are five chapters on the basics of communication, three chapters on dyadic communication, three chapters on small groups, and five chapters on public speaking. Such an array of chapters allows both the teacher and the student to use this book with a variety of course syllabi.

Two very special features of the book are the "Your Turn . . ." and "F.Y.I." boxes—more than 80 located throughout the text. These are integrated into the chapters to help the reader learn more about communication. Unlike boxes in other books, these boxes propose ideas and exercises that can be completed by the student alone. Thus, they can be handled immediately. For instance, the "Your Turn . . ." boxes contain quizzes and exercises that test the reader's understanding of the material or ask the reader to apply the concepts under study. The "F.Y.I." boxes summarize interesting research findings and suggest practical ideas for future use. Both types of boxes relate to and are an integral part of the material being discussed. Consequently, they should not be skipped over by the reader. Rather, the reader should look forward to each one.

For some authors, writing a textbook is an onerous task, one that is compounded by disrespectful deadlines, overzealous editors, and blatant disagreements with reviewers. Such was not the case for me. I enjoyed every moment working on this book. And my pleasure was extended because I worked with such a fine professional as Kevin Howat, my editor at Wadsworth. I thank him for his insight, encouragement, and good fellowship as we rode the tides of producing a textbook together. He is a good man to have in the boat with you.

Likewise, I thank my reviewers who provided the criticisms needed to improve the book. They include Jerrold Anderson, Southwestern College, Chula Vista; Dorothy Bishop, Northern Illinois University; David Branco, Northern Illinois University; Diane Breitwieser, St. Louis Community College at Meramec; Catherine Cummings, Marshall University; Richard A. Filloy, University of Southern California; Martha K. Goodman, Central Virginia Community College; H. Rodman Jones, The University of Tulsa; Larry Kraft, Eastern Washington University; Patrick McDermott, University of Wyoming; Michael McDonald, Volunteer State Community College; Sandra Purnell, California State University at Los Angeles; V. A. Smith, Texas A & I University; Dr. Paul Walwick, East Tennessee State University; and Gary Wilson, Pacific Lutheran University.

I should also acknowledge Mary Arbogast and Toni Haskell who helped with the editing and the production aspects and MaryEllen Podgorski who is responsible for the interior design. The quality of their work is apparent on each page of the textbook.

Lastly, I want to thank Carol, my wife, and my two daughters, Angela and Melissa, for putting up with a husband and father who often forgot to "practice what you preach" as he was working on this project. Ah, even professional communicators fall short from time to time.

Blaine Goss

# I

# SOME BASICS
# OF COMMUNICATION

Communication in everyday life occurs in many settings, but there are some basic principles that apply to all kinds of communication. These principles relate to the process of communication, the verbal and nonverbal aspects of communication, listening, and the characteristics of the communicators.

Part I of this text is like a short course in communication theory. It begins in Chapter 1 with a model of communication. The next four chapters fill in the basic variables that are present in all settings of communication. When you have finished the first five chapters, you should have a good understanding of the basics of human communication. Later in the text, Parts II, III, and IV will expand your knowledge to show how these basics fit into dyadic, small group, and public speaking situations.

# THE PROCESS
# OF COMMUNICATION

**Importance of Communication in Everyday Life**
Pervasiveness of Communication
Communication in Your Personal and Professional Lives

■

**How You Use Communication**
Defining Communication
Why People Communicate

■

**Communication Models**
SMCR Model
Scheidel Model

■

**Elements of Communication**
Source/Receiver
Encoding
Message
Decoding
Interpretation
Feedback
Levels of Communication
Relationship
Context
Reviewing the Goss Model

■

**A Skillful Communicator**

■

**Summary Propositions**

■

**References**

■

For centuries, communication has been a significant part of everyday life. As early as the 4th century B.C., students were formally trained in oral communication skills. Furthermore, these skills were not only used in school, they were part of the "on-the-street" news reporting, policy making, entertaining, and politicking that characterized early Greek life. Today these same everyday skills are important, but we have widened our ability so that we can communicate with many people, across great distances. However, even in our modern world of communication technology (television, radio, telephone, and newspapers), people still need training in face-to-face communication skills. No matter what your role in life, you need effective communication skills, and you need these skills every day.

## Importance of Communication in Everyday Life

Communication plays a large part in your everyday life. You use communication more than you realize. Society is woven together by communication. Burgoon and Ruffner (1978) suggest that "communication, like water to a fish, surrounds us" (p. 3). There is so much communication going on that you cannot escape it for very long. You are constantly being bombarded by communication from your friends, your relatives, television, radio, newspapers, classroom lecturers, and so on. You can hardly turn around without finding someone asking for your attention. As Burgoon and Ruffner remind us, you and I are living in a "sea" of communication.

### PERVASIVENESS OF COMMUNICATION

Just how pervasive is communication in your everyday life? Are you really engulfed by it? What percentage of time in any given day do you spend communicating? To answer these questions, researchers asked 130 residents of Oklahoma to recall their communication activity of the day before. This unpublished survey produced some interesting results.

After tabulating the number of minutes that each person spent speaking, listening, writing, and reading, the researchers found that the respondents spent approximately 93 percent of their waking hours in some kind of communication activity. Translated into hours per day, these findings suggest that you and I spend 15 hours a day communicating. Of the Oklahoma residents' time, 47 percent was devoted to listening, 31 percent to speaking, 17 percent to reading, and 5 percent to writing. But the more impressive statistic is that which suggests you spend 93 percent of each day communicating. This means that for every minute—60 seconds—you escape communication for five seconds. Is communication pervasive in your daily life? You must agree that it is.

If you are like those interviewed, you probably spend more of your time listening and speaking as compared to time spent reading and writing. But, which do you *prefer* to do the most? Which do you *prefer* to do the least? Rank order the four categories, using 1 for the most preferred and 4 for the least preferred, with the others ranked 2 or 3.

_____ Listening

_____ Reading

_____ Speaking

_____ Writing

Now that you have ranked your preferences, how do they match your actual communication activity? Are you doing what you prefer, or does your situation demand that you do what you dislike? Knowing how well your actual communication behavior matches your preferences for communication behavior is the beginning to understanding yourself and your world of communication.

What is it that makes communication so pervasive in your life? Is it that people like to talk a lot? Perhaps. But a better answer to the question comes from the instrumental nature of communication. Communication is instrumental in that people *use* it to accomplish a number of goals. And the utility of communication is evident in many aspects of your everyday life.

## COMMUNICATION IN YOUR PERSONAL AND PROFESSIONAL LIVES

There are two sides of your life in which communication plays a crucial role: your personal life and your professional life. For in-

Everywhere you turn, you encounter communication. (Photos courtesy of B. Goss (top right, bottom left and right) and the Norman Transcript (top left).)

stance, in your personal life, you can write letters to relatives, make a date over the telephone, argue with your neighbor about politics, and seek directions from a gas station attendant when you are lost in a strange city. You can even use communication to build and maintain important personal friendships. As Ma Bell says, you can "reach out and touch someone."

Likewise, you use communication in your professional life. How you get along with co-workers depends on your communication skills. When you interview for a job, you need effective communication. Delicate treaty negotiations depend on the careful communication skills of the participants. In essence, the quality of your professional life depends, in part, on the quality of your communication.

## How You Use Communication

Before exploring the reasons for communicating, we need to define the term *communication*. The word itself is used in a number of different ways that are often misleading. For instance, some people think that communication is the same as messages. A letter to home, then, is a communication. This textbook is a communication. A beautiful painting communicates, according to this loose perspective of communication. These ideas about communication are somewhat inaccurate because they focus on the product of communication (messages) and not on the whole process of communication (the activity that produces messages). For the purposes of learning about the process of communication, you need a more action-oriented definition of communication.

### DEFINING COMMUNICATION

*Communication occurs when two or more people interact through the exchange of messages.* The key to this definition is the idea of "interaction." Communication is a dynamic activity that requires at least two people. At times you may communicate with yourself, but that is a matter for another study. The purpose of this text is to explore how communication takes place between people. Thus, the study of human communication is the study of how people interact with each other through messages. These messages are tools for interaction. They are part of the process, not the whole process. An interaction occurs when people exchange messages, not simply produce messages. The essence of communication, then, lies in the activity of communication, that is, interaction.

As you will discover later, messages do not have to be verbal. They can be nonverbal as well. In fact, skillful communicators care-

How do you see yourself in terms of your overall communication style? Are you a talker? Or do you prefer to let the others do the talking? On another dimension, are you willing to share your emotions with others? Or do you prefer to keep your feelings to yourself?

In the matrix below place an X in the square that best describes your overall style of expression.

talkativeness

low    moderate    high

emotional self-disclosure

high

moderate

low

There is no correct way to answer these questions, but it is interesting to observe the correlation between talkativeness and emotional self-disclosure. Usually, people who are talkative are also willing to share their feelings with others. Likewise, the quiet ones tend to keep their emotions in check.

fully manage both the verbal and nonverbal messages in order to accomplish their goals. Let's explore some of these goals, that is, why people communicate.

## WHY PEOPLE COMMUNICATE

Unquestionably, there are many reasons for communicating. Your ability to use verbal and nonverbal channels of communication provide you with many personal and social benefits. For the sake of economy, however, the most common reasons for communication can be grouped into three categories.

First, you communicate *to express yourself*. Being able to express yourself is crucial to your well-being. It is easy to take for granted the fact that you can talk and listen. But if you couldn't express what you feel inside, you would experience many frustrations. When you express yourself, you establish your social existence. People notice you, as you make your presence known. Most of us discovered this fact early in life when we realized that by talking we could make other people pay attention to us. For a child learning to talk, this insight helps speech development.

Through communication, not only do you express your internal needs and feelings, you also discover how effective you are in social life. In other words, you test your persuasiveness. If people acknowledge, understand, and believe what you say and do, then you have had an impact on them—you are effective.

We use communication, therefore, to let others know that we are around and that we are to be reconciled with. Imagine what it would be like to go through life without being able to express yourself. I suspect that you would tire very quickly of a world that talks to you, if you could not reciprocate.

The second general reason for communication is *to learn and to grow*. By communicating with other people, you learn about your world. They bring to you experiences that you have never had and points of view that are unique. In fact, a good discussion is often defined as one in which the participants learn many new things from each other.

You also use others to test the quality of your ideas. You check with others to see if they view the world the same way you do—sometimes called reality checking. A good example of this would be two friends who go shopping together so that each can seek the other's opinion about certain purchases. By discovering how your friends feel, you can reassure yourself about your own feelings.

As people explore the world through communication, they increase their chances for intellectual growth. As you interact with others, your understanding of the world expands and changes. Without others, your intellectual world would be small indeed. In fact, people who opt for limited contact with others create a hermitlike world of communication that makes it difficult for them to learn and to grow. If you want to develop intellectually, you must expose yourself to many different sources of information.

The third general reason for communication is *to enlist the cooperation of others*. One of the nice things about communication is that you can use it to engage others in cooperative activity. You can ask for help from others, ask for opinions, issue commands, or simply seek agreement on a point you are making. In fact, some things would be nearly impossible to do without communication. For instance, a group of people who are disarming a bomb need to communicate with one another for their own safety. Likewise, a planning committee needs to have open communication lines so that all members can do their jobs. Cooperation calls for communication.

Cooperative communication is a two-way street. For instance, each time that I cooperate with you, and you with me, we build our relationship. Our relationship will become stronger the more we engage in cooperative communication. Consider your best friends.

Sometimes we learn by interacting with others. (Photo courtesy of Peter Vandermark/Stock, Boston, Inc.)

When was the last time you asked one of them to run an errand for you, or to let you borrow a book? It is through cooperative communication that interpersonal relationships develop. If you couldn't communicate with other people, you would have difficulty building interpersonal relationships.

In summary, you use communication to express yourself, to learn and to grow, and to engage others in some kind of cooperative activity. These reasons may seem a little egocentric and selfish, but communication is, in many ways, selfish. As Brooks (1978) notes, being able to communicate effectively improves the quality of your life.

## Communication Models

In order to understand the process of communication, we must examine the main ingredients of interaction among people. This can be done through a study of communication models. A model is nothing more than a graphic representation of the process being studied—in this case, communication. A model is not the real thing, but rather someone's ideas about the essential components. In the communication models that follow, you will learn how three different scholars of communication envision the important elements of communication. It is important to realize that no model is correct or necessarily more

| S SOURCE | M MESSAGE | C CHANNEL | R RECEIVER |
|---|---|---|---|
| communication skills | content | seeing | communication skills |
| attitudes | elements | hearing | attitudes |
| knowledge | treatment | touching | knowledge |
| social system | structure | smelling | social system |
| culture | code | tasting | culture |

**Figure 1.1** SMCR Model of Communication (From The Process of Communication by David Berlo. Copyright 1960, Holt, Rinehart and Winston. Reprinted by permission.)

accurate than others. Each model has its strengths and weaknesses, but each identifies some of the necessary parts of communication and how those parts go together.

## SMCR MODEL

One of the more popular models of communication is the SMCR model (Berlo, 1960). Figure 1.1 shows that this model contains a source (S), message (M), channel (C), and receiver (R). The source and the receiver typically refer to the people in communication. These people have five personal characteristics: *communication skills* (their abilities to speak, listen, read, and write), *attitudes* (their feelings about the speaker and the topic), *knowledge* (the amount of information each person has that is relevant to the communication interaction), *social system* (each person's roles in life, social standing, groups to which each person belongs, and upbringing), and finally, *culture* (the communicators' origins, ethnic backgrounds, and home countries).

The message in the SMCR model is an encoded idea. Messages contain words, gestures, and other signs arranged in such a way as to communicate an idea. Messages are a systematic set of symbols that denote a thought (content) in a certain way (treatment) in a particular language (code). In creating messages, communicators can use both verbal and nonverbal codes to express an idea.

Finally, the channel refers to our five senses (seeing, hearing, touching, smelling, and tasting). Most of the time, we use seeing and hearing as the primary channels for communication, but the other three channels are available as well.

As a model of communication, the SMCR is useful for an initial understanding of communication, but it doesn't illustrate very well the dynamics of interaction. And since interaction is the center of human communication, the SMCR model leaves a bit to be desired. Consequently, a number of writers have attempted to improve on the SMCR model to account more for interaction.

## SCHEIDEL MODEL

One such attempt to improve the SMCR model is Scheidel's model of communication (see Figure 1.2). Scheidel (1976) describes speech communication as "speaking/listening agents who interact within a context" (p. 16). Like Berlo's model earlier, this model has sources and receivers (agents) using channels (sights and sounds) to produce messages. Scheidel calls the communicators "agents" because he feels that neither person is exclusively a source or a receiver, but rather both persons act in both capacities. *Agent* then is a neutral term that allows the people to be sources and receivers simultaneously. Furthermore, the Scheidel model emphasizes interaction and context. Here is the real strength of the model. Interaction refers to the dynamic interchange of messages between agents. Context denotes the social and psychological settings within which agents interact. Scheidel's model, then, is an explication of his definition: agents interacting within a context.

The Scheidel model is simple and focuses on the concept of interaction. Its simplicity makes the model easy to remember, but it also makes the model incomplete. There are some important ele-

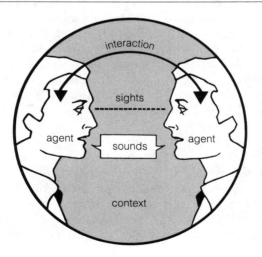

**Figure 1.2** Scheidel Model of Communication (From Speech Communication and Human Interaction by Thomas M. Scheidel. Copyright © 1976, 1972, Scott, Foresman and Company. Reprinted by permission.)

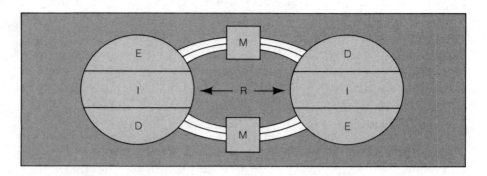

**Figure 1.3** Goss Model of Communication

ments of communication missing. The model proposed in the following section has been devised to illustrate the process of communication more adequately.

## Elements of Communication

Both the SMCR model and the Scheidel model are good beginnings for your understanding of communication. But neither is sophisticated enough for a more complete knowledge of communication, especially the interaction aspect of communication. In order to dissect the communication process a little more and to graphically illustrate interaction in communication, I am proposing a model that is an adaptation of a famous model developed a few decades ago.* My model includes the following elements: source/receiver, encoding, message, decoding, interpretation, feedback, levels, relationship, and context. It is presented in its entirety in Figure 1.3, but each element will be discussed separately.

### SOURCE/RECEIVER

The model begins with two people. They are each called source/ receiver because both serve as sources and receivers throughout the interaction. Whenever you interact with someone, you not only take turns talking, you listen as well. And so does your partner. Thus both communicators simultaneously play the roles of source and receiver.

---

* Wilbur Schramm, *The Process and Effects of Mass Communication* (Urbana, Ill.: University of Illinois Press, 1954).

## ENCODING

Whenever you have an idea that you wish to share with someone else, you must find the right words and expressions to say what you want. This is encoding. Encoding refers to your ability to speak and to write. It is putting your thoughts and ideas into a symbol system.

You have been encoding most of your life. This is one of the skills that a child must learn early in order to communicate efficiently. Furthermore, we probably never cease working on our encoding skills, even if we are only adding new words to our vocabularies. Our encoding skills, hence, are never complete or perfect. But then, they don't have to be to communicate. For instance, an infant making certain distinguishable sounds is communicating, as long as someone is able to make sense out of the utterance and respond appropriately. In fact, sometimes you don't even have to "speak the language" to communicate. Some of my students who have traveled to Europe have shared many encounters in which their language encoding was grossly inarticulate (and at times humorously incorrect) but sufficient for them to meet the basic needs of daily existence.

The symbol system that we often use to encode our ideas is our language. Most of us have been using language so long that we take it for granted. Yet, one of the most amazing feats facing a very young child is to learn language. By learning language the child will be able to encode ideas more efficiently and more precisely. The learning process, however, is not simple. For instance, in order to learn a language, encoding skills must develop in at least three ways— phonetically, syntactically, and semantically. In other words, children must learn to make the sounds correctly (phonemes), use appropriate grammar (syntax), and have meanings for their words and sentences (semantics). Children learning a language are often faced with a dilemma when these three facets do not develop correspondingly. For instance, children may have meanings (semantics) for things long before they can correctly say them (phonemics) or put them into sentences (syntactics). Leaving the San Antonio airport one afternoon, I noticed a little boy who became so excited seeing a Boeing 727 airplane that he pointed and said, "Look, a pane!" The little boy knew what he saw (plane), but he simply couldn't say it correctly (a common linguistic error for three-year-olds). Even adults face encoding difficulties from time to time. When was the last time you stared at the typewriter, paper rolled in place, but found yourself unable to make your fingers move over the keyboard in a meaningful way? Sometimes putting ideas into words is more difficult than thinking of those ideas in the first place. Encoding skills, then, are crucial to communication.

## MESSAGE

Once an idea is encoded, it becomes a message. Messages are products of encoding and can include such things as speeches, memos, newspapers, articles, letters, songs, and so on.

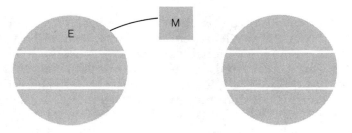

Messages can have many purposes. Some messages may be primarily ceremonial. They are uttered for the sake of acknowledging others. "Hello, how are you?" is an example of a ceremonial message. Other messages are intended to relay specific information. "There will be a meeting at 8 o'clock tonight" is a message designed to inform—its content is important. In general, messages can serve either expressive or informative purposes. If a message is created for expressive purposes, the actual words of the message are not as relevant as the fact that they were encoded. When I say, "How are you?" I am really not inquiring about your health. Rather, I am acknowledging your presence and encouraging you to talk with me. However, if I say that there is a meeting tonight at 8 o'clock, I expect you to pay close attention to the content of my speech and respond consciously to my words.

Knowing the purpose of the message is part of responding in an appropriate way. Breakdowns in communication can occur when people misinterpret the intent of the message. A friend of mine found out that his message was misinterpreted when he concluded a conversation with a former colleague by saying, "It has been great seeing you again. Stop by the house and have dinner with us sometime." That evening he had an unexpected dinner guest! This kind of mix-up occurs when the people talking do not see the intent of the messages in the same light. Some messages should be taken literally; others are only ceremonial. It is a good idea to know the difference.

## DECODING

Before a message can be interpreted, it must be decoded. Decoding is the ability to translate the message code into signals that the brain

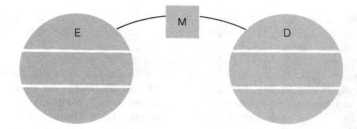

can process. In verbal communication, decoding refers to our skills in listening and reading. In everyday communication, we have available to us messages received by all five senses. But we rely most often on the information provided through hearing and sight.

Like our skills in encoding, we often take for granted our abilities to decode. People who are hard of hearing are perhaps more sensitive to the key role that listening plays in communication. You can interpret only what you decode. If you don't see or hear a message offered by someone else, you probably won't even know it transpired. As you might suspect, the reasons for failing to decode a message range from legitimate physical impairment to not-so-legitimate psychological blindness. In any event, we process what we think we hear rather than what may have actually occurred. In most instances, fortunately, what we process is what was there.

## INTERPRETATION

A decoded message needs to be interpreted. Hence, interpretation is the act of assigning meaning to the message that was decoded. At the interpretation stage of communication you apply your past experiences, knowledge, attitudes, expectations, and feelings in order to

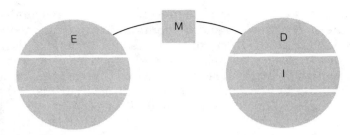

infer what the speaker means. In doing so, you often add to the message and go beyond what is said. Interpreting messages, then, is more than searching your mental dictionary for the meanings of the words. Interpretation includes applying all that you know and feel about the topic to the current message.

Sometimes breakdowns in communication occur at the interpretation stage. Two people may think that they are talking about the same thing, only to discover later that they were not.

One reason for this is the vagueness that is inherent in our language. Some words have fairly clear meanings. For example, words such as *paper clip, coffee,* and *bison* have reasonably clear referents. Other words, however, are not so clear. For instance, words such as *object, stuff, item,* and *implement* are so vague that without further explanation it is difficult to know what the speaker is talking about.

How many times do you assume that your listeners know what you are talking about? It is too easy to think that your listeners are of "like mind" with you, and when this occurs, communication can break down.

## FEEDBACK

Now that the message is encoded, decoded, and interpreted, it is time to complete the cycle of communication with feedback. Just as I am able to encode messages, so are you. And this begins the important feedback cycle. As we interact, we are constantly sending and receiving messages. (This feedback occurs at several levels as we will see momentarily.) Although feedback is not a necessary condition for communication to occur, it is extremely useful for gauging the success of communication. One of the problems facing me as the author of this text is that I am unable to observe your immediate feedback. TV shows, newspapers, and people writing letters have the same problem. Delayed feedback is one of the things that slows down the assessment of communication.

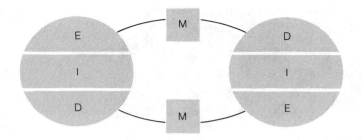

Feedback also has a facilitating effect on communication. It increases accuracy in a problem-solving task. This was demonstrated by Leavitt and Mueller (1951) who had students reproduce a simple line drawing based on the verbal instructions given by a classmate. Four separate feedback conditions were employed, ranging from free feedback (where the students were able to ask questions as the instructions were given) to zero feedback (the students were not permitted to ask questions). The results showed that when the students were allowed to ask questions, their drawings were more accurate than were the drawings of students who were restrained in asking questions. Leavitt and Mueller also found that the students were more confident in their drawings when working under the free feedback condition. The cost of this free feedback, however, was time. It took longer to complete the task when the respondents were able to interrupt the speaker and ask questions. When feedback flows freely, interactions (conversations) become longer, but feedback helps increase the accuracy of understanding among the participants.

*To ask or not to ask!* Sometimes feedback is limited because people won't ask questions when they are confused. In 1978, a college professor reported that 70 percent of her students never asked a question in class, even when they didn't understand part of the material being presented.

It is amazing how many times people withhold questions because they don't want to be embarrassed or to appear ignorant. Yet without such feedback, it is impossible for the teacher to know whether or not you understand the information.

From a communication standpoint, withholding feedback kills the communication cycle. There is simply no way to interact if we do not offer feedback to one another. So if you are confused, ask questions.

C. Patterson, "Teaching Children to Listen," *Today's Education* 67(1978):52–53.

Messages also serve some historical value, reminding us of past events and people. (Photo courtesy of the <u>Norman Transcript</u>.)

## LEVELS OF COMMUNICATION

In many social situations, people can communicate on more than one level at a time. In other words, meanings can be encoded into a number of different messages simultaneously. For our purposes here, three levels of communication are noted:

1. Language: communicating with words

2. Paralanguage: communicating with vocal inflections

3. Kinesics: communicating with gestures

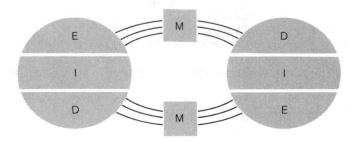

In face-to-face communication, all three levels of communication are used. When talking directly to someone else, you communicate with your words, your body, and your voice. On the telephone, you use the language level and the paralanguage level, but kinesics is missing. When you write a letter, you depend on language without the assistance of paralanguage or kinesics. Thus, the number of levels employed in communication is dependent on the situation.

You wouldn't think that people talk any differently on the telephone than they do in ordinary conversations, but they do. Giles and Powesland (1975) report that there are a number of differences between phone conversations and face-to-face conversations. For instance, people on the phone use longer pauses, repeat more questions, have more "ah" type speech disruptions, and are likely to be more formal.

Why we have these differences is unknown, but there must be something about the telephone that encourages such changes in our speech patterns. Perhaps it is the fact that people cannot see each other and that the phone is often used to conduct business. Maybe people feel suspicious that others may be listening and therefore are more cautious in what they say. Who knows? Future research may tell us more.

H. Giles and P. Powesland, *Speech Style and Social Evaluation* (London: Academic Press, 1975).

In general, the more levels of communication that are operating, the more likely the receivers will understand what the speakers mean. By being able to attend to your words, actions, and tone of voice, your listeners can more accurately assess your meaning. Furthermore, if you are interacting face-to-face, feedback can flow freely. This means that you can correct one another immediately as misunderstandings occur. All of this simply reinforces the benefits of face-to-face communication, when compared to other situations wherein the levels of communication may be inhibited.

## RELATIONSHIP

One of the most socially significant by-products of human communication is that people form relationships as a function of interacting together. The nature of the relationship between the communicators greatly affects how they talk with one another.

There are two ways in which the nature of the relationship between communicators is important. The first deals with differences in roles and status. For instance you should communicate differently with your friends than you do with your professors. You speak differently to your parents than you do to children. Who you are talking

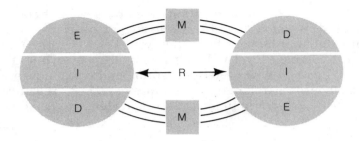

with makes a difference, and sensitive communicators adjust their communication style accordingly.

The second important aspect of the relationship concerns its history. Conversations between strangers are often different than conversations between intimates. The more you know someone, the more your conversational style is personalized. In fact, best friends often have a unique style of communicating with each other that is reserved only for their interactions. In Chapter 6 you will learn more about interaction between intimate communicators.

Sometimes the relationship between the communicators can choke the flow of communication between them. For instance, Likert (1967) found that subordinates in an organization were generally unwilling to talk to their bosses about problems, because the boss was perceived as their superior.

Sometimes students will not approach professors because of the perceived status difference in their relationships with the professors.

When the subordinate-superordinate role relationship becomes more important than the task at hand, it can inhibit the upward flow of communication. Do you ever have difficulty talking to the boss because of the status difference?

R. Likert, *The Human Organization* (New York: McGraw-Hill, 1967).

## CONTEXT

The last variable to be added to this model of communication is the context. Communication does not occur in a vacuum. It always happens sometime, somewhere, and for some reason. Context, in essence, refers to the social and psychological setting in which communication is taking place. Different contexts call for different communication strategies.

Occasionally there is time in your professional life for reading. (Photo courtesy of the Norman Transcript.)

There are two aspects of context that significantly affect communication and communication strategies. The first is the social setting. Some settings are public; others are private. When you are in a public social setting, your communication behaviors will be governed by the existing social norms. Thus it would be inappropriate to yell at a funeral, but you can yell at a football game. Likewise, it is impolite to read a newspaper while your professor is lecturing, but you can read a newspaper while riding a bus.

The second significant aspect of context is the psychological setting. Here we are concerned with the purpose of the communica-

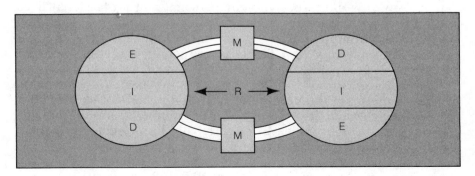

tion event. If you notice two people engaged in an intimate conversation—for example, two businessmen working out a personal problem between them—it is inappropriate to interrupt them with a trivial question such as asking the time. Likewise, it would be ill-mannered for a physician to joke about a child's illness when counseling the parents about the risks of upcoming surgery.

## REVIEWING THE GOSS MODEL

Like any other model of communication, mine is incomplete. There are so many variables that make communication work that it is impossible to include them all. But I believe that the variables included in my model represent the essential elements of human communication. Hopefully, you have come to understand more about the basic ingredients through studying my model of communication. As a review, here again is a list of the elements in the model:

1. Source/receiver

2. Encoding

3. Message

4. Decoding

5. Interpretation

6. Feedback

7. Levels (language, paralanguage, kinesics)

8. Context

## A Skillful Communicator

By now, you should have a fair idea of the pervasiveness of communication, how it is enmeshed in your personal and professional lives, and how it can be defined and modeled. You should also recall how people use communication. Now you might ask, "How am I going to use this information? What should be my goal in studying communication in the first place?"

Your main purpose in studying communication should be to become a more skillful communicator. You become a skillful communicator by studying the process in books and by practicing your communication skills under the direction of a knowledgeable instructor. But what is a skillful communicator?

A skillful communicator is one who speaks and listens effectively, and can do so in a number of different communication settings. Consequently, this book is written to familiarize you with the basic communication skills of speaking and listening. Both verbal and nonverbal aspects will be covered. Furthermore, we will look at communication as it operates in the dyad (two people), in the small group (three or more people), and in public speaking situations (speaker-audience). Skillful communicators will not only be good speakers and listeners, they will also know how to adapt to a number of situations found in their personal and professional lives.

## Summary Propositions

This chapter has emphasized that communication is a major part of everyday life. Thus, most people are very familiar with the processes of communication. However, even though you may be quite accustomed to communication, it is still worth your while to study it carefully in order to improve your own understanding and skills. Communication is defined as the process of two or more people interacting through the exchange of messages. As the three models of communication illustrate, this process involves many variables.

1. You use communication in your personal and professional lives.

2. You spend most of your waking hours communicating in one form or another.

3. Communication occurs when two or more people interact through the exchange of messages.

4. There are three purposes for communicating:

   a. To express yourself

   b. To learn and to grow

   c. To enlist the cooperation of others

5. As you communicate, you are a source and a receiver simultaneously.

6. Encoding is your ability to translate your ideas into words, gestures, and so on.

7. Messages produced when you interact with others generally serve either expressive or informative purposes.

8. Decoding is your ability to decipher a message.

9. Interpretation is the meaning you assign to the decoded message.

10. Feedback completes the cycle of communication and serves as a gauge of your success as a communicator.

11. Communication can take place at three levels:

    a. Language level (communicating with words)

    b. Paralanguage level (communicating with vocal inflections)

    c. Kinesic level (communicating with gestures)

12. As people interact through communication, they build relationships with each other.

13. All communication takes place within a social and a psychological context.

14. A skillful communicator is one who speaks and listens effectively, and who is able to do so in a number of different settings.

# References

**Berlo, D.** *The Process of Communication.* New York: Holt, Rinehart & Winston, 1960.

**Brooks, W.** *Speech Communication.* Dubuque, Iowa: W. C. Brown, 1978.

**Burgoon, M., and Ruffner, M.** *Human Communication.* New York: Holt, Rinehart & Winston, 1978.

**Giles, H., and Powesland, P.** *Speech Style and Social Evaluation.* London: Academic Press, 1975.

**Leavitt, H., and Mueller, R.** "Some Effects of Feedback on Communication." *Human Relations* 4(1951):401–410.

**Likert, R.** *The Human Organization.* New York: McGraw-Hill, 1967.

**Patterson, C.** "Teaching Children to Listen." *Today's Education* 67(1978): 52–53.

**Scheidel, T.** *Speech Communication and Human Interaction.* Glenview, Ill.: Scott, Foresman, 1976.

**Schramm, W.** *The Process and Effects of Mass Communication.* Urbana: University of Illinois Press, 1954.

# 2

# VERBAL
# COMMUNICATION

**Everyday Speech**
Spontaneous Speech
Planning and Monitoring
What It Sounds Like

■

**Using Language**
Language Symbols
Speaking and Writing
Listening and Reading

■

**Meanings**
The Meaning of Meaning
Denotation and Connotation

■

**Summary Propositions**

■

**References**

■

Communication between people can be both verbal and nonverbal. This chapter will deal with verbal communication, and the next chapter with nonverbal communication. In verbal communication, people use speech and language to elicit meanings in one another. In other words, we use speech and language to communicate.

After considering everyday speech and all its aspects, you will learn in this chapter how people use language and how meanings operate in human communication. Remember that speech is the oral manifestation of language, and people use language to express meanings and to understand one another's meanings. Speech, language, and meanings, then, are mutually related.

## Everyday Speech

The kind of speaking that you do every day with friends and associates is an informal style of speaking called everyday speech. Conversations at dinner, talking with friends on the phone, swapping stories in a pub, are all instances when you use your normal, everyday style of speech. Later, in Part IV, you will learn about formal public speaking, but this chapter is on everyday speech. So let's see how you do it.

### SPONTANEOUS SPEECH

Your everyday speech is produced in an impromptu fashion. Unlike formal speeches, you don't carefully plan your sentences, develop outlines, and research your points before you speak. When two friends are talking over the phone, they say what's on their minds and don't speak from a set of notes. This makes everyday speech spontaneous speech.

By definition, spontaneous speech is the act of creating your words and sentences at the time you are speaking. It is choosing your words just before you say them. Every day you use spontaneous speech to express your meanings and engage others in informal conversations. And you do so without much difficulty.

If you use spontaneous speech daily, and if you are reasonably successful with it, how do you do it? How is it that you are able to talk without extensive prior planning? Why is it that most people feel comfortable talking with friends, but fall apart when it is time to give a public speech?

**EXPERIENCE** There are two reasons why spontaneous speaking is easy for most people. One is experience. You have been producing spontaneous speech most of your life. You have little experience with formal public speaking (by comparison), but you have days, months, and years of experience in speaking spontaneously. The more experience you have with a skill, the more you can polish that skill to make it effective.

**RULES** The second reason that spontaneous speech is easy is its rulelike nature. When you speak spontaneously, you automatically combine your understanding of the language with a set of speech conventions and an idea to be communicated to someone. These three elements together help you say things that are grammatically correct, relevant to the conversation, and sufficient to express your internal meanings. In all three of these factors, there is a set of known rules that help you accomplish the act of speaking spontaneously. First, you know the rules of grammar that permit you to construct understandable sentences. Second, you are also aware of certain rules about interacting with others in speech. For example, you know that you should wait for your turn to talk; you know that your remark should be related to something just said in the conversation. Third, you also know that what you have in mind (your meaning) can be expressed by choosing the words that best signal your meanings. All three of these systems (language, speech, and meaning) are rule governed in such a way that if you understand the basic rules of each, you can put together meaningful sentences in a spontaneous fashion. And that is how spontaneous speech works. It is the on-the-spot combination of the rules of language, speech, and meaning.

## PLANNING AND MONITORING

As you speak spontaneously, you do two things that help you make sense. You plan and you monitor. Spontaneous speech is no accident; it is planned. But because it is spontaneous, it cannot be planned far in advance. Therefore, when you speak you do not plan your sentences in their entirety. Rather, you plan by phrases. The reason for this is that many sentences are long and have more than one thought in them. Since most people plan their speech by thoughts, and since sentences can contain more than one thought, it is believed that people plan in phrases more than in entire sentences. These phrases are easily organized into sentences as you speak. In fact, a single phrase can be turned into a sentence as you talk. Since it is easier to plan phrases with one thought in each, rather than plan sentences that may each have more than one thought, people plan their sentences through planning the phrases.

Another aspect of spontaneous speech is monitoring. As you speak spontaneously, you listen to yourself, thereby making it possible for you to correct your mistakes as you make them. Monitoring, then, is listening to your own speech to check it for accuracy. As long as you hear what you expect to hear, you keep talking. If you hit a speech error, you must correct it, on the spot, before proceeding. Monitoring, then, is a self-feedback system. Just as you can use feedback from others to determine how well you are doing, you can listen to your own feedback and make adjustments in your speaking pattern.

Everyday speech, in summary, is characterized as spontaneous speech. It is impromptu. You decide on your words while you are speaking. You do not plan your sentences in their entirety. You plan phrases. When you speak spontaneously, you retrieve an idea from memory and then use your understanding of the rules of language and speech to form utterances that are grammatically correct, relevant, and meaningful. As you talk, you listen to yourself and correct your speech errors as you make them.

## WHAT IT SOUNDS LIKE

Although you have a lot of experience speaking, many of you are probably self-conscious of your speech. When I ask my students what they dislike most about their speaking abilities, their responses are often:

> "I sometimes get my words tangled up because I talk too fast."

> "I occasionally use the wrong words without realizing it. It's embarrassing."

> "I have several words that I can't pronounce correctly. I try to avoid them."

> "I sometimes get lost when I talk. I forget something, or lose my place. Then I just stand there in silence. I feel dumb."

Do any of these sound familiar? Each of them is centered on fluency, that is, error-free speech. Many believe that being fluent is the main goal of learning to speak effectively. Fluency is certainly important, but natural fluency is not as "fluent" as you might think. Natural speech is not error-free speech. In fact, natural speech is rarely a smooth, continuous stream of talk. There are many characteristics of natural speech that you may not be aware of. Let's review some of them.

**LENGTH OF UTTERANCE** How long do you think the average expression lasts? How long do you talk when it is your turn in a conversation? Most people overestimate the amount of time that each interaction takes in a conversation. In an excellent article, James Deese (1978) reported that most utterances in conversations are rather brief. Deese tape-recorded conversations and then timed the length of each interaction. He found that 20 percent of the statements made by the conversationalists lasted for one second or less. Of the thousands of interactions recorded, 90 percent of them lasted less than 10 seconds. This means that your turns at talking are rather brief. In any given conversation, lasting at least one minute, you can expect a number of turns to talk. A good rule of thumb about the length of a turn in a conversation is that if you take more than 45 seconds to make your point, you are giving a speech rather than interacting (Lashbrook and Lashbrook, 1974). Given the brevity of normal speech turns, a sensitive communicator will be careful not to talk too long.

**SPEAKING RATE** In terms of number of words, what is the average rate of speaking? The answer depends on the situation, but most of the time people average about 150 wpm (words per minute). Some people speak faster than others, but this is a function of their different personalities. And some situations cause us to speed up or slow down our speaking rates. But if we vary too much from the 150 wpm norm, we might give others unfavorable impressions (Giles and Powesland, 1975).

**PAUSING** This is one characteristic that people may misunderstand. Please note that pausing is natural in speech. Some people mistakenly think that pausing indicates a mental shortcoming in the speaker. As you will see, we need pauses both when we speak and when we listen.

Two kinds of pauses occur in everyday speech. One is called a grammatical pause. This pause serves to punctuate speech. These pauses are like periods, commas, and exclamation points in writing. They tell the listener when you have completed a thought. They mark your speech and give your sentences order. The second kind of pause is the cognitive pause. This pause is a thinking pause, designed to hold the floor while the speaker thinks about what to say. These pauses often occur in the middle of thoughts. They are also charac-

For many people, speaking is so natural that they don't pay much attention to it. (Photo courtesy of the Norman Transcript.)

terized by time-filling sounds such as "ah," "uh," and so on. Both grammatical pauses and cognitive pauses are useful to you as a speaker. They help order your speaking and allow time for planning your next thought.

Unless you use rather lengthy pauses in your speech, you should not change your style of pausing as you talk. Pauses are natural and give rhythm to speech. Without pauses, speech would be a nonstop, continuous stream of sound. Wouldn't that be difficult to listen to?

**NONFLUENCIES** How often do you foul up a sentence when you talk? Do you experience a lot of nonfluencies when you speak? Most people think that they make speech errors more often than they really do. Deese (1978) found that fewer than 2 percent of all the sentences spoken in a conversation were truly fouled-up sentences. Most of the time, speakers are able to correct their mistakes immediately after making them. Furthermore, it is unnecessary to have perfect fluency. You can mispronounce a word, or have trouble finding the right words to say, without destroying your credibility with your col-

There are a number of speech styles that people display when they talk. Some are seen as more attractive than others. When you think of speaking style, what attributes come to mind that make a person an effective speaker?

Below are four possible characteristics of an effective speaking style. Write a plus sign (+) next to the one you feel is most important. Place a minus sign (−) next to the one that is least important.

_____ Clear (easy to hear, not nasal or mumbly)

_____ Lively (animated voice and gestures, not monotonic)

_____ Organized (easy to follow, not all jumbled up)

_____ Unique (interesting vocabulary, clever phrasing)

Obviously it is to the communicator's advantage to be strong in each of these, but everyone has one that needs more attention. How about you? Which one of these do you need to work on?

leagues. In fact, research shows that perfect fluency (no errors) is probably undesirable (Miller and Hewgill, 1964). Speakers who talk without error may not be trusted because they are perceived as unnatural. An occasional nonfluency is part of normal conversations. Natural speech is spoken by natural people, not by polished public showmen.

What does everyday speech sound like? It is fairly brief, spoken at about 150 wpm, includes two kinds of pauses (cognitive and grammatical), and is not always free from errors. Thoughtful communicators understand the naturalness of spontaneous speech and do not place undue demands on others to speak perfectly.

Earlier, I mentioned that speech and language are intricately related, as speech is the oral manifestation of language. The next section explains how people use language to communicate.

## Using Language

The English language contains about half a million words, yet probably no one uses more than 60,000. Most of us use even fewer. How people use language is, indeed, an intriguing subject. In fact, just learning language may be one of the most amazing feats you have ever accomplished. For instance, when you were two years old, you made little sense to anyone except your parents. But by the time you

If not properly coordinated, too many messages can be overwhelming. (Photo courtesy of the Norman Transcript.)

were five or six, you were using your language well enough to attend school. In three to four years, you developed from an inarticulate toddler into a talkative kindergartner, ready to take on the world of scholastic learning.

What is language? It is a system of communication. More specifically, language is defined as your knowledge and performance of a set of rules that allows you to communicate verbally with other people. Language has three parts: sounds, syntax, and meanings. The sounds you produce are formed into words. These words are arranged according to a set of grammatical rules (syntax) to make sentences. And finally, these sentences are designed to represent what you mean. You are using language when you exercise your understanding of these three parts of language.

According to linguists, languages depend on symbols. In other words, as you use your language to communicate with others, you manipulate the symbols of language to elicit a meaningful response from your receivers. Any study of language, then, must include some consideration of language symbols.

## LANGUAGE SYMBOLS

One of the most interesting features of language is that it is a symbol system. A symbol, by definition, is something that stands for something else. Applied to language, this means that you use words and sentences to symbolically represent your internal meanings. And since your meanings are mental events that cannot leave your brain, you need symbols by which you can talk about your ideas.

Most of the symbols you use are conventional. That is, most people in your country use the same words that you use, thus enabling the people to communicate with one another. Sometimes, however, groups create unique words to meet their particular needs. For instance, CB'ers have a jargon all their own. Waiters, waitresses, and chefs in a restaurant have special words for salads, colas, and coffee. As long as you understand the symbol system, you can use the language. If you don't speak the jargon, you will have difficulty understanding the talk.

Do you know which English word is used more than any other in everyday language usage? To find out, Kucera and Francis (1967) took 500 samples of written materials (books, newspapers, journals, and so on) and tabulated the frequency of occurrence of all the words.

With computer assistance, they were able to determine that most words appeared infrequently, but that a select few were used over and over again. The top five words in terms of frequency of usage were:

1. *the*
2. *of*
3. *and*
4. *to*
5. *a*

The most popular verb was *is*, and the most frequent personal pronoun was *he*. The first 50 words were monosyllabic (one syllable).

Overall, the results showed that the more a word could be used in a number of different sentences, the more frequently it would be used. Thus, words that serve grammatical functions in constructing sentences are used more than content words (nouns, verbs, adjectives, and adverbs).

H. Kucera and W. Francis, *Computational Analysis of Present-Day American English* (Providence, R.I.: Brown University Press, 1967).

Because of the symbolic nature of language, language can be used as a tool both to express meanings and to understand someone else's meanings. By itself, language is not very interesting, but as a tool for encoding and decoding meaning, it is very useful. Psychologists tell us that until children discover the utility of language, they will not bother to learn it (Smith, 1975). As sources and receivers of communication, we must recognize the value of language as we encode (speak and write) and decode (listen and read) messages.

## SPEAKING AND WRITING

As encoding systems, speaking and writing are not the same. They are different in form and style. Writing is not speech in print, nor is everyday speech simply vocalized writing. In fact, writing and speaking are built on two different sets of elements. When you write, you use the alphabet. When you speak, you use the phoneme system (speech sounds). The alphabet and the phoneme system do not even correspond very closely. For instance, the words *cuff* and *rough* sound alike in the vowel sounds, but they are spelled differently. Thus they are phonemically similar but alphabetically different. Likewise, the word *tear* can sound one way in one sentence and another way in another sentence:

1. The man shed a tear.

2. The boy had a tear in his shirt.

In this case, there is alphabetic similarity but phonemic dissimilarity. If speaking and writing were interchangeable systems, these discrepancies would not occur.

Speaking and writing differ in many other ways as well. As a rule, speaking is simpler in style than is writing. When you speak you use shorter words than when you write. Your sentences are typically quicker in speech than in writing. There is more slang in speech—it is less formal. Speaking is often more assertive, without qualifications. Writing, in contrast, has a more careful style. That is, you are more likely to qualify your statements when you write than when you speak. As you boldly talk, you say what's on your mind and then correct yourself (modify your position) if the feedback from your listeners indicates that you should. In essence, then, speaking is simpler, more casual, and bolder than writing.

From a language perspective, speaking and writing differ in the uses of the various parts of speech. More specifically, speaking is characterized by more personal pronouns, more verbs and adverbs. Writing contains more abstract nouns and more adjectives to modify the nouns.

All in all, the differences between speaking and writing involve

One way to discover how different speaking and writing are from each other is to tape-record a brief conversation between two people. Then go home and transcribe (word for word) the conversation. You will find that what you wrote down will look very strange when you read it later. This is the reason that executives who use dictating machines must talk as if they are writing in order for the secretary to reproduce what is said on the tape as a letter or memo.

the different elements upon which each is built (phonemes versus alphabet), the different styles (of simplicity, casualness, and boldness), and the parts of speech used (personal pronouns, verbs, and adverbs versus abstract nouns and adjectives). Certainly some writing is more speechlike than other writing, and some speeches sound more like written presentations. But, overall, there are dependable differences between speaking and writing that suggest that they are different encoding skills.

## LISTENING AND READING

The counterparts to speaking and writing are listening and reading. You need the decoding skills of listening and reading in order to comprehend messages. In Chapter 4 I will discuss listening in detail, but for now I wish to consider some of the differences between these two forms of decoding.

Some differences are obvious. For instance, you can read a book faster than you can listen to someone talk because most speakers talk more slowly (150 wpm). Likewise, if you miss something that you are reading, you can go back and reread it. When listening, you don't have the privilege of going back, unless, of course, you are tape-recording the speech.

Other differences between listening and reading are not so obvious. These differences are related to the forms in which words are presented, and to the presence or absence of nonverbal cues. In terms of word form, listening and reading require some flexibility on the part of the receiver. When listening, you must allow for the speaker's accent or dialect. Since no two speakers have the same vocal patterns, the listeners must adjust as soon as possible to the speaker, in order to simplify the listening task. Readers must also be prepared for variation in word form. Sometimes words are printed in block letters; other times, words are written in longhand, as in personal letters. In brief summary, speakers vary in accent and dialect, while written materials vary in print and longhand.

The daily newspaper is an important part of everyday life. (Photo courtesy of B. Goss.)

Listening and reading also differ in the use of nonverbal cues that help the listener understand the message. For example, you listen for thoughts by noting the speaker's pauses and other nonverbal gestures (hand motions, changes in the voice, and so on) that indicate the beginnings and endings of ideas. In reading, you don't have as many cues. Punctuation marks (commas and periods) help, but the useful nonverbal cues that come from seeing and/or hearing the speaker are missing. And as Smith (1975) notes, the nonverbal cues are more immediately useful to a receiver than are the punctuation marks on a page.

There are also differences between listening and reading as vehicles for learning information. Research shows that how you decode information (listening or reading) may affect the quality of your recall later. For instance, information that you read will be recalled with more precision (exact wording) than will information you hear. Your recall from reading may not be complete, but what you recall will be closely similar to what was written on the page. In contrast, recalling information that you heard will be more complete (more total information retained), but it will contain more errors (false inferences, twisted facts, and so on). That is, recall from listening is more complete than from reading, but it has more errors in it. Obviously, it would be better for you to get your information through both listening and reading. In this way, you would have the completeness of listening and the accuracy of reading.

In review, you have seen how language is a system of communication that uses symbols for both encoding (speaking and writing) and decoding (listening and reading). Your understanding of language permits you to express your meanings and to infer what the other speaker means. Many people have only one language, but there are four ways to use it. Speaking, writing, listening, and reading are related yet independent language-using skills. And as most of you have come to realize, each skill must be developed through training and practice.

## Meanings

Language is designed to express and reflect the meanings of the language users. When you encode through speech or writing, you are expressing your meanings. When you decode by listening or reading, you are trying to decipher the speaker's or author's meaning. When you communicate with language you must realize that meanings are not transferred between people. Rather, your language symbols serve as signals for meanings. Just as clouds can signal rain, your words can elicit meanings in other people. But your words themselves do not carry meaning. Meanings reside in people; they are not in words. The words on this page would be meaningless if you were unfamiliar with them. My words can only remind you of meanings that you already know. If I am an effective communicator, I will choose words that I think you are already familiar with.

### THE MEANING OF MEANING

What is meaning? Meanings are all the learned experiences that you have associated with the usage of words, phrases, gestures, and so on. There are two parts to this definition that deserve special attention. The first is "learned experiences." Many people think that meanings are mental definitions. They are not. Definitions appear in dictionaries and textbooks, but not in people's heads. What you have stored in memory is a set of experiences that are associated with particular words. The more experiences you have with a word, the more meaning that word can trigger when you encounter it. Your meaning for, say, *college education* is a function of your experiences with colleges and with hearing others talk about college education. If you had no experiences associated with *college education*, you would have no meanings for it. Furthermore, your experiences do not have

To see how the context can affect the intended meaning of words, consider how the meaning intended by *run* differs in each of the following contexts:

1. Hosiery

2. A baseball game

3. A track meet

4. Pancake syrup

5. Delivery of pizza

In each of the contexts, the meaning shifts. Listeners need, then, to know the context in order to know what the speaker means.

Just for fun, consult a current dictionary and see how many different entries there are for the word *run*. You might be surprised by the number.

to be firsthand. You can experience something by hearing people talk about it. A person does not have to have cancer to know meaning for *cancer*.

Meanings, gained firsthand or from others, are learned and used in contexts. You learn your meanings by observing the contexts (settings) in which certain words are used. Thus, certain things are said under certain circumstances. The meaning of *thank you* is learned when you discover that is what people say when they wish to express appreciation. You also learned that the context can change the meaning. In one setting, *honey* is a sweet liquid that is spread on toast; yet in another context it is a romantic term. The context, then, helps determine the appropriate meanings that are intended by the speakers. Inappropriate language usage occurs when people use the wrong words at the wrong time. Fortunately, this occurs infrequently.

The second important part of the definition of meaning is the phrase "associated with the usage of words, phrases, gestures, and so on." You have meaning when you see the connection between a word, phrase, or gesture and the experience it signifies. The key is association. You must realize the connection between the experience (event) and what it is called. I remember once trying to teach my oldest daughter the names of the objects pictured in the little book she was "reading." I sat down beside her and thumbed through the picture book, pointing to the pictures and saying the appropriate words. She seemed to enjoy this activity very much. When I handed her the book and said, "Here, honey, you do it," she gladly complied and proceeded page by page, pointing to the pictures but not saying a thing! To her, the object of the game was to point to the pictures and turn the pages. She didn't realize the connection between the words I said and the objects pictured. In other words, this experience taught her more about pointing than it did about language. Until she makes an association between the words and the objects, she has experiences but no meanings. You don't have meanings until you tie your experiences to symbols.

Meanings, then, are learned and are associated with units of language—such as words, phrases, and sentences—and with gestures. Meanings also come in many forms or kinds. The two most prominent kinds of meanings that people have are called denotative meaning and connotative meaning.

## DENOTATION AND CONNOTATION

The denotative meaning that you have for something is similar to a dictionary meaning (but not a definition). For instance, if you go to a dictionary and look up the word *table,* you will find how people use the word. You will discover that a table has certain formal and functional attributes. It might say that a table is a piece of furniture consisting of a flat slab supported by legs, and that it is used for eating meals or decorating a room. This entry describes the formal aspects (furniture, slab, legs) and the functional aspects (eating meals, decorating) of *table*. Denotative meaning is essentially a description of the formal and functional properties of the word being used. It is not the "correct" definition of the word, but rather it is the most common usage of the word.

Now let's change the example a little and see what happens to the meaning of *table* when I make the term *operating table*. Do your meanings shift a bit here? I suspect so. You should have felt two changes. First, you should have a narrower denotative meaning now that I am talking about operating tables. Second, you should have a subtle emotional change as well. The original term *table* was fairly neutral. A table is a table is a table, and so on. But an operating table is another matter. The emotional shift you experienced is called your connotative meaning. Connotative meaning refers to your attitudes and feelings that are associated with your understanding of the words.

Whenever you think of an idea (or meaning of an expression) you have both denotative and connotative reactions to it. It is difficult to think of something without having some feelings about it as well. These feelings, your connotative meanings, are governed by your past experiences and attitudes. If you have positive feelings toward something, you will have positive connotative meanings about it. If you have negative feelings, you will have negative connotations.

It is quite possible for two people to have similar denotative meanings but different connotative meanings. Unlike denotative meanings, there are few conventional connotative meanings, that is, meanings that most people have. For some of you, *operating table* may connote very positive feelings; for others, it might stimulate very negative feelings. It depends on your past experiences. As long as people have different experiences and different attitudes, they will have different connotative meanings. That is one of the reasons that we don't have a dictionary for connotative meanings. It would be voluminous, because it would have to account for everyone's personal feelings and experiences.

In summary, then, meanings are all the learned experiences that you have associated with the usage of words, phrases, sentences, gestures, and so on. Meanings come in two general forms: denotation and connotation. Every time you think of a word or idea, you have both a denotative and a connotative reaction to it. Finally, you should keep in mind that meanings are in people. They are not in dictionaries.

## Summary Propositions

The most common form of verbal communication is spontaneous speech, that kind of informal speaking that characterizes our daily interactions. Unlike the formal speaking patterns in public speeches, spontaneous speech is simpler, is more assertive, and is created as the speaker is talking. In spontaneous speech we can see and understand the dynamics of interaction as presented in the communication models in Chapter 1. The materials of verbal communication are language and meanings. As we encode our ideas into messages, we use language. As receivers decode our messages and interpret them, they use their understanding of the language and meanings to make sense of what they heard or read.

1. Speech is the oral manifestation of language. People use language to express meanings and understand others' meanings.

2. Everyday speech is produced spontaneously—you make it up as you talk.

3. Spontaneous speech is planned by phrases, and you are able to correct your speech as you are saying it.

4. Everyday speech is characterized by:

   a. Short utterances

   b. A rate of approximately 150 wpm

  c. Cognitive and grammatical pauses

  d. Infrequent speech errors or nonfluencies

5. Language is a system of communication made up of symbols.

6. You use your language to express (speaking and writing) and to comprehend (listening and reading).

7. Compared to writing, speaking is more informal, more assertive, and simpler.

8. Compared to reading, listening is slow. But listeners have many nonverbal cues to help them listen, whereas readers have only the words.

9. Meanings are all the learned experiences that you have associated with the usage of words, phrases, sentences, gestures, and so on.

10. There are at least two kinds of meanings: denotation and connotation.

## References

**Deese, J.** "Thought into Speech." *American Scientist* 66(1978):314–321.

**Giles, H., and Powesland, P.** *Speech Style and Social Evaluation.* London: Academic Press, 1975.

**Kucera, H., and Francis, W.** *Computational Analysis of Present-Day American English.* Providence, R.I.: Brown University Press, 1967.

**Lashbrook, W., and Lashbrook, V.** *PROANA 5: A Computerized Technique for the Analysis of Small Group Interaction.* Minneapolis: Burgess, 1974.

**Miller, G., and Hewgill, M.** "The Effects of Variations in Nonfluency on Audience Ratings of Source Credibility." *Quarterly Journal of Speech* 50(1964):36–44.

**Smith, F.** *Comprehension and Learning.* New York: Holt, Rinehart & Winston, 1975.

# 3

# NONVERBAL COMMUNICATION

**Uses of Nonverbal Communication**
Symbolic Displays
Metamessages
Structuring the Interaction
Self-Presentation
Manipulating Others

■

**Paralanguage**
Vocal Perceptions
Vocal Styles

■

**Kinesics**
Facial Expressions
Eye Contact
Gestures

■

**Proxemics**

■

**Summary Propositions**

■

**References**

■

A number of years ago, comedian Red Skelton was asked to perform in front of an audience composed of people from several different countries. Knowing that he would be facing an audience that spoke different languages, Skelton had a problem. He wanted to do something that everyone would understand and enjoy. He also knew that having several translators on stage with him would ruin the timing of his comedy routine. What did he do? He did pantomime. Why? Because it is a form of dramatic nonverbal communication that needs little translation to be understood. Was he successful? You bet. Through pantomime Skelton acted out events and situations that were amusing, and he was able to spice his act with a number of emotions common to all people through the use of facial expressions, body gestures, and so on. In other words, Skelton used nonverbal communication to communicate with his international audience.

As communicators we are capable of using not only words for communication but several kinds of nonverbal behavior as well. In fact, we sometimes can't turn off our nonverbal gestures. I was reminded of this when I found myself waving my arms and hands as I was talking over the phone with a friend 200 miles away. There was no way that Bob could see my gestures, but I used them anyway.

The human propensity for both verbal and nonverbal communication is more than a simple accident. The human brain is apparently wired for both kinds of communication behavior. It has been known for some time that the left side of the brain (for most of us) controls verbal skills, while the right side of the brain controls nonverbal perceptions. In other words, you process words and sentences on the left side, while you process facial expressions and bodily cues on the right side. You should not, though, be left with the impression that the left or the right side does not know what the other side is doing. They do. The two sides are connected by fibers that allow cross-communication to take place as information is being processed in the brain. In fact, it is this ability of the brain to act as a whole, even though it has two halves, that makes it possible for you to understand simultaneously both what people are saying (verbal) and what they are doing (nonverbal).

In everyday life, your verbal and nonverbal behaviors reinforce each other. Thus, *what* you say is supported by *how* you say it. In this way, your gestures, facial expressions, and vocal inflections coordinate with the content of your speech. At least, that is how it should be. If your verbal behavior and your nonverbal behavior do not agree, most people will believe what you are saying nonverbally, rather than verbally. In other words, your actions will be seen as more honest than your words. Fortunately, discrepancies between a speaker's verbal and nonverbal communication are rare, and occur only when the speaker is lying rather poorly or is trying to be funny.

F.Y.I.

How much of a speaker's meaning is carried by the verbal message compared to the nonverbal messages? Mehrabian and Weiner (1967) use the following formula to determine the relative weights that each part plays.

$$\text{speaker's attitude} = \text{words (7\%)} + \text{tone of voice (38\%)} + \text{facial expression (55\%)}$$

If this formula is accurate, that means that over 90 percent of your attitude is communicated nonverbally. Given this, you should be careful to watch not only *what* you say, but also *how* you say it.

A. Mehrabian and M. Weiner, "Decoding Inconsistent Communications," *Journal of Personality and Social Psychology* 6(1967):109–114.

Research in nonverbal communication is typically divided into at least three subdivisions: paralanguage, kinesics, and proxemics. Before exploring these areas of nonverbal communication, you need to know how people use nonverbal communication in general, without reference to any particular area.

## Uses of Nonverbal Communication

Judee Burgoon (1978), an expert in nonverbal behavior, suggests that people use nonverbal communication in at least five ways: for symbolic displays, for metamessages, for structuring the interaction, for self-presentation, and for manipulating others. These uses, or functions, can apply to all kinds of nonverbal behavior. For example, a wave of the hand can have many uses ("hello," "I'm next, please," "over here," and so on). Keep this in mind as you go through the five functions of nonverbal communication.

## SYMBOLIC DISPLAYS

When people use nonverbal behavior for symbolic displays, they are emitting cues that are conventionally understood by others. Sometimes called emblems, symbolic displays are like nonverbal words in that they can stand by themselves and be meaningful. They need no verbal explanation. For example, when you are happy, you smile. Laughter tells us that something is humorous. Other examples are more graphic. An extension of the forefinger and the middle finger to form a *V* was a sign for peace in the turbulent 1960s. A clenched fist raised above the head is used as a sign for "right on," but it began as an emblem for "black power." Bumper stickers often have symbolic displays in the form of emblems (the Christian fish figure, or a logo for a labor union). We even have an international highway sign system so that travelers from around the world can read the road signs. The same is true for airport signs that direct passengers to various areas in the terminal.

In brief, then, symbolic displays (including emblems) are used when you want your nonverbal gestures, expressions, and movements to communicate a specific meaning. They are like nonverbal words.

## METAMESSAGES

Sometimes you use nonverbal gestures, expressions, and movements to augment what you are saying. In other words, you use nonverbal behaviors to directly support your verbal point. When you do this, you are using nonverbal communication as metamessages. Metamessages are sometimes called illustrators because they illustrate verbal behavior. A good fish story often needs extended arms to talk about "the one that got away." Whenever you ask someone for directions, the response will often include pointing as a means to show you the direction you need to travel. Likewise, people can use their voices as metamessages. Trained actors are able to offer a quivering voice when they are portraying the sad part of the script, and yet they can turn around and sound boisterous and bawdy in the barroom brawl in the next scene. Whenever you vary your nonverbal actions to match your verbal communication, you are using your nonverbal communication to serve a metamessage purpose.

## STRUCTURING THE INTERACTION

A third way that people use nonverbal behavior, according to Burgoon, is to structure interaction. Sometimes the structuring takes place through the arrangement of furniture. For example, you might have your living room furniture arranged in a pattern that promotes face-to-face conversations. People structure the conversations when they use eye contact to maintain the other person's attention while talking. Some Latin Americans often will not start a conversation until they are holding the other person's forearms. You can also raise your voice if you notice your partner's attention waning. All of these devices are useful in structuring the interaction. Furthermore, we often do these things without knowing why.

## SELF-PRESENTATION

The fourth function of nonverbal behavior is self-presentation. By using nonverbal communication carefully, you present an image of yourself for others to observe. Your physical appearance can provide clues to your self-image. How you dress, style your hair, and walk can indicate the kind of person you see yourself as being. You can even control your speech in order to sound intelligent, or masculine, or feminine. Cosmetic companies, auto manufacturers, travel agents, and liquor distributors all use self-images as a means of selling their products. Such image building through nonverbal channels is common in people and in advertising.

## MANIPULATING OTHERS

The final and fifth function of nonverbal communication is manipulating others. When people use nonverbal messages to manipulate others, they typically are trying to persuade. Persuasion, however, is not just used in advertising and sales, it is used every day by nearly everyone. For instance, during a conversation you might nod your head in agreement or shake it in disagreement as your partner is talking. These head motions will, no doubt, affect your partner's subsequent conversation with you. When children are misbehaving in public, parents often send a forbidding stare, hoping that the children will see it and respond accordingly. Restaurants and clubs are designed to nonverbally manipulate people into spending more money. For instance, the furniture, greenery, lighting, and colors create a comfortable environment to encourage the customers to linger and perhaps spend more money. Sommer (1974) calls these kinds of environments "soft" surroundings. According to Sommer, soft surroundings are more personal, and thus are likely to be more comfortable than hard surroundings, such as gymnasiums or many college classrooms. Whenever you change the surroundings to alter the mood, you are using nonverbal channels to manipulate others.

In summary, the five functions of nonverbal behavior are: symbolic displays, metamessages, structuring interaction, self-presentation, and manipulating others. As with other kinds of functions, the nonverbal functions can operate simultaneously within any act. For instance, you can nod your head to structure the conversation (keep it going, or indicate that you want to talk next) and at the same time use these nods as symbolic displays (yes, you agree with the speaker). Finally, you should realize that you are probably not even aware of many of your nonverbal behaviors. Nonverbal gestures, expressions, and movements are so natural that it is easy to overlook the ways that we use them.

Now that you understand the overall functions of nonverbal behavior, let's look at the specific areas of nonverbal communication.

# Paralanguage

Communication research typically divides the study of nonverbal behavior into three areas: paralanguage, kinesics, and proxemics. Sometimes called "tone of voice," paralanguage refers to all the ways speakers can vary their voices (volume, rhythm, pitch, and so on). Most of you realize that you can say the same words a number of different ways and imply different meanings by doing so. Likewise, your listeners pay attention to vocal variations as they figure out what you mean.

In this part of the chapter, you will learn how people make inferences about you based on listening to your voice. Then you will discover how everyone has a different vocal style that makes each person unique.

## VOCAL PERCEPTIONS

Whenever you speak, people "read into" your voice various emotional states and personality traits. David Addington (1968) conducted a well-known study in which he discovered that listeners were quite willing to make personal judgments about speakers without even seeing the speakers or knowing anything in advance about them. Addington played audio tape recordings of a number of different speakers and had the listeners rate each speaker on such characteristics as age, enthusiasm, physical appearance, and so forth. The various recordings differed from each other in qualities such as nasality, tenseness, thinness, and so on. These differences in vocal quality produced markedly different inferences about the speakers. The results showed that people formed separate stereotypes for each different voice they heard. For instance, breathy, female voices were judged as coming from people who were pretty and effervescent. Slow, nasal voices were heard as coming from a "slow" person, probably low in intelligence.

Addington's work is supported by other researchers as well. Smith et al. (1975) found that speakers who talk at slower-than-normal rates are perceived by others as lower in intelligence as well. Miller and Hewgill (1964) found that too many vocal nonfluencies ("uh," "ah," "you know") cause listeners to doubt the speaker's personal competence. Finally, certain data indicate that louder-than-average voices are perceived as more sociable and more likeable (Scherer, 1979). Extreme loudness, however, is considered annoying.

All of this research points to the fact that people listen to *how* you talk and then make decisions about your emotions and your personality. Sometimes their judgments are flattering; other times, they are not. The point remains: How you talk makes a difference.

For some of us, it is not very comforting to know that others will make judgments about our personalities based on our voices. Such stereotyping, based on such minute data, seems unfair. Yet, most of us must confess that we too judge others based on their voices. For instance, have you ever tried to "size up" a person over the phone? Maybe it was a blind date, or a prospective client. Whoever it was, you probably developed an image of that person as you were talking. Like it or not, the voice communicates.

Some people believe that you can tell when others are lying by observing their eyes and listening carefully to the paralanguage.

Unfortunately, research does not bear this out. Hocking et al. (1979) conclude that people are not as good at detecting a liar as they think they are. In fact, they found that the nonverbal behaviors helped conceal lying more than it helped to expose it.

So, while the voice communicates, it is difficult to know whether it is telling the truth. One might ask: Have we as communicators learned to lie so well that most people can't tell when we are doing it?

J. Hocking et al., "Detecting Deceptive Communication from Verbal, Visual, and Paralinguistic Cues," *Human Communication Research* 6(1979):33–46.

## VOCAL STYLES

Whether you recognize it or not, you have a unique vocal style. Your voice is like a fingerprint. No one talks exactly as you do. Your rate of speech, your rhythm, your dialect, and your particular articulation skills—combined, these all make up your personal vocal style. People recognize your voice and know your style sometimes better than you do.

You acquired your style from your surroundings. For instance, how you say certain words is a function of which part of the country you learned to talk in. In the Southwest, automobiles, trucks, tractors, and mobile homes all ride on "tars" (tires). New Englanders have a way of mixing the *r* sound and the *a* sound. To some degree, even loudness is a function of your surroundings. Some homes are loud homes. The family members really speak up when they talk. Other homes are quiet homes—the members speak very softly.

Without realizing it, we inherit speech patterns from people who are important to us. For instance, you might sound more like your mother than does your sister. Or you may have recently picked up some mannerisms of the people you work with.

As you think about your vocal style, whom do you sound like? Who in your family sound alike? Write down the names of your family members and pair them together according to how closely they act and sound alike. Do they share any other commonalities as well?

Common vocal styles are prevalent in your professional life as well as your personal life. Many people believe that bankers should talk like bankers, ministers should talk like ministers, professors should be professing, and so on. Even the corporate image seems to have a style. Dale Carnegie salespeople are always enthusiastic. Funeral directors should not be frivolous. The list could continue on and on. The point is this: People establish their vocal styles based on their surroundings and their upbringings, and on the roles they seem to be playing.

## Kinesics

The second area of nonverbal communication is kinesics. Kinesics is the study of how people use their bodies to communicate. Some people call kinesics "body language." Whatever you call it, it is the study of how you move your facial muscles, eyes, arms, and legs to say things to others.

In face-to-face communication, three aspects of kinesics are fundamental: facial expressions, eye contact, and gestures. Let's look at each one independently.

### FACIAL EXPRESSIONS

Many people believe that the human face is a map of the emotions. By looking at someone's face you can tell whether the person is happy, sad, afraid, surprised, disgusted, or frustrated. In fact, photographers delight in catching the right moment on someone's face when they are taking pictures of people in action. Apparently, the face communicates more than we may realize or like.

Look at the picture below. From the woman's facial expression, what is going on? Is she happy, sad, surprised, afraid, or what?

Photo courtesy of Tom Dunning, Ok-lahoma Daily.

What you see above is only part of the original photo. Turn to page 289 in Appendix A and you will learn why she is responding the way she is.

The face does communicate, but you often need the context ("the rest of the story") to know what a particular expression means.

In a systematic study of the human face, Boucher and Ekman (1975) gave a number of photographs of people's faces to a group of respondents and asked them to guess the emotion being displayed in each photograph. Not only could the people accurately judge the emotions, they could do it with only one part of the face revealed in each picture. Furthermore, it was discovered that certain emotions are easier to discern from some parts of the face than from other parts. For instance, surprise was best noted around the eyes, whereas disgust was best detected in the lower part of the face around the cheeks and the mouth. This study points out that the face communicates, and that different parts of the face make good sources of information about the person's feelings.

Using the face to mirror one's emotions seems to be a universal trait among people around the world. Boucher and Ekman (1975) remind us, however, that even though people from different countries smile, frown, and change their facial expressions in similar ways, not all emotions are expressed in identical fashion across cultures. But cross-cultural differences in emotional expression do not mean that people don't have similar emotions. Emotions are universal.

It is interesting to note that people don't necessarily *learn* how to make faces when feeling sad, happy, frustrated, or otherwise. As Davis (1973) points out, even blind children laugh, cry, pout, and show anger, fear, and sadness in their faces without ever having seen anyone else do these things. Facial expressions are natural; they do not have to be learned.

## EYE CONTACT

When most people interact, they often glance at each other. When they each look at the other's eyes, they establish eye contact. In face-to-face communication, eye contact is used for turn taking. In other words, if we were conversing, when I am about to finish my turn talking, I can look you in the eyes to signal that your turn is coming up. Likewise, you can be watching me to see if I am in fact finishing my turn. As a means of structuring interaction, eye contact is very important and quite natural in everyday conversation, especially in North America.

In a study of how people use eye contact in everyday interaction, Kendon (1977) concluded that people engage other people in eye contact either to affiliate with them or to challenge them. That is, we can use our eyes to arouse feelings of friendship within others or to arouse feelings of being threatened. If we were meeting, it would be very easy for me to change the emotional meaning of my words simply by changing how I look at you. For instance, if I come up to you, shake your hand, and say, "Nice to see you," while at the same time I am looking over your shoulder to see what's going on behind you, you would have every right to question my sincerity. But if I look you in the eye, you should feel that I am glad to see you.

*Not* looking at someone also communicates nonverbally. In the greeting example, you would question my sincerity if I didn't look at you. But I may be having another problem that makes it difficult for me to look at you—stress. In many ways, the eyes are an index of stress. The more uncomfortable you become, the less likely you are to make eye contact with others; and vice versa. Cegala et al. (1979) found that people avoid eye contact when they are experiencing difficulty talking. And often difficulty in talking is preceded by some other difficulty that makes it hard to talk. Have you ever noticed how awkward you feel when you are talking with someone that you want to impress? Feelings of intimidation are frequently accompanied by downward gazes. A good test of how comfortable people are when talking with you is to watch how often they look downward to avoid eye contact.

Sometimes the hands alone carry messages, revealing how we feel. (Photo courtesy of the Norman Transcript.)

## GESTURES

Nonverbal gestures are movements of the hands, arms, legs, torso, and other major muscle groups of the body. The most obvious gestures are hand gestures, but we communicate with the rest of our bodies as well. Just about any body movement can be used as a gesture. Furthermore, gestures can be used within any of the five functions of nonverbal behavior. For example, you can touch together the ends of your thumb and your forefinger to show an OK sign (symbolic display), or you can recline your body backwards in your chair to show an informal style (self-presentation).

The use of gestures is universal, but the particular gestures vary from culture to culture. Even in the continental United States, gestures for the same meaning vary. American Plains Indians often point not with their hands and fingers, but with their faces and lips. In other words, if you asked, "Where are you going?" the Plains Indian might turn his or her face with pursed lips in the direction of travel. American Indians also have specific hand motions for saying "yes" to a question.

How do you feel about spitting? For most Americans, spitting in public is vulgar. But in the East African tribe of Masai, spitting is a gesture of respect. Thus, when two Masai tribesmen meet, they spit at each other to show respect and friendship. They also use this gesture as a means of greeting one another.

M. Vogel, *The Big Book of Amazing Facts* (New York: Waldman, 1980).

There are also differences in how American men and women use gestures when they interact. Ekman and Friesen (1971) found that women use gestures less often than men. They also discovered that women use more eye contact than men. The significance of these findings may be difficult to determine, but they do point out that there are potential intracultural differences in nonverbal gesturing habits.

**INTERACTIONAL SYNCHRONY** Perhaps more than for any other reason, gestures are used to provide interactional synchrony, that is, using gestures (not just hand gestures) to conduct a conversation. If you watch closely when two people are interacting, not only do they coordinate their verbal behavior, they coordinate their nonverbal behavior as well. Condon and Ogston (1966) observed that as one person moves during a conversation, so does the other. It is almost like a dance. Furthermore, each person moves in anticipation of what the other person will say. This means that, to some degree, we actually control the physical movements of one another through our speech. At first, this may be difficult to imagine, but if you simply watch two people talking you will see how both vary their movements to produce changes in each other. For instance, suppose we were talking together. Then you start to move away from me while I am talking. I am likely to move closer to you, talk a little louder, and attempt to reestablish eye contact so that you will turn back toward me.

Over time, interactional synchrony looks like a silent movie. The communicators move, lean, shift, and generally change positions in synchrony with the conversation. Thus, they interact nonverbally as well as verbally.

## Proxemics

In essence, proxemics, the third area of nonverbal behavior, refers to how humans use and distribute space among one another. The study of proxemics considers such issues as conversational distance, ter-

**Table 3.1 Spatial Zones of Social Interaction\***

| Zone | Type of Interaction |
|------|---------------------|
| Very close (3 to 6 in.) | Soft whisper; top secret |
| Close (8 to 12 in.) | Audible whisper; very confidential |
| Near (12 to 20 in.) | Soft voice; confidential |
| Neutral (20 to 36 in.) | Soft voice, low volume; personal subject matter |
| Neutral (4.5 to 5 ft.) | Full voice; impersonal information |
| Public (5.5 to 8 ft.) | Slightly overloud; information for others to hear |
| Across the room (8 to 20 ft.) | Loud voice; talking to a group |
| Hailing distance (20 to 24 ft. indoors, 100 ft. outdoors) | Loud voice to shout; departures and calls |

\* E. Hall, *The Silent Language* (Greenwich, Conn.: Fawcett Publications, 1959).

ritoriality, and privacy. Every society seems to have its norms about how close people can stand to each other when they talk, how crowded people can be and still live peacefully with one another, and so forth. Apparently, the amount of space among people makes a significant difference in how they communicate with one another.

There are many ways that proxemics enters into human communication. We vary the distance between ourselves and others, depending on how much intimacy we want. We arrange offices to promote certain kinds of communication and discourage others. But the most obvious use of proxemics is conversational distance. In the Western world, we have norms about the appropriate distance between speakers. These distances are determined by the type of interaction taking place. Hall (1959) offers the chart shown in Table 3.1 to illustrate the most common spatial zones (interactional distances). Supposedly, a well-mannered communicator will observe these norms.

You should realize that the chart does not prescribe what is correct; it only describes how people communicate. But if the zones are broken, as in a very crowded elevator, people are treated as objects rather than persons. When you look at the back of a person's head in a crowded elevator it is easy to make that individual a nonperson, but what would happen if people were jammed in face-to-face? In order to treat the others as nonpersons, each would have to avoid eye contact. Once you make eye contact, you make personal, not nonpersonal, contact.

We build fences not only to mark our boundaries, but to ensure some privacy. (Photo courtesy of B. Goss.)

We not only have zones for interaction, we seem to readily establish territories as well. These territories may be for status reasons, such as first-class seating versus coach seating on airplanes, or executive parking versus staff parking at work. We can also stake out territories for ownership reasons, such as building fences to mark property lines. More territory seems to mean better status since more space costs more money. Larger apartments and larger lots are associated with having more wealth. Status and ownership, then, are often measured by the quantity of space as well as the quality. When you move to the better side of town you tend to get more space, both inside the dwelling and in the distance between units. There is nothing inherently better about having more space; it is simply a North American norm.

This may sound a bit selfish to you and perhaps disgusting that we would have this penchant for more space. Maybe you don't have these same desires. But when was the last time you spread your papers and books on a table in the library only to have a stranger intrude, causing you to move your books and thus diminishing your space? Think about your living arrangements. Do you feel that you have a right to a certain amount of space? Would you divide that space evenly with your roommate? Would it matter?

**YOUR TURN...**

How you arrange your own space and territory not only may be affected by your proxemic needs, but also may be affected by your concern for visibility.

For instance, where you choose to sit in a classroom will be guided, in part, by your desires for interaction. Sommer (1969) found that students who were seated near the center of the room were more likely to get involved in discussions with the instructor than those who chose the low-profile seats on the sides and in the back.

What this means is that some people may choose a more or less prestigious location in order to be more or less visible. It depends, obviously, on the person and the immediate needs.

R. Sommer, *Personal Space: The Behavioral Basis of Design* (Englewood Cliffs, N.J.: Prentice-Hall, 1969).

Closely akin to territoriality is the issue of privacy. Americans seem to have a need for a certain amount of privacy. Our architecture is designed for this need. We build homes with private bedrooms, private baths, and so on. Yet in prisons we deny the inmates the right to privacy by placing unenclosed stools in the jail cells. To some, this is another form of punishment. To all, it is an invasion of privacy. Perhaps we have been taught to expect a certain amount of space just for ourselves, without others intruding. This, then, may be the reason that we value privacy.

No matter how you look at the issues, the significance of territories and privacy cannot be denied. As Burgoon (1978) so cogently concludes (after reviewing a number of studies), "It is clear that people have strong spatial needs and strong reactions to violations of their personal space or territory. As a result, proxemic variations can serve as a very powerful communication vehicle" (p. 134).

## Summary Propositions

Nonverbal communication is how people use their voices, bodies, and surroundings to send messages to other people. You can communicate through paralanguage, kinesics, and proxemics. Since nonverbal communication is thought to be more involuntary than verbal communication, people will watch your nonverbal behaviors to discover your true feelings. In most cases, however, your nonverbal behavior will endorse your verbal behavior, unless you are being a poor liar or are trying to tell a joke.

Nonverbal communication functions in five ways: as symbolic displays, as metamessages, for structuring interaction, for presenting yourself to others, and for manipulating others. Research into paralanguage, kinesics, and proxemics demonstrates how nonverbal behaviors can actually communicate. All in all, whenever people construct messages they can use both verbal and nonverbal channels.

1. Just as you can use words to communicate, you can use your voice, body, and environment to communicate in a nonverbal sense.

2. Judee Burgoon (1978) suggests five ways in which people use nonverbal messages:

   a. Symbolic displays (like nonverbal words)

   b. Metamessages (augmenting the words)

   c. Structuring the interaction (guiding how people interact with each other)

   d. Self-presentation (displaying your personal image through clothing, actions, and so forth)

   e. Manipulating others (mood setting and persuasion)

3. Paralanguage is the study of the speaker's voice.

4. People make judgments about the speaker based on hearing the speaker's voice.

5. Every speaker has a unique style of voice.

6. Kinesics is the study of how people use their bodies to communicate.

7. Your facial expressions often tell others how you feel.

8. You use eye contact to manage conversations as you take turns talking in a conversation.

9. People use gestures not only to augment their speech but also to regulate the flow of the conversation.

10. Proxemics is the study of how people use space as they communicate.

11. We have spatial zones that vary according to the kind of communication that is taking place.

12. In addition to establishing territories, people can arrange furniture and other parts of the environment to establish desired patterns of interaction.

# References

**Addington, D.** "The Relationship of Selected Vocal Characteristics to Personality Perception." *Speech Monographs* 35(1968):492–503.

**Boucher, J., and Ekman, P.** "Facial Areas of Emotional Information." *Journal of Communication* 25(1975):21–29.

**Burgoon, J.** "Nonverbal Communication." In *Human Communication*, by M. Burgoon and M. Ruffner. New York: Holt, Rinehart & Winston, 1978.

**Cegala, D.; Alexander, A.; and Sokuvitz, S.** "An Investigation of Eye Gaze and Its Relation to Selected Verbal Behavior." *Human Communication Research* 5(1979):99–108.

**Condon, A., and Ogston, W.** "Sound Film Analysis of Normal and Pathological Behavior Patterns." *Journal of Nervous and Mental Disease* 143(1966): 338–347.

**Davis, F.** *Inside Intuition.* New York: McGraw-Hill, 1973.

**Ekman, P., and Friesen, W.** "Constants across Cultures in the Face and Emotion." *Journal of Personality and Social Psychology* 17(1971):124–129.

**Hall, E.** *The Silent Language.* Greenwich, Conn.: Fawcett, 1959.

**Hocking, J.; Bauchner, J.; Kaminiski, E.; and Miller, G.** "Detecting Deceptive Communication from Verbal, Visual, and Paralinguistic Cues." *Human Communication Research* 6(1979):33–46.

**Kendon, A.** *Studies on the Behavior of Social Interaction.* Bloomington: Indiana University Press, 1977.

**Mehrabian, A., and Weiner, M.** "Decoding Inconsistent Communications." *Journal of Personality and Social Psychology* 6(1967):109–114.

**Miller, G., and Hewgill, M.** "The Effects of Variations in Nonfluency on Audience Ratings of Source Credibility." *Quarterly Journal of Speech* 50(1964): 36–44.

**Scherer, K.** "Voice and Speech Correlates of Perceived Social Influence in Simulated Juries." In *Language and Social Psychology,* edited by H. Giles and R. St. Clair. Baltimore: University Park Press, 1979.

**Smith, B.; Brown, B.; Strong, W.; and Rencher, A.** "Effects of Speech Rate on Personality Perception." *Language and Speech* 18(1975):145–152.

**Sommer, R.** *Personal Space: The Behavioral Basis of Design.* Englewood Cliffs, N.J.: Prentice-Hall, 1969.

**Sommer, R.** *Tight Spaces: Hard Architecture and How to Humanize It.* Englewood Cliffs, N.J.: Prentice-Hall, 1974.

**Vogel, M.** *The Big Book of Amazing Facts.* New York: Waldman Publishing, 1980.

# LISTENING

In Shakespeare's play *Henry IV,* Falstaff laments that he gets into trouble because he doesn't listen well: "It is the disease of not listening . . . that I am troubled withal" (part II, act I, scene 2). Failing to listen is not an actual disease, but it can cause discomfort, as Falstaff learned. Everyone is guilty of faulty listening at one time or another. You can, however, correct faulty listening and become a more responsive or a more critical listener.

In this chapter, you will learn a number of things about listening. After distinguishing listening from hearing, this chapter will explain how people listen, the reasons for poor listening, how to be a responsive listener, and how to be a critical listener. After reading this chapter, you should not only understand the listening process, but also discover ways to improve your own listening.

## Hearing versus Listening

Hearing and listening are related, but not identical, processes. To listen, you have to hear. But you can hear without listening. The reason for this is that listening goes beyond hearing. Listening requires the interpretation of sounds, not just the reception of them. Thus, you can hear others yet choose not to listen to them. Even though hearing and listening are related, there are some essential differences that are worth noting.

First of all, hearing is basically an involuntary process of sensing sounds. You don't have to choose to hear; it occurs automatically if a sound is audible (loud enough to be heard). Audible sounds are measured in decibels. The scale begins at zero (0) for inaudible sounds and goes over 100 decibels for very loud sounds. In average conversations, the speech sounds register around 50 decibels. Since most speech sounds fall comfortably within our normal range of hearing, hearing is usually not as much a problem for communication as is listening.

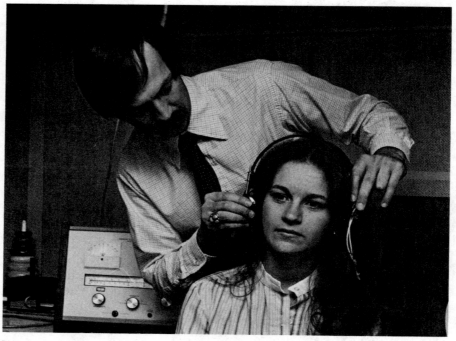

People don't have their hearing checked as often as they have their vision checked. (Photo courtesy of the Norman Transcript.)

Listening, by contrast, is more than sensing sounds; it is interpreting the sounds as well. Thus, listening is an act of perception. When you listen, you are taking what you hear and assigning meaning to it. There are no apparent physical limits to listening other than those associated with hearing, but there may be some psychological barriers that cause poor listening (for example, not understanding the words the speaker is using, or disagreeing with the speaker).

The second difference between hearing and listening is a quantitative one. Of all the sounds that you hear, you listen to only some of them. Theoretically, it should be possible to listen to everything you hear, but if you did, you would go crazy. Since more mental energy is needed to listen than is needed to hear, most people choose not to listen to everything. Thus, the domain of listening is smaller than the domain of hearing. Later in this chapter, you will learn why this is so.

The third feature of listening, compared to hearing, is its selectivity. When you listen, you choose from among those sounds you hear the ones you wish to focus on. Often, your choices are determined by your attitudes and expectations. Thus, if you expect a person to say stupid or inane things, stupidities and inanities are all you will listen for. Likewise, if you really like a speaker, you may not see the faulty logic being used in the speech. Later, in Chapter 5, you'll

Everyday sounds vary in intensity. Here is a list of common sounds placed on the decibel scale.

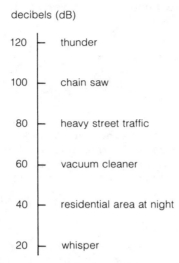

decibels (dB)

| | |
|---|---|
| 120 | thunder |
| 100 | chain saw |
| 80 | heavy street traffic |
| 60 | vacuum cleaner |
| 40 | residential area at night |
| 20 | whisper |

For your own safety, you should know that continuous exposure to sounds exceeding 100 dB can cause damage to your ears. It is a good idea, then, not to expose yourself for long periods of time to very loud noises (such as some rock concerts).

Also, note that conversational speech (50 dB) falls below the level of a running vacuum cleaner. Have you ever raised your voice to be heard over a vacuum cleaner?

learn more about selective perception, but for now let's agree that listening entails a certain amount of selectivity.

By now it should be obvious that you have more control over your listening than you do over your hearing. This control is important. If you could not selectively listen, you would be at the mercy of a very noisy and demanding world. By focusing your attention on certain messages while ignoring others, you might miss some important information, but you will be better able to understand the messages you are attending to. The selectivity of listening, then, becomes a problem only when you choose the wrong message to attend to.

## How You Listen

The act of listening is no simple task. Sometimes people listen energetically to one message, and at other times they divide their attention among many different messages simultaneously. How in-

One of the ways you can understand the difference between hearing and listening is through homophones. Homophones are words that sound alike but are different in meaning. For instance, say aloud the following pairs of words:

*stare, stair*

*weight, wait*

*four, fore*

*pier, peer*

You will hear each pair of words as the same sounds, but because they refer to different things, you must listen to (interpret) them differently.

When you listen, you need more than hearing. You need to know what the speaker is talking about so that you can assign the proper meaning.

---

tensively you listen to a message is determined by many factors. But just being able to listen (at any level of intensity) requires three things.

## REQUIREMENTS FOR LISTENING

*1. Isolating the Message*  You are surrounded by a world of sounds, some of which are relevant messages while others are simply noise. As a listener, you have to decide when a sound is noise (irrelevant input) and when it is a message (relevant input). This decision is what makes the domain of listening smaller than the domain of hearing. Your decision depends on your immediate task and needs. For instance, while you are reading this book (your immediate task) you can screen out the extraneous sounds coming from outside (people laughing, dogs barking, and so on) because those outside signals are not helpful in reading. Isolating the message, then, means that you can focus your attention on the important message, making it stand out from all the other sounds impinging on your ears. This isolation occurs on two levels.

First, you need to recognize a speech sound apart from the other sounds. In other words, you must identify a sound as a verbal message, as opposed to being part of the world of noise. This may seem like a trivial point to you, but you have been listening most of your life and it is easy to forget that recognizing speech sounds is an ability. For a very young infant, being able to isolate speech sounds from all other sounds in the world is a major step in learning language.

The second level of isolating the message is zeroing in on one message at a time. You are surrounded by a multitude of messages. If you attend to all of them with equal energy, you will not only experience the frustration of overload, you may become confused as well. Somehow, you must filter out those messages that you wish to deal with and leave the others behind. If you have too much input to cope with, your comprehension may suffer.

One of the reasons that I do not take my classes outside on beautiful sunny days is that we (myself included) often find other things more interesting than the topic of discussion. Someone is always watching the people walk by. Someone else is juggling a pebble. Another is peering at the strange-sounding bird in the trees above us. Although I agree that it is more pleasant to sit on the lawn than it is to sit on the hard wooden chairs in the classroom, it is harder to teach class amid the passing people, pebbles, and penguins. Listening requires that you isolate the message, primarily by removing distractions and focusing your attention on the message. Listening is so much easier when you are paying attention.

One person's noise is another person's message. When thinking about noise in the environment, be careful not to assume that a particular sound is always regarded as noise. For instance, the humming sound made by an air-conditioner may tell a repair person that the unit is working well. Yet the employee whose desk is located near the air-conditioner may hear it as distracting noise. Likewise, the noisy children in the backyard may annoy a neighbor, while those same sounds are "music" to the parent who realizes that the children are happily playing.

   In essence, then, a sound is neither a noise nor a message until the receiver decides it is. Before that, it is only a sound.

B. Goss, *Processing Communication* (Belmont, Calif.: Wadsworth, 1982).

2. *Being Ready to Respond*  Identifying a message for listening is really just the beginning. Next you must be ready to do the work of listening—that is, you must be ready to respond to the message. Readiness involves two factors. First, you must be in the proper frame of mind to receive a message. You should be aware that someone is talking to you, and you should have an idea about what is going on. A listener who is unaware that a message is coming will be caught off guard. Have you ever started a conversation without first checking to see if your receiver is ready to listen? Do you remember what happened? You probably had to start all over when you realized that your listener had not been ready to listen. As a speaker, then, you should make sure that your listener is ready to listen before you begin your message. Likewise, as a listener, you can't expect to understand the speaker until you turn your attention to the message being sent. Thus, being in the proper frame of mind is important to listening.

Have you ever noticed that at a noisy party you can be involved in one conversation and still listen to others?

Colin Cherry, a communication expert, calls this the "cocktail party problem." His research suggests that people can actively listen to one message, but monitor other messages enough to keep track of what's going on. This is a form of selective listening. The problem with selective listening, though, is that you cannot recall all the different messages with equal accuracy. Those messages to which you actively listen will be recalled more accurately than those messages you simply monitor while listening to the main conversation.

This shows us that accurate recall requires active listening. So remove the outside distractions or ignore other people when you must listen for accuracy.

C. Cherry, *On Human Communication* (Cambridge, Mass.: The M.I.T. Press, 1966).

The second factor in readiness pertains to personal energy. You cannot have an energy shortage when it is time to listen. Listening is work and you need to be alert to listen. To understand how fatigue affects your listening, consider the nights when you doze off while watching TV. As you fall asleep, your ears still hear the TV, but you don't bother to listen because you are too tired. Likewise, as you tire during the day, you become a less effective listener. I'm sure that you have nodded your way through more than one lecture or sermon because you didn't have the necessary energy to stay alert.

In summary, listening readiness requires that you (1) focus your attention on the message and (2) have a sufficient amount of energy to listen to what is being said. If you have problems with either, you will not listen very effectively.

*3. Decoding and Assigning Meaning* Now that you have isolated the message and are ready to listen, you can do the main part of listening. That is, you must decode (decipher) the message into its principal parts, and then assign meaning to the parts. In the communication model presented in Chapter 1, this is called decoding and interpretation. When the messages are verbal, the listener must segment the stream of speech sounds into words, phrases, and sentences. Then the listener can interpret the decoded message by assigning meanings to the units in the message.

Let me illustrate how decoding and assigning meaning occur. Suppose you hear the following: "Itrainedlastnight." What was said? At first, it seems like one long word. But a careful inspection reveals that there are four words. As a listener, you must decode this stream of speech into its parts before you can decide what the speaker means. Once you have established that the words are *it rained last night,* you can assign meaning to them. Assigning meaning is done in two ways.

The first way that you assign meaning is at the individual word level. As the listener, you analyze each unit of the message, recognizing those words that elicit immediate meanings in your mind. Thus, if you know what rain is and if you know night from day, you will be well able to handle the words.

But there is more to understanding *it rained last night* than simply responding to the words. The second way that meaning is assigned is in knowing the complete thought expressed in the message. In other words, the message *it rained last night* is an assertion about reality. The speaker is talking about something, some time. If you properly assign meaning to the complete expression, you know not only the words, but also what happened (it rained) and when it happened (last night).

Like so many of our daily habits, we take for granted our abilities to decode and assign meaning to language. But without these skills, you couldn't follow a normal conversation. Young children often have trouble following adult conversations at the dinner table, not because they don't hear what is said, but because they don't recognize some of the words being used or they don't have the proper meanings to assign to the words they recognize. They have a listening problem, not a hearing problem.

The requirements for listening—isolating the message, being ready to respond, and decoding and assigning meaning—are certainly

Listening plays a key role in learning. (Photo courtesy of University of Oklahoma Instructional Services Office.)

crucial. But meeting these three requirements does not ensure that you will listen accurately. It only means that you have completed the act of listening. How well you listen is another matter that will be dealt with later in this chapter. Furthermore, these requirements for listening represent the necessary components of listening, but they do not describe the main strategy for listening. This is where forecasting comes in.

## FORECASTING

As I mentioned earlier, listening is a complex task. Exactly how you attach meaning to words that you have decoded is still being investigated by researchers. But it is generally understood that listening is an active, not a passive, process. That is, listeners must be assigning meaning at the same time the speaker is speaking.

When you listen, you don't just sit back and let the speaker fill your ears and your mind with words. Nor do you even wait to hear the whole message before you interpret it. You actually assign meaning to the message as it is being communicated. Cole and Jakimik (1978) suggest that when listening to a speaker, listeners are no more than one or two words behind the speaker as they comprehend what is being said.

If listening takes place while the other person is speaking, how is it done? The answer involves forecasting. Forecasting is a listening strategy in which the listener predicts what is coming up in an ongoing message. You forecast when you guess what the speaker is about to say. Then you wait to see if you are correct. Forecasting follows a predict-then-confirm pattern. A good example of forecasting is when a friend who is talking has difficulty thinking of the "right" word in the middle of a sentence. To help your friend, you volunteer the word you think he or she is searching for. Most of the time, you guess correctly. What allows you to predict successfully is the fact that you have been mentally forecasting during the conversation. Sometimes you hit the right word; other times, you miss. But even if the word you offer is not the exact one the speaker was groping for, your choice may be quite satisfactory if it conveys the right thought.

Because forecasting is such a rapid process and because we forecast without much conscious effort, many people doubt whether or not there is enough time to forecast while listening. In actuality, though, there is time to forecast and to listen to the current words being spoken. Effective listening, then, is an active, two-part process of forecasting and hearing at the same time. This is why listening takes so much energy.

Finally, you should understand that forecasting is cyclical. As people listen to each other and forecast what's coming up, they check their predictions to see if they are confirmed. If the speaker says what

comprehension

confirmation          prediction

**Figure 4.1** The Cycle of Forecasting

they expect, then their predictions are confirmed. These confirmed predictions, then, lead to more comprehension. And this cycle continues throughout a conversation. Figure 4.1 illustrates the cyclical nature of forecasting.

Although forecasting is a natural process in listening, it is not always accurate. Faulty forecasting, and faulty listening, can be caused by a number of things, not the least of which is whether or not the listener is paying attention to the speaker and to the conversation. People commonly get lost in a conversation when they are distracted by extraneous messages or negative feelings about the speaker. Poor listening habits can cause a breakdown in listening. And whenever listening breaks down, communication breaks down. That is why it is important to understand what causes poor listening.

## Reasons for Poor Listening

Poor listening habits not only cause breakdowns in communication, they can cause breakdowns in memory. In other words, if you do not listen carefully to a message, you might not be able to recall it later (during an exam, for example). Thus, poor listening affects both the present conversation and future situations. The reasons for poor listening are many, but they can be economically grouped into three categories: distractions, disorientation, and defensiveness.

### DISTRACTIONS

A real nemesis to listening is a distraction—something that draws your attention away from the message. For instance, during a lecture on communication arts, you may be thinking about your date last night. Or you might notice that the sky outside is clouding and you wonder if it is going to rain. These kinds of distractions make effective listening more difficult.

Distractions have two general origins: internal and external. An internal distraction is an irrelevant thought that comes into your mind while someone is talking. It may be something that you have been worrying about. Perhaps you are thinking about your dinner plans for the evening. Maybe you can't get the lyrics of a song out of your mind. Whatever the distraction, it leads to daydreaming and inattention to the speaker.

External distractions, in contrast, do not start in your mind. They come from the environment. In a classroom, an external distraction may be a giant fly that is making the rounds in the room. Maybe the lights are flickering as the bulbs are about to burn out. Perhaps someone has fallen asleep and is snoring loud enough to be heard throughout the room. These are all examples of external distractions.

The key point to remember is: If a distraction causes you to divert your attention away from the speaker long enough to miss an important idea, then the distraction will be detrimental to your comprehension. Obviously, it is a good idea to avoid distractions whenever possible.

## DISORIENTATION

Disorientation occurs when listeners become lost and feel out of the mainstream of thought in a conversation or lecture. Not knowing what is going on is a form of disorientation. This lost feeling is caused by confusion, boredom, and/or reflections.

Do you ever have problems listening to foreigners speaking English? Do their accents make it hard for you to understand their words?

The key to listening to a foreigner speaking English is twofold: Pick up the rhythm and listen primarily for the content words.

Sometimes an English-speaking foreigner imposes his or her native accent on the English grammar. This causes a timing problem for untrained listeners. But it doesn't take long to catch on to the rhythm that is created by the accent. This process is made easier if you focus on the content words (nouns, verbs, adjectives, adverbs, and so on) as you are attending to your foreign friend.

Finally, take comfort in the fact that you are not the only one who has trouble understanding the accented English, and your foreign friend realizes this too. Don't be afraid to show your confusion, and don't be afraid to laugh at your own inadequacies. Many foreigners are used to being misunderstood.

Confusion can occur when the material being covered is too difficult to understand, or not well organized. No matter how listeners become confused, their disorientation will interfere with their understanding of the message. In fact, when listeners become confused, they can overreact to their disoriented state and "tune out" the speaker.

Boredom is another source of disorientation. Exactly how people become bored is hard to specify. But it is an accepted fact that listeners can think faster than speakers can talk. So a listener could easily become bored with a speaker simply because the spoken word is too slow for the brain. Boredom can also be an attitude problem. For instance, you may have decided beforehand that the speaker was going to be boring. Consequently, you listen as though you are bored. Like confusion, boredom interferes with effective listening.

Finally, reflections cause disorientation. As a listener, have you ever been stimulated by a speaker to think more deeply about a point raised in the message? More than once, I have had my mind triggered by a speaker, causing me to reflect about the idea while ignoring the fact that the speaker has gone on to another point. Once I return my attention to the speaker, I realize that I missed a part of the presentation. Sound familiar?

## DEFENSIVENESS

In a listening situation, you might not feel distracted or disoriented, but you may feel defensive. Defensiveness occurs when people feel threatened by either the speaker, the message, or the situation. For instance, you may dislike the speaker, thereby making it hard for you to listen attentively. Or perhaps the speaker said something that you strongly disagreed with, and this caused you to "turn off" the speaker. Or maybe you are an involuntary participant, "roped into going to this meeting." No matter what the cause of your defensiveness, these negative feelings can inhibit your listening abilities, making it possible for you to ignore the speaker, or to refute point for point everything said without giving the speaker a fair hearing. Whenever your negative attitudes interfere with accurate listening, you are a defensive listener. In Chapter 6, you will learn more about defensiveness in communication.

## Responsive Listening

A responsive listener is an empathetic, other-oriented listener. To listen responsively, you have to set aside your opinions about the topic and the speaker, and then listen for the speaker's feelings. For instance, a sympathetic parent may listen for his child's feelings about an incident that took place at school. An engineer who listens responsively will discover her client's feelings about a project, even when those feelings are not openly expressed.

Responsive listening, though, is really more than lending a sympathetic ear to another person. It involves active strategies in which you talk as well as listen. Stewart and D'Angelo (1975) propose two specific responsive listening strategies: paraphrasing and parasupporting.

## PARAPHRASING

Paraphrasing is the act of listening to a speaker and then responding in such a way that you restate in your words what the speaker just said. For instance, suppose we were conversing and I said that I was tired and in need of sleep. You might respond by saying something such as, "I'll bet you're tired. The sleep will do you some good." By paraphrasing, you show that you are, in fact, listening and that you understand my feelings. If done tactfully, paraphrasing will be appreciated by the speaker.

## PARASUPPORTING

Parasupporting is similar to paraphrasing, but goes further. When you parasupport, you not only rephrase the speaker's point, you carry the point a step further. Let me illustrate. If I say that I am tired and in need of sleep (as before), you might parasupport me by saying, "Yes, I'm sure you are tired. You have been working very hard lately. You deserve the rest. Why don't you go lie down?" Such a response on your part shows that you listened responsively and that you agree with my feelings. That is, you support me.

Both paraphrasing and parasupporting are positive listening strategies. They promote goodwill and help build relations between people. Both are responsive listening strategies that endorse people's feelings. The crucial difference between them is that paraphrasing *acknowledges* the speaker's thoughts and feelings, while parasupporting goes on to *advocate* those thoughts and feelings.

Being a responsive listener through paraphrasing or parasupporting is not as easy as it seems. Not only is it easy to forget to be a responsive listener, it is difficult to listen responsively when you have a point that you want to make. Many people don't listen long enough to paraphrase or parasupport effectively. To do it well, you must be paying attention to the speaker, not to your next point.

If you are known for being a responsive listener, people will actively seek you out, asking you to listen to their ideas and feelings. Furthermore, the more responsive you are with others, the more they will tell you things you don't know or expect. In essence, responsive listening produces more responsive speaking. How you listen can determine how other people talk to you.

# Critical Listening

There are at least two sides to effective listening. As responsive listening is essential for everyday life, so too is critical listening. In critical situations such as listening to a lecture, a political speech, or a sales pitch, or interviewing for a job, you must be able to analyze carefully the speakers' messages so that you are not unfairly persuaded or deceived in some way. You need critical listening skills.

What is a critical listener? A critical listener is one who listens objectively to a speaker in order to analyze the points and arguments advanced in the message. The critical listener isolates the content of the message from the speaker's attractiveness, the situation, and other nonmessage factors so that the validity of the message may be tested. Therefore, the critical listener must know the difference between facts and opinions, and also know that people sometimes say things they cannot prove.

Listening critically does not negate listening responsively. Good listeners are able to do both simultaneously. Every message has both a subjective side and an objective side. Effective listening is both subjective (responsive) and objective (critical). It takes a lot of energy to do both, but it's worth it.

Most people, however, think that critical listening is difficult, so they require more training in this kind of listening. But what does this training entail? What should a critical listener look for? This is where standards for accuracy and acceptability are important.

## ACCURACY AND ACCEPTABILITY

Critical listeners do not accept blindly whatever the speaker says. They assess the message in terms of accuracy (how fairly is the information reported?) and acceptability (how reasonable are the drawn conclusions?). If the speaker mistreats the information or attempts to distort the facts, the critical listener will reject the message on the grounds of inaccuracy. Likewise, if the speaker draws unwarranted conclusions, given the evidence presented, the critical listener will reject the message as unacceptable. Thus, critical listeners listen for facts and appropriate conclusions, and they also evaluate those facts and conclusions along the way. Uncritical listeners are likely to overlook the facts and conclusions, and therefore agree with the speaker, whether they should or not.

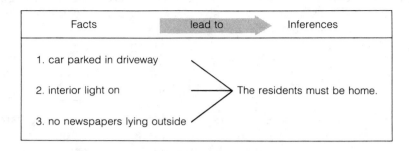

| Facts | lead to | Inferences |
|-------|---------|------------|
| 1. car parked in driveway | | |
| 2. interior light on | | The residents must be home. |
| 3. no newspapers lying outside | | |

**Figure 4.2** Facts Leading to an Inference

If you want to sharpen your awareness of facts and justifiable conclusions, you need to learn more about the differences between facts and inferences.

## FACTS VERSUS INFERENCES

Not all statements in a message are alike. Some are dominated by the speaker's attitudes and feelings and are thus judgmental (for example, "I think this food tastes awful"). Other statements are declarative sentences designed to report the facts honestly ("The capital of California is Sacramento"). Still other statements are conjectures or guesses about reality ("You look like you are ready to go home"). Good critical listening requires that you know the differences among such sentences, especially the difference between facts and inferences.

To understand the difference between facts and inferences, consider the following example. Assume that you are preparing to leave for a two-week vacation to sunny Siberia. Since your house will be vacant during your absence, you want to take whatever precautions are necessary to keep it safe. The police department recommended that you lock all doors and windows, have a neighbor collect your mail and your newspapers every day, have a light inside the house turned on during evening hours, and, if possible, leave a car parked in your driveway. You do these things so that potential intruders will conclude that you are home and not out of town. But notice that the conclusion is an inference. All the facts indicate that you are home, but the person making the inference does not know for sure (and may not even question it). (See Figure 4.2.)

This example demonstrates the difference between facts and inferences. Facts are observable aspects of reality that are empirically verifiable. For instance, if someone says that there are five magazines on the coffee table, you can look for yourself to see if that is correct. If incorrect, the speaker has falsely represented the facts.

Whether or not a statement is a fact or an inference sometimes depends on who is saying it. The speaker who is in a position to know can speak factually. But the speaker who doesn't know for sure makes some statements that are only inferences.

Below are three statements that I am making concerning you and this book. Place a check mark next to the statements that are inferences on my part. Leave the facts blank.

_____ You have been reading this entire chapter.

_____ You paid for this textbook.

_____ You are enrolled in a course that uses this book as a text.

If you were careful, you checked all three statements. From my perspective, each statement can only be an inference. I don't know for sure what you have been reading, who paid for this book, which course it is used in. Furthermore, all of the statements could turn out to be false. I just don't know. So what may be facts to you are only inferences to me.

Unlike facts, inferences may or may not be verifiable. It depends on what the inference refers to. For instance, if people pass by your home and see the lights on and a car parked in the driveway, they can check their inference that you are home by knocking on your door, calling your name, or peering in your windows. One or all of these three tests should reveal whether or not you are, in fact, home. An inference such as this one is verifiable because your presence at home can be physically observed.

Other inferences cannot be verified because they refer to unobservable feelings that people hold (attitudes, motives, and desires). The statement that "my family loves me" is one such inference. Although I do not doubt my family's love for me (I believe it), there is really no way to observe, objectively, the state of love. It is a subjective experience, based on feelings, not on facts. And the love is part of my personal world, more than my physical world.

As you can see, facts and inferences are different, but not opposite. Many inferences become facts, through verification. Likewise, you can use facts to derive inferences, such as when you prepare your house before you leave for vacation. Facts and inferences, then, work together.

A critical listener realizes, then, that messages will contain both facts and inferences. Such a listener will listen for these and decide which inferences are justifiable (potentially verifiable) and which are not (are untestable). Knowing how to treat facts and inferences is part of being a skillful listener.

## Summary Propositions

Listening is an important decoding skill that assumes more than simply hearing the message. In order to listen effectively, you must be prepared to do so. This means that you can recognize the speech signal, are ready to respond, and have the ability to respond meaningfully to the message. People with poor listening habits are often hampered by distractions, disorientation, and/or defensiveness. Effective listeners listen responsively and critically. But there are times when effective listening calls for more responsive than critical skills; other times, the reverse is true. A good listener, then, can practice both responsive and critical listening and knows when each is needed the most.

1. Hearing is sensing; listening is perceiving.

2. There are three requirements for listening:

   a. Isolating the message

   b. Being ready to respond

   c. Decoding and assigning meaning

3. As you listen, you forecast the ideas that you think are coming up.

4. Forecasting is cyclical—you predict, confirm, comprehend; predict, confirm, comprehend; and so on.

5. In addition to not asking questions when they should, people have poor listening habits because of:

   a. Distractions

   b. Disorientations

   c. Defensiveness

6. Responsive listening calls for one of two listening strategies: paraphrasing or parasupporting.

7. Critical listening implies that you pay attention to the speaker's main points and analyze them for validity.

8. A critical listener knows the difference between facts and inferences, and is able to test the believability of the message.

## References

**Cherry, C.** *On Human Communication.* Cambridge, Mass.: The M.I.T. Press, 1966.

**Cole, R., and Jakimik, J.** "Understanding Speech: How Words Are Heard." In *Strategies of Information Processing,* edited by G. Underwood. London: Academic Press, 1978.

**Goss, B.** *Processing Communication.* Belmont, Calif.: Wadsworth, 1982.

**Stewart, J., and D'Angelo, G.** *Together: Communicating Interpersonally.* Reading, Mass.: Addison-Wesley, 1975.

# 5

# COMMUNICATOR CHARACTERISTICS

**Self-Concept**
Defining Self-Concept
Origins of the Self-Concept
Changes in Self-Concept
Low Self-Esteem
Improving Your Self-Esteem

■

**Perception**
Filters
Selective Perception
Attitudes and Values

■

**Needs**
Maslow's Hierarchy of Needs
Schutz's Interpersonal Needs

■

**Summary Propositions**

■

**References**

■

Successful communication not only depends on the quality of the verbal and the nonverbal messages, it depends also on the quality of the communicators. Any shortcoming or limitation in the sources and the receivers of communication will manifest itself in the process of communication. Although we humans have created machines capable of rapid and precise information processing, we creators rarely meet these high standards ourselves. We have the potential for communicating without error, but we don't often fulfill it.

Why are humans less efficient than machines in many circumstances? The answer lies in the nature of the communicators. When we humans interact, we bring to every communication exchange personal expectations and biases that contribute to the distortion of information. These biases are a function of each person's self-concept, perceptions, and needs. Each of these characteristics of communicators is worthy of closer attention.

## Self-Concept

Have you ever heard: "Gee, you sure made a good point in the discussion this morning." Or, "you must really understand this material, given the way you asked questions in the meeting." Compliments such as these not only make you feel good, they bolster your self-concept. And this is important because your self-concept affects how you communicate.

### DEFINING SELF-CONCEPT

Bear with me a moment while I make a necessary distinction before defining the term *self-concept*. There is a difference between your physical being and your psychological being. You can see, hear, touch, and generally sense your physical existence, but your psychological existence—your self—is not so obvious. It is based on your

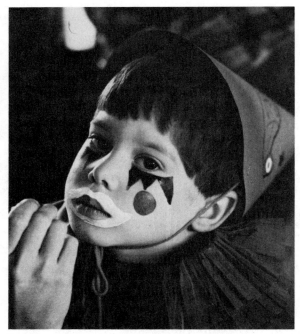

There is often a difference between who we are and who we would like to be. (Photo courtesy of the Norman Transcript.)

feelings. You cannot touch it, but you know you exist, have a mind, and have a self.

In learning about your self, you observe yourself in action. You are aware of how you talk, what you think about, how you feel, and how others react to you. How you evaluate yourself on these things constitutes your self-concept. Your self-concept, then, is your attitude about you as a person. It is your bundle of perceptions of how well you do things, how people respond to you, and what you think about yourself.

## ORIGINS OF THE SELF-CONCEPT

Where does your self-concept come from? Is it simply your innate personality? To some extent, your self-concept is governed by your personality, but your self-concept is much more.

You may be born with particular personality features, but your self-concept must be learned. You must discover it by watching yourself in action. As you observe how you behave, you make inferences about yourself based on your performance. For instance, you might discover that you have trouble giving public speeches, thus leading you to conclude that you are a lousy public speaker. Or you may observe that every time you are introduced to an attractive guy or gal, your hands sweat, your heart races, and you can't think of anything to say. Such nervous reactions may cause you to classify yourself as socially inept. In either case, you will not have a healthy self-concept. And unfortunately, such attitudes about ourselves are not uncommon. Furthermore, the reality of the situation (whether you truly are a poor speaker or socially inept) may not be as important to you as your attitude about it. In essence, you can teach yourself who you are by judging your own actions.

Part of your self-concept is how you view yourself as a communicator. Below are three brief statements by different students. Which one best describes you?

*Chris:* "I like to talk to people. I even enjoy giving public speeches."

*Sam:* "Me? I am the quiet type. People are OK, but I work best alone. There is no way that I would volunteer to give a speech."

*Jan:* "I really don't know how I feel about speaking in public. Frankly, I've never given a speech in my life. It looks a bit scary."

If you chose Chris, then you are confident in your abilities. That's good. If you chose Sam, you probably have a high degree of stage fright. Hopefully, this course will help you. If you chose Jan, you are like most people. And like most people, you can benefit from more training in communication.

You also learn your self-concept by noticing how other people react to you. If you notice that people listen attentively as you talk, you should conclude that you are a socially effective person. Likewise, if others compliment you on a job well done, you should interpret those remarks as a personal strength for you.

To further understand how the self-concept is formed, consider an exercise I conducted in class recently. I asked my students to write on paper the answer to this question: "Who are you?" After everyone finished, we discussed the answers, and one student volunteered this answer: "I am a student, a woman, a Baptist, a pre-med major, a part-time electrician, a redhead, and a numismatist." After a quick check in my pocket dictionary to be sure of the public propriety of the last item mentioned (numismatist), I engaged the class in a discussion about her answers. We decided that her list was composed of her attributes and roles in everyday life. Others concurred that they, too, used such terms to describe who they were. Through such a listing of personal interests, skills, beliefs, and social qualities, people categorize themselves.

But where do these labels and categories come from? I asked my willing student how the labels listed applied to her. She told us that they had evolved over her lifetime (even her red hair—she was born a blond). For instance, she knew that she was a Baptist because she attends a Baptist church. She knew she was an electrician because she works for the phone company in that capacity. In fact, for each item listed she knew who she was because of her own observations and the observations of others about her.

The crucial part of learning a self-concept lies in the amount of reinforcement you receive from others. If others see you as you see you, your chances of learning that aspect of your self-concept are enhanced. In contrast, if the world continually presents contradictory information to you, your self-concept will be more difficult to learn. For instance, if my students don't recognize me as a professor, then I cannot be a professor. Furthermore, I cannot be a good professor unless I earn teacher evaluations that are better than at least one other professor's. So having a self-concept means more than having certain attributes and roles. Others must recognize you for those things. You cannot clinch your learning of your self-concept until you receive the recognition from others.

Thus, feedback becomes very important in everyday life. How people react to you provides critical data about your self-concept. If their reactions agree with your feelings about yourself, then your self-concept will be reinforced. If you receive contradictory feedback, then changes in your self-concept may be necessary.

## CHANGES IN SELF-CONCEPT

Most of us have had experiences that caused us to reevaluate our self-concepts. Perhaps you didn't do as well as you expected on an exam in your favorite class. Maybe you allowed someone to persuade you to do something you weren't quite sure was ethical. Whatever the occasion, it is quite possible to have a significant interaction with someone else that causes you to reassess yourself. When these encounters occur, one of four things can happen to your self-concept.

First, the encounter can *add* to your self-concept. This occurs when you try something new and discover that you can or cannot do it well. Learning to water-ski on one ski rather than two may add to your self-concept. Discovering that you have the periodical table of chemicals memorized before anyone else in class can add to your self-concept. Likewise, if you fail in these tasks (water-skiing and learning the periodic table), you learn that these are not your strengths, thus adding to your understanding of your limitations.

Second, your self-concept may be *clarified* by an encounter. For instance, you may be unsure of your ability to learn statistics, but you discover after the first exam that you did better than you expected.

Thus your feelings about yourself as a statistician may be clarified for you by the exam.

Your self-concept can change in a third way as well—through *doubt*. Sometimes an event can cause you to doubt your abilities or to reassess your interests. College students who change majors often undergo periods of doubt about their self-concepts as they change majors.

Finally, your self-concept may undergo a *major alteration*. This occurs when you make a major change in your life. Religious conversions cause major alterations in self-concepts. Finding a new major in college that seems to fit your abilities often leads to new goals and new images of yourself in a newfound career. Being promoted at work or transferred to a new job location can cause you to alter your self-concept. Perhaps you have experienced a major change in your life recently. If so, you know how it can cause a major alteration in your self-concept.

## LOW SELF-ESTEEM

Closely related to your self-concept is a more general feeling about your self-worth called your self-esteem. Your self-esteem is your attitude about your overall self. People who have low self-esteem do not value themselves very highly. In fact, McCroskey and Wheeless (1976) suggest that "people with low self-esteem lack confidence in their ability . . . and tend to accept other people's views readily be-

---

Here's a list of words that describe people. Look them over and then of the three words in each set, circle the one that best describes you.

1. *enterprising, affable, anxious*

2. *confident, tactful, kind*

3. *hot-tempered, cool, warm*

4. *withdrawn, sociable, active*

When you are finished, you should have four words circled.

Now go through the list again and underline the words that your parents would choose if they were describing you.

As I mentioned earlier in the chapter, how you see yourself is a function of how others see you. If you noted any discrepancies when scoring yourself compared to guessing how your parents would score you, ask yourself why. Do you believe one thing about yourself but act in another way?

cause they consider their own views to be of less value. . . ." (pp. 130–131). Goss et al. (1978) found a strong correlation between students' self-esteem and their levels of communication apprehension. People with high communication apprehension (stage fright) tended to have low self-esteem. Thus, the more unsure you are about yourself, the more susceptible to influence you will be, and the more concerned you will be about your communication skills.

Problems with low self-esteem manifest themselves in self-fulfilling prophecy. This refers to the phenomenon in which people behave according to how they label themselves. Thus, if you see yourself as a poor public speaker, you will communicate like one. If you believe you have never been good at math, you might have extra trouble mastering a statistics course. In contrast, if you apply positive labels to yourself, you might perform accordingly. For instance, you may be able to develop a better method of filing if you believe you are a well-organized worker. In any case, the label given you can determine how you act. Thus, we need to be careful how we label ourselves and others. People often try to live up to their labels, even those that are inappropriate.

## IMPROVING YOUR SELF-ESTEEM

Just about everyone can use an occasional boost in self-esteem. In fact, it is healthy to feel good about yourself, and you can accomplish this through three processes (Brooks, 1978): self-acceptance, accepting others, and choosing supportive people to interact with.

The first process, self-acceptance, is saying to yourself, "I'm OK." It is the process of acknowledging your own worth because you are human and have human feelings. You are important—this is something that I try to remind my children of from time to time. The ability to say, "I'm OK, and that's what matters the most," is one of your best defenses against mental depression.

The second process is accepting others, that is, assuming that they are OK too. The image that you have of other people often affects how you communicate with them. If you feel that "the world is out to get me," you will show that attitude in your dealings with people. Most people don't like being treated suspiciously. In order not to invite such dislike, you can assume that other people are friendly and worth knowing. By assuming that others are acceptable, you may realize that you are acceptable as well, thus enhancing your own self-esteem. In this way, acceptance of others and acceptance of yourself work together. So, unless you know for sure that a particular person should be avoided, you should approach all people in a positive manner.

The third process for improving your self-esteem is choosing supportive people to interact with. This means that you actively

You see what you are ready to see. What do you see here? Answer in Appendix A on page 290. (Photo courtesy of the Norman Transcript.)

search for those people whom you enjoy being around. Make friends with those who will listen and be sympathetic to your feelings. But be sure that you find people who can help you with accurate assessments of your self-concept as well. If you surround yourself with uncaring "yea-sayers," who offer no critical advice but only false praise, you might end up worse than you started. Whatever you do, be realistic in choosing your friends.

## Perception

A number of years ago, a controversial football game was played between Dartmouth and Princeton. During the game, many fouls occurred; some were called by the officials, others were not. At the end of the game, the fans from both sides of the stadium were upset, each side accusing the other team of cheating.

Because of the intensity of the game, two researchers (Hastorf and Cantril, 1954) surveyed the fans about their feelings. Using questionnaires and film playbacks, Hastorf and Cantril found that Dartmouth fans saw many more fouls committed by Princeton

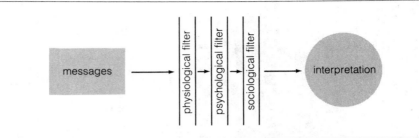

**Figure 5.1** Perceptual Filters

players than did the Princeton fans, and vice versa. Given the conflicting reports of the game, you might wonder if they all saw the same game. What happened?

The answer to this question lies in the perceptions of the fans. No doubt, there were uncalled fouls by each team. But the fans, armed with personal biases and expectations, saw only what they wanted to see.

By definition, perception is making sense out of what you see, hear, smell, taste, and touch. Perception is part of the decoding and interpretation stages of the communication model in Chapter 1. Perception not only operates in football games, it operates in communication as well.

## FILTERS

The biases and expectations found in perception are governed by three personal filtering systems: physiological, psychological, and sociological. Figure 5.1 illustrates these three filters.

The physiological filter includes the five senses, the central nervous system, the brain, and so on. The psychological filter contains your attitudes, feelings, emotions, and so forth. The sociological filter represents your cultural background, values, basic beliefs, and so on. As a receiver, you interpret messages according to your filters. Even though everyone has these three filters, it is impossible for everyone to see the same thing in every instance because the contents of their filters vary. Thus, as long as people have different experiences recorded in their filters, they will have different perceptions.

## SELECTIVE PERCEPTION

Because information is filtered before it is interpreted, perception is selective. Some information gets through the filters; some does not. Selective perception, then, is simply choosing what you want to see as you witness an event such as a football game. Because perception is selective, it is necessarily biased. The fans at the football game saw what fit their filters. They did not see contradictory information.

Selective perception usually involves two subtle tendencies that most people overlook. One is called closure; the other, familiarity. Let's consider each.

*Closure* means that we tend to see things as complete wholes rather than incomplete configurations. With the smallest amount of data, we make major inferences about the whole. The following figures illustrate this point.

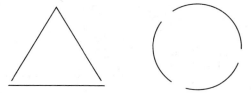

Most people see the figures as a triangle and a circle. Yet neither is presented in its complete form. *We* do the completing.

*Familiarity* means that we identify input as representatives of things with which we are familiar.

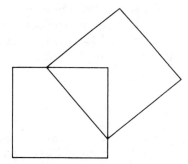

In the preceding figure, what do you see? Two overlapping squares? Could there be three figures, all irregular in shape? Since we are more familiar with squares than we are with odd-shaped figures, we perceive two squares.

Taking our analysis of perception a step further, we discover that over time we develop habits of perception that make it diffi-cult to objectively analyze such tasks as:

What do you see here? Did you read this as "Paris in the Spring"? Did you notice the duplication of *the*? Many people don't. The reason is that you probably know the expression and therefore ignore the improper grammar. If you have never heard of the expression, you might more readily notice the grammatical error.

What do you see in the following shapes?

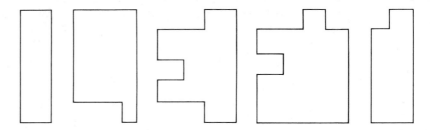

Depending on how you organize the figure-ground relationship of the illustration, you will or will not see the word *LEFT*. Now that you have the knowledge (internal information) of the preceding illustrations, you should not make the same mistakes again. That is, of course, if your memory serves you correctly on your next encounter.

These exercises are designed to show how normal people have perceptual biases that lead them to expect particular ideas. It is amazing how many people "fall" for these exercises. All of us have biases, often without being aware of them.

F.Y.I.

Some researchers believe that your perceptions are dependent on your language. Thus, it is reasoned that because Eskimos have more than a dozen words for snow, they are better equipped to perceive actual differences in snow than are most English-speaking people (Whorf, 1956).

Likewise, professional photographers look at photographs and see many aspects of them that Grandmother overlooks as she thumbs through the family album.

This same effect would be true for architects, artists, and musicians as they survey buildings, paintings, and symphonies, respectively.

Obviously the more you are trained in a profession or hobby, the more critically you can perceive objects of your field.

B. Whorf, "Science and Linguistics," in *Language, Thought, and Reality*, ed. J. Carroll (Cambridge, Mass.: John Wiley and Sons, 1956).

## ATTITUDES AND VALUES

It is difficult to talk about perception without considering attitudes and values. Attitudes (part of the psychological filter) and values (part of the sociological filter) play significant roles in how you perceive ideas, messages, and other people.

Attitudes are commonly defined as your predispositions to respond favorably or unfavorably to ideas, objects, or people. Attitudes are evaluations. They are the internal opinions that you hold. They are usually thought of in terms of a positive-negative continuum. For instance, you might have a negative attitude toward conscription (the draft). At the other end, you might have a positive attitude about tennis. Your roommate may hate classical music; if you like that kind of music, this could affect when and where you play your classical music tapes and records.

Values are similar to attitudes, except that they are long-term standards of judgment that apply to many situations in your everyday life. You can have many attitudes (one for each topic of discussion), whereas you only need a small set of values. Examples of values

This sign is at the corner of Poplar and Magnolia. What's wrong with it? (Photo courtesy of B. Goss.)

What's wrong here? (Photo courtesy of B. Goss.)

would be honesty, fair play, self-preservation, frugality, and so forth. Each of these values can be used as standards through which you can assess the desirability of any act or idea. If you value fair play, for instance, then your dealings with people should reflect such a value. Cheating people would then be behaving inconsistently with your values.

Attitudes and values are important in how they influence perception. If you have a positive attitude about something, you will see the good qualities of the object and overlook what is bad about it. Thus, if you enjoy your sports car (a positive attitude), you might overlook the fact that repair bills are higher on such cars and good mechanics are hard to find. Likewise, if you dislike a professor, you might have trouble noticing his or her admirable qualities. Furthermore, it can be demonstrated that your attitudes affect your memory. For some reason, yet unknown, memories about positive things are easier to recall than memories of not-so-positive events. All in all, the stronger your attitudes and values, the more they will affect how you perceive your world.

# Needs

Communicators not only bring self-concepts and perceptions to the communication exchange, they bring needs as well. Needs are drives that motivate people to behave in particular ways. There are a lot of specific needs in your life, but rather than listing them, let's consider two popular theories about human needs.

## MASLOW'S HIERARCHY OF NEEDS

Abraham Maslow (1968) maintains that humans have five types of needs, arranged in a hierarchy. These needs are related to the biological and psychological welfare of the person. Figure 5.2 illustrates this hierarchy.

*Physiological* needs are for those things basic to life. You need food, water, oxygen, and so forth. Without these essentials, you cannot survive. *Safety* needs refer to things that make you secure, such as clothing, shelter, and so on. When people lock their doors before going to bed at night, they are responding to their need for safety. *Belonging* needs are related to your desires to feel wanted, to be a part of a group. The fourth type of need, *self-esteem,* refers to your wanting to feel important or worthy of respect. People want others to think favorably of them. The ultimate need is for *self-actualization.* This is a need to become all that you can. The need for self-actualization is the hardest to satisfy but the most important to the total self. Self-actualization is the ultimate in self-fulfillment.

Sometimes our perceptions of people hinder our actions. This is especially true when we deal with those who are different from us, such as the physically handicapped. For many nonhandicapped people, dealing with those who are blind, deaf, or confined to a wheelchair is an awkward task.

One special problem that occurs is when someone tries to help a handicapped person accomplish some task such as finding the library or locating the exit in a building. *How* you offer to help a handicapped person is important. Here are some suggestions:

1. Get consent to help before you boldly come to the rescue. ("May I help you?")

2. Ask exactly how to help. ("What is the best way for me to do this?")

3. Adopt a matter-of-fact attitude.

Helping a handicapped person is a nice gesture, but many handicapped people resent badly planned gestures on the part of those without such handicaps.

Three points are important to understand as you consider Maslow's hierarchy of needs. First, these five types of needs are ordered. Consequently, a person must be satisfying the lower needs before attending to the higher ones. A starving man is not likely to be interested in a self-help seminar or any other higher-order activity until he is fed. Likewise, a homeowner will install locks on the doors and

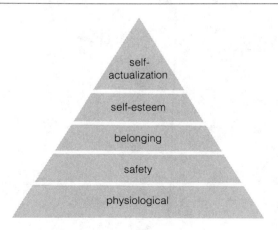

**Figure 5.2** Maslow's Hierarchy of Needs

windows of the house before investing in a swimming pool for the backyard. Second, it is not necessary to satisfy each lower need completely before working on higher ones. As long as a person is also taking care of the lower needs, then he or she can step up and work on a higher need. Finally, you should understand that the ultimate need is the top one—self-actualization. A fully developing person will be trying to fulfill this need, seeking experiences that expand and stretch his or her personal development, so that the potentials may be discovered. People who do not stretch themselves do not know their limits. But, as Maslow says, unsatisfied lower needs often interfere with the self-actualization need.

## SCHUTZ'S INTERPERSONAL NEEDS

Maslow's needs are primarily personal (related to the individual), while Schutz's needs are interpersonal (related to the self and others). According to Schutz (1958), people need to develop satisfying relationships with others. This produces three interpersonal needs: for inclusion, for control, and for affection.

*Inclusion* refers to the need to belong to groups. It is similar to Maslow's need for belonging. Apparently, people desire to be with others. We like to be affiliated. This need for inclusion varies in inten-

People find ways to meet their interpersonal needs even at an early age. (Photo courtesy of B. Goss.)

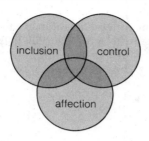

**Figure 5.3** Schutz's Interrelationship of Needs

sity from individual to individual, but our basic gregarious nature implies that each of us has some need for inclusion. The need for *control* springs from our wanting to be effective in our everyday lives. People expect to be effective—they want to have some social power. They do not want to be subject to pressures from others without being able to exert their own pressure. In other words, most of us enjoy being influential with others. Finally, the need for *affection* is related to the desire to love and to be loved. Like wanting to belong and wanting to feel influential, the need for love is strong. People who feel unloved or incapable of loving often have difficulty with intimate communication. Consequently, their social lives are underdeveloped and characterized by impersonal, formal relations with others.

Unlike Maslow's needs, the needs for inclusion, control, and affection are not hierarchically arranged. Instead, they are all inter-related (see Figure 5.3). You can be working on all three needs at once. You don't have to fulfill one before the others can be satisfied.

Whether you are considering Maslow's five types of needs or Schutz's three needs, both theories point out that human behavior is not without purpose. As Ruffner and Burgoon (1981) state, "People engage in certain behaviors because they are motivated to do so" (p. 35). Any understanding of the characteristics of the communicators must include the realization that needs are important to human communication. So who you are (your self-concept), how you view the world (your perception), and what motivates you (your needs) all contribute to how you will behave when you are communicating. As these things change, so will your communication behavior.

## Summary Propositions

At the beginning of the chapter, you learned that humans rarely communicate with the efficiency and accuracy of computers. Our self-concepts, perceptions, and needs all color how we interact with one another. If we think poorly of ourselves (low self-esteem), or if we

Not everyone feels the same amount of intensity for the three needs posited by Schutz. Some people rank affection as their highest need. Others prefer inclusion. Still others see control as their greatest need. How about you? Rank order the three needs for you:

_____ Inclusion

_____ Control

_____ Affection

Now think about your daily communication habits. Do they help you meet your needs? Or have you developed some habits that work against your needs? For instance, if you have been very busy lately, not talking much to others, this may be interfering with your need for inclusion. (That is, you may not be talking enough to others to feel part of the group.) Perhaps you have communication habits that are not very affection-oriented. If you are "all business" with others, they will in turn act that way with you, thus minimizing the exchange of affection that humans need.

have faulty perceptions about the speaker and the message, or if we have needs that are not being adequately met (needs for food, approval, and so on), we may not communicate very effectively. Even when communicating under the most crucial circumstances (such as working on an important technical project at work), you cannot expect people to communicate without error. Human error is present in all aspects of everyday communication, both at home and at work.

1. Your self-concept is how you feel about you as a person (it is your attitude about yourself).

2. You learn your self-concept through observing your actions and the reactions of others toward you.

3. Any particular encounter can cause one of four changes in your self-concept:

   a. Addition to your self-concept

   b. Clarification of your self-concept

   c. Doubt about yourself

   d. Major alteration in your self-concept

4. People who suffer from low self-esteem are susceptible to influence and anxious about their abilities to express themselves.

5. Perception is making sense out of what you see, hear, smell, taste, and touch.

6. How you interpret any message is a function of three perceptual filters:

   a. Physiological filter

   b. Psychological filter

   c. Sociological filter

7. Selective perception is characterized by closure and familiarity.

8. Your attitudes and values affect how you perceive the world.

9. Maslow suggests that everyone has five types of needs: physiological, safety, belonging, self-esteem, and self-actualization.

10. Schutz proposes three interpersonal needs: for inclusion, for control, and for affection.

11. Who you are (your self-concept), how you view the world (your perception), and what motivates you (your needs) all contribute to how you communicate.

## References

**Brooks, W.** *Speech Communication.* Dubuque, Iowa: W. C. Brown, 1978.

**Goss, B.; Thompson, M.; and Olds, S.** "Behavioral Support for Systematic Desensitization for Communication Apprehension." *Human Communication Research* 4(1978):158–163.

**Hastorf, A., and Cantril, H.** "They Saw a Game: A Case Study." *Journal of Abnormal and Social Psychology* 49(1954):129–134.

**Maslow, A.** *Toward a Psychology of Being.* New York: Van Nostrand, 1968.

**McCroskey, J., and Wheeless, L.** *Introduction to Human Communication.* Boston: Allyn & Bacon, 1976.

**Ruffner, M., and Burgoon, M.** *Interpersonal Communication.* New York: Holt, Rinehart & Winston, 1981.

**Schutz, W.** *FIRO: A Three-Dimensional Theory of Interpersonal Behavior.* New York: Holt, Rinehart & Winston, 1958.

**Whorf, B.** "Science and Linguistics." In *Language, Thought, and Reality,* edited by J. Carroll. Cambridge, Mass.: John Wiley, 1956.

# II

# PERSONAL AND PROFESSIONAL DYADIC COMMUNICATION

Think about the conversations that you have had recently. How many people, other than yourself, were involved? In some instances, you were talking with a group of people; but in the majority of cases, you probably were talking with only one other person. Of all the forms of face-to-face communication (dyad, small group, and public speaking), we usually spend most of our time conversing one-on-one.

This kind of one-on-one, dyadic communication is common in both your personal and your professional life. From a bull session with a friend to a phone call to your boss, you use dyadic communication skills daily.

In this part of the text, you will learn about the important elements of dyadic communication. Then you will read about two very special kinds of dyadic communication: conflict management and interviewing. To be a skillful communicator, you should know how to handle such situations.

# 6

# ELEMENTS OF DYADIC COMMUNICATION

**Impression Formation**
OICE
Attributing Causes
Public Impressions

■

**Interpersonal Sensitivity**
Mutual Trust
Mutual Understanding

■

**Defensive Communication**

■

**Interpersonal Relationships**
Stages of Development
Continuing a Relationship

■

**Summary Propositions**

■

**References**

■

Communication can take place between two people, in groups, or in public meetings. When it occurs between two people, it is called dyadic communication. Over time, two people can develop a very close relationship, and their communication can become quite intimate. However, not all dyadic communication is intimate communication. Likewise, not all dyadic relationships are personal. Some are professional. Dyadic communication, then, varies in terms of intimacy and in terms of whether it occurs in your personal or your professional life. One common factor in all dyads, though, is that they depend on communication. Without communication, it is difficult to establish, maintain, and/or change a relationship. Communication and relationships seem to go together.

Building relationships through dyadic communication depends on several interpersonal skills. Whenever people engage in dyadic communication, they form impressions of one another, they display varying amounts of interpersonal sensitivity, and they sometimes become defensive with each other.

## Impression Formation

In your personal and professional lives you have contact with many different people. Some you know well, others you know hardly at all. With all of them, however, you are forming impressions of what they are like. You have an idea (impression) of each person at work, of your neighbors, of your fellow members at church, and of your colleagues on your softball team. Likewise, those people are forming impressions about you. So whether you are dealing with a friend or with a client, impressions are forming.

How do people form impressions of you? What do they look for? Forming impressions is a continuing process that appears to have four steps. I call this OICE.

## OICE

OICE stands for observing, inferring, classifying, and expecting. Each is a separate step in impression formation.

**OBSERVING (O)** This is the initial data-gathering step in forming impressions of others. You watch others in action, and they watch you. People watching is a common pastime at football games, in shopping centers, at meetings, and at home. Wherever there are people, there are people watching.

What do people look for when they watch you? Two things are generally noticed: (1) how you look, and (2) how you behave. Your physical appearance (clothing, hair style, posture, physique, and so forth) provides evidence for others as they form impressions about you. Your actions (how you talk, walk, and move about the room) can also indicate things about your personality. Even your laugh can be used as evidence in forming impressions of you. In fact, from a communication standpoint, your verbal and nonverbal communication behaviors serve as clues to your personality. Consequently, it is a good idea to be in control of your communication behavior when you want to impress people in certain ways. For instance, you may have a nervous habit that distracts those who are listening to you. Perhaps you are a foot bobber when you cross your legs while sitting. Maybe you have a strained voice that is not clearly audible. You might even (as many people do) develop places to scratch that don't really itch. Whatever the nervous habit, it could be sending undesirable messages to your audiences. Fortunately, though, people observe all of your actions, not just your nervous acts.

**INFERRING (I)** This is the second step in impression formation. People take the data observed and then guess what those data mean. In impression formation, inferences are guesses about the reasons that people do what they do. For instance, you might be at a shopping mall and you observe a young man running toward an exit door. You might infer that he is running because he is late for an appointment, or you might think that he is chasing someone that you didn't see. Perhaps he just robbed a store and is fleeing the scene of the crime. All of these reasons are inferences. Until you investigate further, you cannot know for sure why the young man is running.

Why do people make inferences about other people? Can't we simply observe other people and not jump to conclusions about their motives? Apparently, we can't. The reason that people make inferences is based in a fundamental assumption about human behavior. This assumption is that *human behavior is basically purposeful;* it is not pointless. When you do something, most people believe that you have a reason for doing so. Your behavior, then, is indicative of your motives. For instance, many people wear a particular style of clothing to project an image to others. Likewise, you may communicate in ways to project a favorable image. How you speak may reflect your upbringing, education, personal values, and so on. If you want people to think that you are happy, you should talk about happy ideas. If you talk about negative things, people might believe that you are a negative thinker. As actors do on a stage, you can present the image you want by playing the part correctly. Because others see your behavior as purposeful, they will interpret your behavior as reflecting your true self. People do play roles in life that help them project the image they want others to have of them. Erving Goffman (1959) called this your "presentation of self in everyday life."

**CLASSIFYING (C)** The third step in impression formation, after observing and inferring, is classifying. When you classify people, you fit them into categories. The purpose of classifying is to differentiate among different kinds of people. You must be able to tell the difference between friends and strangers, between co-workers and bosses, between intimate confidants and gossipers. People categories, then, are useful for understanding others and how to react to them. These categories are useful if they remain flexible. But if they become frozen or unchangeable, such as some stereotypes, then the categories can create interpersonal obstacles.

Psychologists call your personal classification system of people your "implicit theory of personality." This personality theory allows you to observe, to make inferences about, and to classify people. For instance, you might have a category in your theory for college professors. In this category can be such features as: wise, gray hair, boring, body odor, and so on. Whatever your list of features is for professors, your stereotype will determine what you look for when you encounter a professor. If you meet a professor that doesn't fit your current category, you may need to adjust the category to produce more realistic expectations.

**EXPECTING (E)** Once someone is classified, the impression formation process would seem to be complete. But it is not. The fourth step in impression formation is expecting. Impressions—once initiated through observing, inferring, and classifying—become the bases for predicting future behavior. Whenever you form an image of another, you will expect that person to behave accordingly. For instance, you may have an image of your best friend as "a wonderful person, but always late in getting things done." Consequently, you would not be very surprised to learn that your friend earned only a C in a course due to a couple of late papers. In fact, your image of your friend might even affect how you plan social events with him or her. If you are planning an outing together, you might ask your friend to meet you by, say, 7:30 when in fact you need to meet by 8:00.

Expecting, then, is an important part of impression formation. And the more two people know each other, the more accurate will be their expectations of each other. If you want to observe faulty expectations, watch the TV show called "The Newlywed Game." The show is based on the notion that newlyweds do not know each other well enough to accurately predict one another's answers. And it is the inaccuracy of prediction that makes the show entertaining.

Although it is difficult to know why people form impressions of one another, we know that they do. And when they do, they execute four steps: observing, inferring, classifying, and expecting. Impression formation occurs in all our interpersonal relationships. The people you work with have impressions of you. Your family members have impressions of you. About the only people who do not have impressions about you, specifically, are strangers.

## ATTRIBUTING CAUSES

Earlier I mentioned that people speculate about the motives for your behavior. In doing so, they are attributing causes to your behavior. Let me illustrate. Suppose that you are a nurse in a large metropolitan hospital. Normally, you are a cheerful person, with a ready smile for everyone. One day, however, you snap back at a patient. Later, the patient explains your behavior by saying to herself, "I think the nurse got up on the wrong side of the bed this morning." What kind of reason is that? Obviously, a trite one. More likely the patient believes in a more serious explanation for your actions. Perhaps the patient thinks that you don't like her, or that you had an argument with your spouse. Whatever the true reason, the patient will attribute a cause to your behavior.

Generally, there are two ways to attribute causes to people's behaviors (Kelley, 1973). The first is called the *disposition* approach. This is when you explain someone's behavior by referring to the personality of the person. You might believe that a certain woman acts that way because she is that kind of person. Your friend, Kris, may be part of the Big Brother–Big Sister program because that's the kind of person Kris is (generous, warm, loving). Whenever you refer to the personal nature of the individual as the main reason for his or her actions, you are using the disposition approach to attributing causes.

The second approach to attributing causes is called the *situation* approach. This is when behavior seems to be caused by the situation and not by the person. As people observe your behavior, they might believe that what you are currently doing is caused by external influences beyond your personal control. For instance, you may be angry because you just discovered that someone stole your car. Or you may have developed into a habitual smoker because everyone else smokes where you work, thus causing you to start. A politician arriving at an airport may stop to greet people because she feels obligated to do so in order to be reelected to office. A father may control his temper at work because he could lose his job, yet at home he becomes a yelling tyrant. In each of these examples, the situation (more than the person) seems to be determining the observed behavior.

After reviewing a few studies on attributing causes to undesirable behaviors, Lefrancois (1980) concludes that "when observing other people's behavior, we are most likely to make dispositional attributions; when observing our own, in many though not all cases, we are more likely to make situational attributions" (p. 580).

If Lefrancois is correct, we tend to blame others personally for their problems, but attribute our own troubles to extenuating circumstances.

How do you feel about this? Do you look for situational excuses to help explain your problems? Do you allow others the same privilege?

G. Lefrancois, *Psychology* (Belmont, Calif.: Wadsworth, 1980).

Whether they use the disposition approach or the situation approach, people at work and at home will attribute causes to your behavior. As long as your behavior is open for inspection, it will be interpreted by others. Those in highly visible, public jobs are especially vulnerable to such inspection and interpretation.

## PUBLIC IMPRESSIONS

People who work in the public eye—such as airline attendants, hotel employees, loan officers, consultants, politicians, agricultural extension agents—must be especially careful of the impressions they leave with the public. How they answer the telephone, how they drive the company cars, where they are seen during off hours, and how they dress, all contribute to their public impressions.

The reason that public impressions are so important is that when you work for an organization, people see you as the organiza-

Public officials like police officers are very cognizant of their public images. (Photo courtesy of B. Goss.)

tion. Thus the actions of a few can give the rest of the group a good or a bad reputation. How many unfavorable impressions have been formed about colleges based on the violent acts of a few students? Consider the public impression of a military base, or of a large industrial firm that has been tarnished by past unfortunate incidents. No matter how official your role may be in an organization, your behavior can be the public reflection of the organization. Thus, your behavior affects two impressions: of you personally, and of your organization.

Let's review. Impression formation follows four steps (OICE): observing, inferring, classifying, and expecting. All throughout the conversation, the people in the dyad are forming impressions of each other. In doing so, they look for what makes the other person "tick." They attribute some of the other person's behaviors to disposition, while attributing the rest to the situation. As a member of an organization, an individual's behavior influences not only others' impressions of the individual but also their impressions of the organization. Dyadic communication, then, is a continuous impression formation exercise. In order to form accurate impressions and to promote positive relationships, the communicators must have a certain amount of interpersonal sensitivity. And that is the next topic of discussion.

Look at this picture. What impressions do you have of the two men?

Why is the man on the left looking that way? What about the man on the right? What conclusions can you make about them? What seems to be going on here?

Obviously, your impressions of others will influence how you interact with them. If you were to meet either of these men, would you like him?

## Interpersonal Sensitivity

Successful dyadic communication depends on a certain amount of interpersonal sensitivity. Interpersonal sensitivity refers to the ability to communicate in ways that take into account the other person and help build relationships with that person. Being interpersonally sensitive means being other-oriented. People who assume an other-orientation set aside their own ideas and stratagems and focus on the needs and ideas of the other person. Insensitive communicators cannot do this; they interact with others selfishly, not paying much attention to the other person.

Interpersonally sensitive communicators realize that successful communication depends on their receivers understanding what they mean. The sensitive communicator, then, works hard to adjust his or her messages to fit the audience. To accomplish such adaptable communication, the communicators in a dyad need mutual trust and mutual understanding.

## MUTUAL TRUST

Mutual trust is a delicate matter. In most relationships it must be built, it cannot be assumed. A certain amount of trust is needed for people to grow closer together. And a certain amount of trust is needed for people to believe what each other says.

What is trust? Dictionaries define trust as confidence, believing, relying, and so on. In human relationships, trust is being willing to place your welfare in someone else's hands. When you go to the dentist, you trust the dentist's ability to repair your teeth. When you trust your parents, you believe that they will help you in time of need. Placing your welfare in someone else's hands, though, involves risks. This idea was made clear to me by the following story.

One sunny afternoon, a tightrope walker strung his rope across the edge of the great Niagara Falls. He then proceeded to cross the raging river on the rope. Soon a crowd formed to cheer him on. Having crossed the falls a half dozen times, he asked the crowd whether or not they thought he could do it again. They responded with a resounding "Yes!" "We believe you. We know you can do it," the crowd cried. At that point, he asked them if they thought he could cross the river with a chair strapped to his back. Again they exclaimed their support for him. Finally, he asked if anyone would be willing to sit in the chair strapped to his back as he crossed the falls. No one volunteered.

What happened? Why didn't anyone step forward? The crowd believed the man, but they didn't trust him. You see, trusting is believing plus investing. And investing in someone is risky. When you trust someone, you do so under the assumption that the other person will not "burn you." The crowd watching the tightrope walker believed in his skills but were unwilling to take the defenseless position of sitting in that chair as he crossed the raging waters.

Do you need that amount of trust in communication? Probably not. There are times when only a minimal amount of trust is needed. When you ask for assistance from a librarian, you don't need much trust, you need competent help. But when two friends are discussing very personal matters, they need to be able to trust one another so that fragile emotions are not shattered. Consequently, each different interaction calls for a different amount of interpersonal trust. But no interaction is devoid of trust altogether.

**BUILDING TRUST** Building trust depends on three skills: positive images of other people, honesty, and empathy. To say that you need *positive images* of other people is simply to affirm what was said in Chapter 5 about your attitude toward people. If you start with the assumption that people are friendly and worth knowing, you have the beginning of a trusting relationship. This implies that you must re-

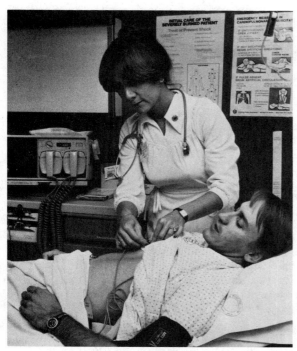

No matter what profession you are in, a certain amount of interpersonal trust is needed on the job. (Photo courtesy of the Norman Transcript.)

move suspicions from your mind and assume that the other person can be trusted. If you approach other people with a skeptical attitude, you will have difficulty establishing trust with people.

The next element required for building trust is *honesty*. The more you trust someone, the more honesty will occur. Likewise, the more you are honest with someone, the more you will be trusted. It may not always work that way, but that's the way it should be.

The opposite of honesty is deception. Deceptive communication, lying, is detrimental to building trusting relationships. If you discover that I have lied to you, I have betrayed your trust, and it will take a long time for me to win back your trust. Like anything else, honesty should be reciprocal if the relationship is to be long lasting. In other words, a trusting relationship requires that both parties be honest with each other. A relationship that is built on deception or on nonreciprocal honesty will not last.

Some people believe that honesty and self-disclosure are synonymous. They are not. It is quite possible to be honest without a great deal of self-disclosure. By definition, self-disclosure means sharing your intimate feelings so that your true self is revealed to someone else. If I do not reveal my innermost feelings to you, I am not necessarily being dishonest. Total self-disclosure is not essential for honest communication. Honesty is telling the truth, not "spilling my guts" to you about my feelings. If you require people to be totally self-disclosing with you, you will have few intimate relationships.

Some people believe that self-disclosure is good for your mental health. They go so far as to say that people need to self-disclose as often as they can. Recent research shows, however, that more self-disclosure does not lead to more happiness.

Chelune and Figueroa (1981) found that people who use self-disclosure too much are just as neurotic as those who refuse to self-disclose. The least neurotic people were those who were moderately self-disclosing. In other words, they were discriminating. They realized that self-disclosure has a time and a place, and that self-disclosure in itself does not produce good health.

A sensitive communicator is aware of the situation and the people involved. He or she takes into account these factors before self-disclosing. Apparently, knowing when to self-disclose and when not to is part of being a well-adjusted communicator.

G. Chelune and J. Figueroa, "Self-Disclosure Flexibility, Neuroticism, and Effective Interpersonal Communication," *Western Journal of Speech Communication* 45(1981):27–37.

Finally, *empathy* is a requirement for building trust. Empathy is the ability to "step into the other person's shoes." You are being empathetic when you can accurately express how the other person feels. Empathy is understanding. Furthermore, empathy does not require sympathy. Sympathy means sharing someone's feelings to the point where you agree with those feelings. It is quite possible to be empathetic with people without agreeing with their feelings. When my daughters become angry with me for punishing them, I can understand their feelings of dislike for me, but I will certainly not agree with them that I am dislikable or unfair.

## MUTUAL UNDERSTANDING

Interpersonal sensitivity depends not only on mutual trust, but on mutual understanding as well. By mutual understanding, I am referring to the degree of accuracy with which each person in a dyad can predict the other person's responses. Thus, two people understand each other when they can both predict accurately how one another will behave under certain circumstances.

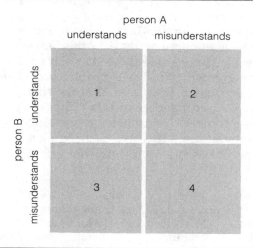

**Figure 6.1** Matrix of Understanding

Let's consider an example. Billy and Angela are friends who have been dating for about six months. Over time, they have come to understand each other through sharing ideas and opinions. For the most part, their relationship has been developing nicely. One Saturday afternoon, Billy comes over to Angela's house and suggests that they go have a pizza. Angela hates pizza, but Billy doesn't know that. Had Billy known that Angela hates pizza, he would have ignored the discount coupon for pizza in the newspaper and suggested that they go shopping instead. But he didn't. Now he has a problem. But notice who is in control of this communication situation. It is Angela. She knows that Billy is unaware of her dislike for pizza. So she can choose how to handle the situation.

The point of the story is that between Angela and Billy there is no *mutual* understanding. Angela understands the situation, but Billy doesn't. Whenever there is no mutual understanding, it is because one person understands while the other doesn't, or because neither understands. The first situation is one-sided understanding, and the second situation is mutual misunderstanding. Figure 6.1 shows that there are four outcomes of understanding between two people in a dyad. In square 1, both A and B understand; this is mutual understanding. In squares 2 and 3, one understands, the other doesn't. In square 4, both misunderstand; this can be chaos.

The importance of understanding in a relationship centers on control. When both understand (mutual understanding), then both parties share control over their situation. They can communicate with one another intelligently and not blindly. They can account for one another's feelings and, hopefully, avoid mishaps. When there is only one-sided understanding, then the misunderstanding person is at the mercy of the understanding person. This is especially true when the one who is understood by the other does not realize that he or she is predictable. Being able to predict someone gives you a lot of power in your relationship. If I can predict you (I understand you) and if you don't recognize that I can do this, then I am at a distinct advantage when we get together to talk. That's why mutual understanding is so much more desirable than one-sided understanding or mutual misunderstanding. Ideally, both parties should be able to predict each other, thus producing mutual understanding.

F.Y.I.

Apparently the way couples talk to each other affects how much they understand each other. Courtright et al. (1979) found that the more dominant the style of communication one spouse uses in a marriage, the less each partner is able to predict one another's feelings. In other words, if the husband or the wife is domineering, it can inhibit their ability to understand each other.

A home that is dominated heavily by one person may be a home wherein people fail to talk openly to discover one another's feelings. Maybe when one spouse says in frustration, "You don't understand me," he or she is really saying, "You dominate me too much." If a dominating style has such inhibitory effects on a couple's ability to accurately predict each other's feelings, then the dominator should reconsider his or her communication style.

J. Courtright et al., "Domineeringness and Dominance: Replication and Expansion," *Communication Monographs* 46(1979):179–192.

In essence, then, interpersonal sensitivity is more than being a nice person. It is something that is created between people. It depends on mutual trust and mutual understanding. Through mutual trust, both persons can have compassion for one another's welfare. Through mutual understanding, both people can share control of the relationship and deal with each other intelligently. The goal of any healthy, ongoing relationship should be the further development of mutual trust and mutual understanding.

## Defensive Communication

Most people realize that dyadic relationships do not always follow a smooth course. There are both good and bad times in interpersonal relationships. In the next chapter, I discuss conflicts in relationships, but for now I wish to look at how defensive communication can strain a relationship.

Jack Gibb (1961) proposes that when people communicate defensively, they start a vicious circle of defensiveness. That is, defensive remarks provoke defensive reactions. According to Gibb, defensive communication produces ill feelings and strains the relationship between the parties involved. He goes on to say that defensiveness causes people to be poor listeners. They lose the ability to empathize, and they look for ulterior motives. Defensiveness is characterized by passing judgment on others, giving orders, manipulating others, not caring, feeling superior, and knowing all the answers. Each of these feelings is selfish. And each one inhibits the growth of the relationship.

To combat tendencies toward defensive communication behavior, Gibb recommends that people replace defensive feelings with the following supportive behaviors:

1. *Be descriptive, not evaluative.* (Withhold judgments, describe what is happening, don't assess it.)

2. *Be problem oriented, not bossy.* (Don't give orders; try to resolve the situation cooperatively.)

3. *Be spontaneous, not manipulative.* (Go with the flow; don't always have a plan of attack.)

4. *Be empathetic, not neutral.* (Care for others' feelings; don't simply ignore them.)

5. *Be coequal, not superior.* (Be a colleague, not condescending.)

6. *Be tentative, not certain.* (Don't pretend that you know all the answers; show flexibility.)

By becoming more supportive and less defensive, according to Gibb, you will improve interpersonal relationships because people will trust you more and not fear you. Defensiveness promotes fear; supportiveness promotes trust.

Let's see how a conversation could be altered from a defensive one to a more supportive one. The following is a hypothetical conversation between two roommates. See if the conversation sounds familiar.

*Terry:* Hey, where is the spatula?

*Jan:* How do I know? You're the one who leaves it out all the time.

*Terry:* Oh yeah? You used it last night for dinner. Now where did you leave it?

> *Jan:* Look in the drawer. I always put things where they be-
> long.
>
> *Terry:* I already looked. If it was there, I wouldn't be asking
> you about it.
>
> *Jan:* Look again.

Have you ever taken part in such a conversation? Too often we let our emotions rule our speech. In the process, we start a vicious circle of defensiveness. Let's try this conversation again, but with a supportive perspective to it.

> *Terry:* Do you know where the spatula is?
>
> *Jan:* I thought it was in the drawer.
>
> *Terry:* I looked, but didn't find it.
>
> *Jan:* Maybe I can help you find it.

Isn't this one better? Notice how each person rephrased his or her remarks so that a defensive reaction could be minimized. If you want fireworks in a conversation, be defensive. If you want cooperation, talk supportively.

YOUR TURN...

In everyday life there will be countless instances of defensive communication. This kind of talk often occurs when people are fighting. In fact, for some people, this kind of communication is routine. Others would rather avoid such intensive communication.

How do you feel about interpersonal arguments? When two of your friends are engaged in a heated argument that is getting personal, do you step in and help them resolve it? Or is your approach one of keeping your mouth shut and letting them do battle?

Answer this question: What is the likelihood that you would actively enter an argument between friends to help settle the dispute?

_____ Very likely

_____ About 50-50

_____ No way; never

Obviously, your answer would depend on the topic, the intensity of the argument, and your relationship with the combatants—but what would you do most of the time?

Write here the reason you answered as you did: _____

_____

_____

_____

# Interpersonal Relationships

In your personal and professional lives, you are involved in many kinds of interpersonal relationships. They range from relationships with strangers to relationships with intimate confidants. And no two relationships are the same. Furthermore, positive interpersonal relationships don't just happen. They take time to create, and they are never finished in their development. Relationships are not static, they are constantly growing—sometimes for the better, other times for the worse. How a relationship grows depends on how the people involved get to know each other.

According to Miller and Steinberg (1975), whenever dyads form, the participants get to know each other through three sources of information. First, the individuals use cultural data (race, language spoken, status, and so forth) to make assumptions about each other. Second, they use sociological data (age, home town, place of employment, and so on). Third, they use psychological data (attitudes, career plans, personal problems). With these three kinds of data, people form impressions of each other.

As a relationship grows, however, the people depend less on the cultural and the sociological data and more on the psychological data. They become more personal, as evidenced by their talk. For instance, at the beginning of a relationship, people share "safe" information about themselves, such as where they work or live, or how many children they have. As the relationship matures, they feel comfortable sharing more intimate, psychologically based information. In fact, it is only when the dyad has transcended the preliminary stage of exchanging demographic data that the individuals are ready for more personal communication. In this sense, then, the nature of the communication (nonpersonal versus personal) determines the stage of development of the relationship.

Miller and Steinberg provide some useful insights into the relationship between communication behavior and interpersonal relationship stages. But their analysis is just the beginning.

## STAGES OF DEVELOPMENT

Altman and Taylor (1973) suggest that when people interact, they use both verbal and nonverbal behaviors in order to control the level of intimacy that they wish in a relationship. Consequently, strangers will restrict what they do and say, while close friends might be very unrestricted in their expressions.

To describe how communication differs at the various stages of development in a relationship, Altman and Taylor propose a four-stage process of developing relationships. The first stage is called *orientation*. This is the earliest stage of development, and it occurs most often with strangers. During the orientation stage, people are presenting favorable images, being polite (not offensive), withholding evaluations of each other, and being careful not to disclose too much personal data. Cautious, yet friendly, interaction might be the best way to describe this stage.

Stage two is the *exploratory affective exchange* stage. You are at this stage with many of your neighbors. During this stage, people interact more freely than before. They carefully let down their guards and begin interacting more spontaneously. They react to each other's remarks, and even evaluate each other a little. In this stage, people feel free to openly share opinions about the topic of discussion and about some aspects of one another's behavior. Still, though, the affection (both loving and attitudinal) is limited. The people are still exploring the boundaries of their relationship, so they must be friendly, caring, but not totally disclosing.

Stage three is the *affective exchange* stage. It is a direct outgrowth of stage two. You are in this stage with your best friends, those that you have known for some time. In this stage, conversations are freewheeling. There is more self-disclosure. Individuals criticize and praise one another regularly. There is also more physical touching and exchanging of affection.

The fourth and final stage is the *stable exchange* stage. This is the ultimate stage. It is also the one you have the fewest relationships in. In this stage is your relationship with your one best friend, your most intimate confidant. These relationships call for a lot of mutual trust and mutual understanding. In these relationships, communication is very efficient. Sometimes the people at this stage don't need to say much at all. This stage of a relationship has a high degree of predictability. The people know each other intimately.

It is important to realize that these four stages of development are not necessarily exclusive—you do not have to leave one stage completely before entering another one. In fact, during the development of a relationship many transitional times will have characteristics of two stages, until the transition is complete. But for the most part, you can tell how intimate a relationship is by observing the interaction and determining which stage the people are in. In this sense, the Altman and Taylor system is useful for sorting out your interpersonal relationships.

## CONTINUING A RELATIONSHIP

Have you ever been involved in a relationship that was doing you no good? Undesirable relationships are usually discontinued or repaired to make them more desirable. Fortunately, most of our relationships are desirable, though not equally so. What makes a relationship desirable? How do you know when to continue in a relationship and

Have you ever had trouble starting a conversation with a new acquaintance? Such awkwardness is common, but not incurable.

For initial contacts, Strain and Wysong (1978) make the following recommendations that center on asking questions:

1. After exchanging greetings, ask questions that focus on the other person. (For example, "I have been thinking about buying a new calculator. What kind do you have?")

2. Keep the other person talking with open-ended questions. ("What should I look for in a calculator?")

3. As the conversation develops, ask probing questions that call for more information. ("Where is the best place to buy calculators?")

Obviously, you should not bring up topics out of the blue. So it is a good idea to share some of your ideas about the topic before you inquire about your partner's ideas. The key, however, is to pursue each topic with questions. This stimulates the conversation, making the awkwardness of the initial encounter more bearable.

B. Strain and P. Wysong, *Communication Skills* (Reading, Mass.: Addison-Wesley, 1978).

when to quit? For most people, the answer lies in the interpersonal profit of the relationship.

By interpersonal profit, I mean the perceived benefits that you see in a relationship after you evaluate the costs and the rewards inherent in the relationship. Equity theorists suggest that people will remain in a relationship as long as the costs are less than the rewards (Walster et al., 1978; Homans, 1961; Thibaut and Kelley, 1959). When one person feels that he or she is paying too much to be a part of the relationship, if that cost exceeds the rewards derived from the relationship, then the person must choose whether or not to continue the relationship.

In order to maximize the benefits, people use communication to promote those things that make the relationship desirable. For instance, a couple may not want to "rock the boat" in their relationship, so they each choose to overlook one another's occasional faults. Business partners may adopt a very encouraging conversational style with each other, knowing that the success of their business depends, in part, on the goodwill between them. They may praise one another openly, and criticize gently. Likewise, two people who truly care for each other will help each other grow. When one person, however, feels that he or she is giving more than the other (higher cost), then the relationship can suffer. Consequently, people use communication behavior as a barometer for the relationship. By keeping track of how each person in the dyad talks with the other, you can keep track of the relationship.

One way to keep such track of a dyadic conversation is to listen for the frequency of the pronouns *we* and *us* compared to *you* and *me*. The collective pronouns (*we* and *us*) indicate a perceived unity in the speaker's mind, thus suggesting a close relationship. Wilmot (1979) found that when married couples wanted to show a united front, they talked about themselves as "we" rather than "she" and "he." Another way to test the quality of the relationship through observing the communication behavior is to look for the presence of supportive communication as opposed to defensive communication. You might also check for gestures of helping in a pair's communication behaviors. If the conversation between two people consists mainly of *telling* the other what to do, without ever *asking* the other for help or offering to help, then the relationship may be sagging. The degree of telling versus asking in a conversation can indicate the strength and desirability of the relationship.

In summary, relationships vary according to their respective levels of development. Early or young relationships will be characterized by more cultural and sociological information, while later relationships will include psychological data. Relationships seem to go through four stages, but never seem to be complete. If the communication behavior in the relationship indicates a togetherness, then the relationship is moving toward intimacy. If the communication behavior shows a detachment between the people involved, then the relationship may be dissolving. In either case, the communication behavior can serve as an indicator of the stage of the relationship.

## Summary Propositions

Dyadic communication takes place between two people. The more two people interact, the more their relationship can develop. As people interact, however, they are forming impressions of one another. The four stages of impression formation are observing, inferring, classifying, and expecting (OICE). Relationships grow as people develop favorable impressions of one another, and have mutual trust and mutual understanding. Defensive communication is a barrier to forming intimate relationships, and thus should be avoided. Finally, all relationships are growing (for better or for worse), and they can be described by stages. People will remain in a relationship if they perceive that it is interpersonally profitable to do so.

1. As people communicate, they build relationships, form impressions of one another, display varying amounts of sensitivity, and sometimes become defensive.

2. When people form impressions about others, they go through four stages of impression formation: observing, inferring, classifying, and expecting.

3. When trying to explain behavior, others use two methods of attributing causes: disposition and situation.

4. Interpersonal sensitivity refers to the ability to communicate in an other-oriented fashion.

5. Interpersonal sensitivity requires mutual trust and mutual understanding. Without them, communication proceeds blindly.

6. Defensive communication occurs when people have selfish motives and behave judgmentally.

7. Relationships are created as people interact, and they are subject to change over time.

8. Altman and Taylor indicate that relationships develop through four stages: orientation, exploratory affective exchange, affective exchange, and stable exchange.

9. The likelihood of continuing a relationship is dependent on the interpersonal profits of the relationship.

## References

**Altman, I., and Taylor, D.** *Social Penetration: The Development of Interpersonal Relationships.* New York: Holt, Rinehart & Winston, 1973.

**Chelune, G., and Figueroa, J.** "Self-Disclosure Flexibility, Neuroticism, and Effective Interpersonal Communication." *Western Journal of Speech Communication* 45(1981):27–37.

**Courtwright, J.; Millar, F.; and Rogers-Millar, E.** "Domineeringness and Dominance: Replication and Expansion." *Communication Monographs* 46(1979):179–192.

**Gibb, J.** "Defensive Communication." *Journal of Communication* 11(1961):141–148.

**Goffman, E.** *The Presentation of Self in Everyday Life.* Garden City, N.Y.: Doubleday, .1959.

**Homans, G.** *Social Behavior: Its Elementary Forms.* New York: Harcourt, Brace, & World, 1961.

**Kelley, H.** "The Processes of Causal Attribution." *American Psychologist* 28(1973):107–128.

**Lefrancois, G.** *Psychology*. Belmont, Calif.: Wadsworth, 1980.

**Miller, G., and Steinberg, M.** *Between People*. Palo Alto, Calif.: Science Research Associates, 1975.

**Strain, B., and Wysong, P.** *Communication Skills*. Reading, Mass.: Addison-Wesley, 1978.

**Thibaut, J., and Kelley, H.** *The Social Psychology of Groups*. New York: John Wiley, 1959.

**Walster, E.; Walster, G.; and Berscheid, E.** *Equity: Theory and Research*. Boston: Allyn & Bacon, 1978.

**Wilmot, W.** *Dyadic Communication*. Reading, Mass.: Addison-Wesley, 1979.

# 7

# CONFLICT
# MANAGEMENT

**Types of Conflict**
Intrapersonal Conflicts
Interpersonal Conflicts

■

**Intensity of Conflicts**
Ego-involvement
Frustration
Coping Abilities

■

**Managing Conflicts**
Joint Problem Solving
Negotiation and Bargaining
Mediation
Arbitration
Force

■

**Family Conflicts**
Healthy Family Fighting

■

**Summary Propositions**

■

**References**

■

A pervasive, but sometimes disheartening, fact of everyday life is the presence of conflict. We are all involved in conflicts, both within ourselves and between people. Whenever people get together, there are bound to be some differences of opinion. And when these differences become acute, a conflict begins.

You cannot resolve conflicts by avoiding them. Avoiding a conflict only postpones the problem. What you need is to be able to manage your conflicts, and to do so in satisfying ways. To help you understand conflict management, this chapter includes information on types of conflicts, intensity of conflicts, managing conflicts, and family conflicts. After reading this chapter, you should better understand how to cope with conflicts in both your personal and your professional life.

## Types of Conflict

Conflicts can be categorized into two major types: intrapersonal conflicts and interpersonal conflicts. Intrapersonal conflicts are those that occur within the individual. You are having an intrapersonal conflict when you are struggling with a decision, or trying to resolve a contradictory set of beliefs and attitudes. In contrast, interpersonal conflicts occur between people. They are characterized by an intensive disagreement between two or more people.

### INTRAPERSONAL CONFLICTS

An intrapersonal conflict can occur when someone is struggling to make a difficult decision. The conflict occurs because a choice must be made. These choices can be frustrating because the alternatives may be equally desirable or undesirable. Intrapersonal conflicts occur most often in important decisions. The more important the decision, the greater the potential conflict can be. In just about all intrapersonal conflicts, the struggle is somewhat painful. That's why people occasionally avoid making decisions—to avoid the pain of conflicts.

Intrapersonal conflicts can appear in many forms. Sometimes two positive alternatives can cause trouble. For instance, looking over a menu in a fine restaurant, you might discover two entrees that you really like. You could order both entrees and avoid the conflict, but such gluttony may be beyond your normal style and your pocketbook. If you choose one, you will miss the other. That's one of the problems with such conflicts: Choosing one alternative means that you can't have the other. Other conflicts develop from two negative alternatives. For instance, you might have to choose between going to the dentist or suffering through a toothache with aspirin as your only medication. No matter which you choose, some pain will be involved.

Whether the choices are positive or negative, the conflict arises because a decision must be made. Once the decision is made, the conflict subsides. Unfortunately, your decision may induce dissonance. Dissonance is a state of intrapersonal discomfort caused by making a difficult decision. Dissonance occurs after your decision. What causes dissonance is the thought of what you are missing because you chose one alternative rather than the other. In the restaurant example, once you receive your entree, you might wonder about the other one as you quietly eat your chosen meal. Likewise, in the waiting room at the dentist's office you might wonder whether the toothache might have ceased if you had simply continued to take aspirin. In either case, you are experiencing some postdecision regret. In order to relieve yourself of this kind of regret, you can focus on the good qualities of the choice you made. In the restaurant, you might comment on how good your meal is and how glad you are that you ordered it. In the dentist's office, you might congratulate yourself on mustering up enough nerve to go to the dentist. Whatever you do, you need to justify your decision, so that you can avoid dissonance.

Intrapersonal conflicts and dissonance go together. The more conflict you experience in making a decision, the more dissonance you can expect. And the more dissonance you encounter, the more you need to be ready to justify your behavior. In many ways, just making a decision can be painful. As you will see later in this chapter, people vary in their abilities to cope with conflicting alternatives.

## INTERPERSONAL CONFLICTS

Conflicts that occur between people can be more painful than conflicts arising from a tough decision. By definition, an interpersonal conflict is when two or more people sharply disagree about something. As Verderber (1978) observes, interpersonal conflicts develop when people have a "clash of opposing attitudes, ideas, behaviors, goals, and needs" (p. 123). Interpersonal conflicts happen in our dyads, in our small groups, and in the larger groups that we belong to. Whenever there are a number of people with different ideas, there is the potential for conflict. But for a conflict to actually arise, two or more people with discrepant feelings must encounter each other. Unless they get together and discover their differences, an interpersonal conflict is not likely to surface.

**YOUR TURN...**

Every day you make on-the-spot decisions concerning how to react to something that someone says or does. How you react can determine how many friends you have. If you choose the wrong reaction, you might destroy some of your important relationships.

Below are three situations, each requiring a strategic response from you. Read each example and circle the response that you would most naturally choose.

1. Your best friend has decided to marry a person that you think is all wrong for him or her. Furthermore, you are suspicious of the reasons for the marriage proposal. What should you do?

   a. Tell your friend how you feel.

   b. Keep your mouth shut and ignore your feelings.

   c. Mention your displeasure in a humorous way.

   d. Support their decision to marry.

2. Someone at work is an overbearing, disruptive, and antagonistic person who has everyone on edge. Since it used to be a happy place of work you should:

   a. Quit your job, even though you like it.

   b. Pressure the boss to straighten out the situation.

   c. Go directly to the offender and explain your feelings.

   d. Pretend that person doesn't exist and do your job.

3. A friend of yours has just insulted you with an offensive joke. The others around you laugh at the joke. How should you react?

   a. Tell the person then and there that you did not like the joke.

   b. Smile politely, then forget it.

   c. Seek other friends.

   d. Tell the person later that you were offended.

Interpersonal conflicts occur in two forms: spontaneous interpersonal conflicts (SIC) and major interpersonal conflicts (MIC). An SIC arises when people have a temporary disagreement. These situations develop quickly and the conflict is immediately brought out in the open. How you handle an SIC is important, because if it is not settled quickly, it can develop into a major conflict. Most of us, when confronted with a spontaneous interpersonal conflict, want to react defensively, but such an approach may only prolong the problem. Let me illustrate.

Suppose that you are in charge of shipping for a business that services a number of large firms. You are busy working on some reports when Mary Cline, vice-president in charge of materials for a large manufacturing firm, calls to complain about some late shipments. When you pick up the phone, you do not know who is calling or what the call is about. Being caught off guard, you are at a disadvantage. You must be ready to handle Cline's complaint so that the conflict can be settled.

Perhaps the fastest way to resolve a spontaneous interpersonal conflict is to try to understand one another's needs and feelings. Conflicts arise from frustrations. Frustrations occur when someone is having difficulty attaining a goal. In order to cope with an SIC, then, you should learn from the other person what he or she wants out of the situation. In Cline's case, she is angry and wants the materials sent promptly. In order to help her with her frustrations, you must uncover her needs and feelings about the problem. This calls for empathetic listening. A defensive reaction will only aggravate the conflict.

I am not suggesting total acquiescence on your part in an SIC. But I am suggesting that the sooner you remove the battle lines, the sooner you can work out a solution. People who manage spontaneous interpersonal conflicts (SIC) well know how to get to the basic frustrations without excessive ventilation of emotions or unnecessary defensiveness. Identifying early the heart of the issue speeds up finding a solution.

On-the-spot interpersonal conflicts such as the one just mentioned are usually short-lived and not necessarily damaging to a relationship. Other conflicts are more serious. They are called major interpersonal conflicts (MIC) because they are more fully developed than an SIC. An MIC is a conflict that has been festering. Due to the long gestation period (building up over time) an MIC is harder to resolve than an SIC. Furthermore, this kind of conflict can reappear if not fully resolved. An MIC, because of its intensity and gestation, can be most detrimental to your interpersonal relationships. People can have spontaneous interpersonal conflicts regularly and still maintain a healthy relationship. But major interpersonal conflicts that remain unresolved can cause a relationship to dissolve. Since these conflicts require more permanent solutions, and since they are

Sometimes conflicts are obvious because they are out in the open. Other times, they are covert—still festering in the minds of the people. When a conflict is brewing, you can usually tell by noticeable changes in the participants' communication behaviors.

Here are some conflict indicators to look for if you suspect your group is having some interpersonal conflicts:

1. *Lack of levity.* If the group normally jokes around and laughs together, a change in the level of fun can indicate a conflict developing in the group.

2. *Less interactive communication.* Sometimes groups, when experiencing conflict, become more formal in style. People interact less and give more orders.

3. *Increase in rumors.* Rumors are a good measure of problems. Nothing spreads faster than gossip. If the group is having problems, rumors will fly.

4. *Increase in memos.* In work groups especially, the more trouble that a group is having, the more management feels the need to take control. New policies surface, more actions are recorded in writing, and so forth.

5. *Avoidance of normal channels.* When there is a problem in a group, the people involved will avoid dealing with each other. They will simply "work around" one another.

6. *Increase in physical separation.* This is a nonverbal sign of trouble. Various members of the group may take longer breaks, or not show up for meetings, or work behind closed doors.

7. *Decrease in productivity.* If there are problems among the group members, these problems will inhibit the amount of work completed. If you notice a drop in productivity, check for an interpersonal conflict.

the hardest to resolve, the rest of this chapter will be devoted to major interpersonal conflicts.

## Intensity of Conflicts

Conflicts, of all kinds, vary in intensity. Some are simply more heated than others, but all major interpersonal conflicts have a certain amount of "steam" associated with them. Exactly how much inten-

**Figure 7.1** High versus Low Ego-involvement

sity a given conflict will have is a function of three factors: ego-involvement, frustration, and coping abilities.

## EGO-INVOLVEMENT

Compared to an MIC, arguments about minor irritations in life are not likely to be very intense. Arguments about strongly held attitudes, beliefs, and values, however, can be very intense. The intensity of an MIC is often determined by the ego-involvement of the participants. The more involved each person is with the issue, the stronger the MIC will be. In general, ego-involvement refers to the degree to which a person holds strongly to an attitude. People who are highly ego-involved hold fast to one position and reject most other points of view. In contrast, people who have a lot of tolerance for other positions are not too highly ego-involved in their own positions.

Figure 7.1 shows an example of two different people, one who is highly involved and another who is not highly involved. As you can

**Figure 7.2** Two Different, Highly Ego-involved Positions

see, there are seven possible positions regarding gun control on each scale. Each person's position is noted by the X on the scale. The other positions that are acceptable are marked A, while the rejected positions are marked R. N marks a position that is neither accepted nor rejected; that is, the person is noncommittal on these positions. Obviously, Alex is considerably more ego-involved with his position than Louise is with hers. Alex rejects more positions than the combined number of those he accepts or is noncommittal about. For Louise, the opposite is true. Her range of acceptable positions is broad, while she rejects only one position. On the topic of gun control, then, Alex is highly ego-involved while Louise is not. Yet they both hold the same position (X).

In most major interpersonal conflicts, however, the participants do not hold the same positions. Their opinions usually differ considerably. If both are like Alex, then they will hold their different positions with great vigor. Figure 7.2 shows such a case. In this situation, a wife and a husband disagree about methods of punishing children. The wife thinks spanking is good; the husband does not. But more importantly, both of them are highly ego-involved in their respective positions. Thus, any discussion of spanking is likely to produce an MIC.

## FRUSTRATION

A second factor that influences the intensity of a major interpersonal conflict is the degree of frustration felt by the participants. Frustration occurs when some form of goal-directed behavior is thwarted. You feel frustrated when you don't seem to be making any progress. Perhaps you are in your car, hurrying to meet someone, and you are stopped at an intersection by a red light. As the light turns green, the car in front of you stalls. Since the car behind you is too close, you can't go around the stalled car. Sound familiar? That is frustration.

Psychologists report that as people become more frustrated they become more aggressive (Lefrancois, 1980). In an MIC, then, high levels of frustration will induce highly belligerent arguments. People will lose their composure, yell, and say things they later regret. This, however, is often beneficial since such temper outbursts can have a cathartic effect. However you look at it, there seems to be a direct relationship between the amount of frustration felt and the intensity of the MIC.

Here's a popular form of frustration. Do you recognize this puzzle? (Photo courtesy of B. Goss.)

## COPING ABILITIES

The third element that affects the intensity of a conflict is the ability of each person to cope with conflict in general. People vary in their abilities to cope with conflict. Some people handle conflicts well; others do not. A person who cannot handle conflict effectively will act in one of three ways: (1) avoid conflicts by becoming reticent (not talking); (2) avoid conflicts by becoming acquiescent (agreeing with everything); or (3) aggressively start arguments (disagree with nearly everything). The first two strategies are avoidance patterns that tend to ignore the conflict rather than resolve it. The third coping strategy is one of overreaction (sometimes called premature defensiveness).

All of these coping strategies are dysfunctional, because they tend to escalate the intensity of the conflict. The first two approaches (reticence and acquiescence) intensify the conflict in a passive manner. By avoiding conflict, you permit it to fester and grow stronger, even though it may not have been completely aired yet. A disagreement that is left to brew can grow into an interpersonal monster before it finally comes out in the open. The third method (overreaction) is an active strategy for fueling an MIC. This technique of fighting back, however, is nondiscriminating—the individual lashes out at any remark that may be threatening. Consequently, this technique encourages the other person to respond in kind. Such a vicious argument can ultimately spiral into irrelevant issues, losing sight of the original issue. In the next section, you will learn about more effective coping strategies.

Psychologists indicate that people have at least two ways in which they can ventilate frustration. Coon (1977) reports that people aggressively display frustration by either direct or displaced aggression.

*Direct aggression* is attacking the source of your conflict (for example, complaining to a waiter in a restaurant about the service, or yelling at your children for being too noisy).

*Displaced aggression* is venting your anger on an uninvolved third party (for example, becoming moody around others, or honking unnecessarily at other drivers).

Apparently, when frustration needs venting, people choose the nearest target, even if the object of wrath doesn't deserve it. Next time you lose your temper with someone, be sure that you are attacking the right person and are not overstating your case due to your temporary frustration level.

D. Coon, *Introduction to Psychology* (St. Paul, Minn.: West Publishing, 1977).

In summary, then, the intensity of a conflict depends on the people involved. The more ego-involved each person is, the more that involvement can stimulate the intensity of the conflict. Also the more frustration people feel, the more their conflicts will be intensified. Finally, how the participants cope with conflict in general can contribute to the intensity of the particular conflict.

## Managing Conflicts

When a major interpersonal conflict arises, it must be managed, brought under control. Unmanaged conflicts continue and create more problems later. In order to manage your conflicts, you need to know your options.

John Keltner (1970) proposes five strategies for managing conflicts. They range from joint problem solving, which is a communication-based approach, to force, which is a warlike approach. The main goal of all of the strategies is a decision, a solution to the conflict.

### JOINT PROBLEM SOLVING

Keltner recommends that, whenever possible, people should solve their interpersonal problems through deliberation. They should meet and discuss the problem and then attempt a mutually agreeable solution. When individuals come together to solve problems, the solutions they produce should be joint decisions. That is, a solution developed through deliberation should be shared and approved by each person. If the conflict involves more than two people, the solution should have the unanimous support of all those involved, if possible. Sometimes, however, this is not possible. But the more numerous the people who endorse the solution, the more the solution will be supported when it is enacted later. Solutions agreed upon by all parties have the greatest chance of succeeding.

### NEGOTIATION AND BARGAINING

If the parties in conflict cannot discuss the problem and arrive at a mutually satisfying agreement, then some form of negotiation and bargaining will be needed. Notice that negotiation and bargaining imply trade-offs. In trading, you give up something you want in order to get something else that you want. Resolving conflicts by trading is obviously not as desirable as reaching a mutually satisfying solution (that does not require trading), but in many conflicts, this is the best approach.

## MEDIATION

When negotiations have failed to produce an acceptable solution, then some form of mediation is needed. The conflicting parties bring in a third person who will help them reach a solution. The mediator serves as a moderator, one who coordinates the negotiation process between the parties without taking sides or favoring one solution over another. As Keltner notes, the mediator has no power to make decisions. He or she simply calls together the conflicting parties and promotes an exchange of communication. Thus, the mediator should have the necessary discussion skills to guide the negotiations toward a workable agreement.

## ARBITRATION

"When the parties are unable to settle a dispute through their own processes or through the assistance of a mediator, they may then turn by mutual agreement to a third person and ask him to make a decision for them" (Keltner, 1970, p. 251). An arbitrator is called in when an impasse has been reached. Unlike the mediator who only guides the decision-making process, the arbitrator is empowered to actually make the decision for the conflicting parties. It is important, then, that the arbitrator be a person who is trusted by those on both sides of

Sometimes force is the only apparent way to solve a conflict. (Photo courtesy of Hap Stewart/Jeroboam, Inc.)

the disagreement. By the time they feel the need for an arbitrator, they will be at the point of highest frustration. Turning over the decision to an arbitrator is a critical step, because it implies that the parties in conflict are willing to forefeit some of their power in the matter. Arbitration, then, is one of the last resorts.

## FORCE

If all else fails, those in conflict can resort to force. Either side can try to beat the opponent through brute strength, either physically or socially. Labor strikes are an example of using force to obtain a decision. War is another example. Cutting off supplies and financial resources is another form of force. The main goal of force is to create enough discomfort in the opposite party so that he or she will be willing to meet the demands. Whenever force is used, the strongest side usually wins. So force is designed to match strength against strength. As a means of resolving conflicts, it is, obviously, very painful.

In most of your interpersonal relationships, you should not need force to resolve conflicts. In fact, American society and its laws are designed to discourage force. We pride ourselves on being able to resolve problems through peaceful means. Furthermore, we believe that peacefully derived solutions will be more lasting than forcefully obtained ones. Joint problem solving, and not force, is seen as your best alternative to managing conflicts.

Have you ever suffered the frustration of not getting a satisfactory response to a complaint you made to a company? Knowing how to complain is an art. Some people complain by letting off steam—they simply get angry, make idle threats they can never keep. Although getting mad may make you feel good, it may not be a good communication strategy.

When you have a legitimate complaint to make to someone, use the following steps:

1. Be specific about the problem.

2. Don't make idle threats.

3. Ask for specific commitments.

By being specific and avoiding poorly conceived threats, you inform the complaint handler that you are in control of the complaint. In asking for specific commitments, you should inquire: what will be done, when it will be done, and how you will know when it is done. Don't settle for, "We'll see what we can do for you."

# Family Conflicts

For some reason the family is a common setting for conflicts. Yet for many of us our family members are the most important people in our lives. Thus, you might think that families would be immune from conflicts, but they are not. In fact, many people report that they fight with family members more often than they argue with friends, associates at work, and strangers. Why?

According to Turner (1970), most serious conflicts occur when the parties have an established relationship with one another. In the family, these relationships can be quite intimate and last for a lifetime. With strangers your relationships are very temporary at best. With the people you work with or go to school with, your relationships can be defined by boundaries of work and time. You can leave work, but it is harder to leave a family.

When a disagreement occurs between casual acquaintances or between strangers, the simplest response for both parties would be one of indifference. Each simply doesn't care that much about such disagreements. In the family, however, this option of indifference is not so available. Conflicts in families are painful because the combatants are bound together in an important relationship. If indifference dominates the handling of conflict, the relationship suffers. In fact, one way to determine whether or not a relationship is in the process of dissolving is to see if the people deal with their conflicts via indifference. Although the indifferent reaction may look peaceful, the underlying feeling of not caring spells disaster for the relationship. Only two totally apathetic individuals could maintain a relationship wherein conflicts are settled by indifference. This would, of course, be highly unlikely since two totally apathetic people would have little to fight about in the first place!

## HEALTHY FAMILY FIGHTING

Since the family is a source of reward and comfort for many people, and since the family is a fertile setting for arguments, it might be helpful to consider some guidelines for healthy family fighting. Families fight (some more than others), but the arguments do not have to be destructive to the family unit. If all the family members adhere to some rules for fair fighting, everyone could be happier. Here are four suggestions on handling family conflicts.

*First, decide what to argue about.* Given the pain associated with arguments, you would be wise to save your more passionate "beefs" for those things that really matter. Too many arguments are centered on momentary irritations. "You're getting on my nerves" is an example of a minor irritable argument. Unless the irritations indicate a fundamental personality difference between the parties, each family member should be able to place into perspective many of the daily irritants that lead to temporary squabbles. The gravity of the argument is often determined by the perceived seriousness of the disputed issue. As long as both parties agree that the issue is minor, the argument will not have catastrophic consequences. Only when you allow minor issues to become major issues do problems emerge. The first thing a family should do, then, is to recognize that many of the arguments are simply not worth the battle.

*Second, disagree without destruction.* A healthy family should be able to argue without inflicting mortal pain on one another. By that I mean that family members should be able to scrap without personally destroying each other's integrity and self-concept. It is quite possible to have a heated disagreement without stripping the "humanness" from the other person. A strong disagreement may not destroy the family unit, but an intensive destruction of the other person's personality will. If winning the battle is so important that you resort to dirty fighting, you might lose the war.

*Third, solve the problem, don't nag.* Families are perhaps most often characterized by reemerging topics for fights. Many of the daily irritations reoccur and thus many of the arguments about them reoccur. If a problem is worth arguing over, it is worth solving. Too many times, people argue to "get it off their chests" without ever solving the problem itself. The trouble with not solving the problem is that it can resurface later. This is how nagging develops. Instead of nagging one another, work to reach a mutual agreement. Solving the problem is better than keeping it around for future battles.

*Fourth, end your arguments.* This one is similar to the third point. You should work to finish an argument, then leave it behind. Whenever possible, the end of an argument should not be simply the end of "round one." This requires three steps: apologizing, forgiving, and forgetting. Let's look quickly at each one.

*Apologizing* means that you express your regret for the misunderstanding. This is often hard because you may feel that you are not responsible for the fight. Most of the time, however, that is not the case. It takes two people to argue—both persons are responsible for the disagreement. Each is responsible for apologizing in the end.

*Forgiving* is also difficult, especially if the quarrel has been a "dilly." But without forgiveness, you cannot end an argument; you can only take a recess from it. If you want to end the argument, you must be willing to forgive.

Finally, there is *forgetting*. Without question, this is the most difficult step. Forgetting means that you don't hold any grudges, or keep that "ace in the hole" to spring on your partner later. Forgetting may be one of the factors that separates children's fights from adults' fights. Kids seem to be able to fight and forget it. Adults fight, then tuck away the dispute in memory for future use. A past fight should never become a future weapon. If you want to truly end an argument, you must forget it.

How do you rate when it comes to ending an argument? Are you able to apologize, forgive, and forget? Which is the hardest for you? Using a 1 to 5 scale (1, easiest; 5, hardest), rate yourself on these three skills.

_____ Apologizing

_____ Forgiving

_____ Forgetting

Your ratings obviously depend on the seriousness of the conflict, but it is interesting to observe that children are better at disposing of arguments than adults are. Children fight and forget. Adults seem to have more trouble with this. How much could your family communication be improved if you would apologize, forgive, and then forget?

## Summary Propositions

Conflict management is a real skill in communication. You experience both intrapersonal conflicts and interpersonal conflicts. Neither is much fun, but both are a part of your personal and professional lives. Interpersonal conflicts vary in intensity. Temporary ones are called spontaneous interpersonal conflicts (SIC). The more enduring ones are called major interpersonal conflicts (MIC). How intense any conflict becomes is a function of the participants' ego-involvement, frustration, and coping abilities. There are several strategies for managing conflicts, ranging from joint problem solving to force. No matter what the conflict, it should be managed. Avoiding conflicts does not solve the problem, and this is especially true in families where people should learn to fight in a healthy way.

1. Conflicts are an unavoidable part of your personal and professional lives.

2. Intrapersonal conflicts occur when you have a difficult choice to make.

3. Intrapersonal conflicts can lead to dissonance.

4. Interpersonal conflicts happen when two or more people have sharp disagreements about something.

5. Temporary interpersonal conflicts are called spontaneous interpersonal conflicts (SIC).

6. An SIC occurs on the spot and is often settled at the time it arises.

7. More enduring conflicts are called major interpersonal conflicts (MIC).

8. The intensity of a conflict is a function of the participants':

   a. Ego-involvement

   b. Frustration

   c. Coping abilities

9. Keltner proposes five strategies for managing conflicts, ranging from joint problem solving to force.

10. Healthy family fighting assumes that the members:

    a. Decide what to argue about

    b. Disagree without destruction

    c. Solve problems (don't nag)

    d. End their arguments

## References

**Coon, D.** *Introduction to Psychology*. St. Paul: West Publishing, 1977.

**Keltner, J.** *Interpersonal Speech Communication*. Belmont, Calif.: Wadsworth, 1970.

**Lefrancois, G.** *Psychology*. Belmont, Calif.: Wadsworth, 1980.

**Turner, R.** *Family Interaction*. New York: John Wiley, 1970.

**Verderber, R.** *The Challenge of Public Speaking*. Belmont, Calif.: Wadsworth, 1978.

# 8

# INTERVIEWING

**Interviewing Defined**

■

**Types of Interviews**
News-gathering Interview
Counseling Interview

■

**Advantages of Interviews**
Efficient Feedback
Topic Development
Impromptu Topics

■

**Questions**
Open-ended versus Closed-ended Questions
Initiating versus Probing Questions
Funneling

■

**Answers**
Honesty
Complete Answers

■

**Employment Interview**
A Proper Perspective
The Three Ms
Presenting Yourself Favorably
Problems You Might Encounter

■

**Summary Propositions**

■

**References**

■

Have you ever applied for a loan? Have you ever been stopped on the sidewalk by a survey taker? Have you ever testified as a witness to an accident? If you answered yes to any of these questions, you have experience in interviewing. Many people believe that, apart from a job interview or two, they have not participated in many interviews. But if you think carefully about it, you realize you have been involved in a number of interviews, ranging from learning at a party about a person's background to more formal interviews such as the job interview.

In this chapter you will learn about the different types of interviews and the types of questions and answers involved in an interview. But the main goal of this chapter is to prepare you for one of your most important interviews—the employment interview. You will learn what to expect, what image you should put forward, and how to present yourself as favorably as you can. You will learn how to handle problems that may arise in the job interview. All of these issues will be dealt with primarily from the interviewee's point of view, that is, as though you are the one to be interviewed.

## Interviewing Defined

An interview is a planned dyadic interaction designed to accomplish specific goals. This means that interviews have structure and goals. They are structured through a previously arranged set of questions to be asked at an appointed meeting time. Their goals are the purposes of the meeting. If two people meet for a job interview, then the goal is centered on the job and the applicant's qualifications. If the interview is for counseling purposes, then the goal is to discover the problem and begin to solve it.

Although an interview has a planned structure and predetermined goals, the actual interview must be performed spontaneously. The interviewer can rehearse the questions beforehand, and the interviewee can rehearse answers to possible questions, but the enacted interview will not be scripted like a drama. Each person, then, must be prepared for the interview and skilled at responding to the spontaneity of an interview in progress.

# Types of Interviews

When most people think of interviews, they envision two types—the job interview and the news-gathering interview as seen on television. Actually there are many kinds of formal interviews, but three are particularly relevant here: the job interview, the news-gathering interview, and the counseling interview. Since the job interview will receive extensive coverage later in the chapter, only the news-gathering interview and the counseling interview will be discussed here.

## NEWS-GATHERING INTERVIEW

If you watch news programs on TV, you are familiar with the news-gathering interview. The main goal of this type of interview is to gather information. For instance, if you are researching a paper on a topic you know little about, it is a good idea to interview someone who knows about that topic. You might interview a professor who specializes in your subject of interest. Or you might interview a civic leader who works with the problem you are researching. No matter who you interview, you want to talk to someone who can give reliable answers to your questions. The credibility of the person you are interviewing is crucial. If that person doesn't know much about your topic, the answers you receive may be of questionable quality.

Consider this example of an interview I watched on television in New Orleans in 1973. It was aired on a 6 o'clock newscast and was presented as a "man-on-the-street" interview. Ten different people were asked the same question: "What do you think of the Watergate situation?" In order to appreciate the last person's response to this question, you need to know that these interviews took place in March of 1973. At that time, the Watergate scandal surrounding the Nixon administration was beginning to leak out of Washington. Also, the Midwest had just experienced one of the largest continuous rainfalls in history. The Mississippi River had crested, wiping out a number of towns upstream from New Orleans. Within this context, then, the question about the Watergate situation brought the following answer from a nice old lady who had lived in New Orleans all her adult life. She said to the reporter, "Son, I hope that they don't open up that

If you are to be the interviewee, a good way to prepare for the interview is to anticipate some of the questions you will be asked. As you do this, keep in mind the goals of the interviewers, because they will ask questions aimed at getting the information they need to know.

For example, what are the purposes of the following interviews? Write your answers in the space provided.

1. Interviewing prospective directors of an inner-city recreation center.

   _____

   _____

   _____

2. Interviewing prospective roommates for an apartment.

   _____

   _____

   _____

3. Interviewing a witness to an auto accident.

   _____

   _____

   _____

By knowing the goals of the interview and realizing what the interviewer is looking for, you can better anticipate the questions you will be asked. You cannot predict every question by doing this, but it should help minimize the surprises you face in the actual interview.

gate. We've got enough water down here as it is!" As I said earlier, it is a good idea to interview people who can give you relevant and useful answers when you conduct news-gathering interviews.

The quality of the news-gathering interview depends not only on the quality of those being interviewed, but also on the types of questions asked by the interviewer. In interviewing you get what you ask for. Your questions should be clear and to the point. Poorly phrased questions will produce poor answers. Let's look at an example taken from everyday life, not a newscast interview.

Assume that you are in a drugstore looking for a cold medicine. After a quick look around the store, you realize that you don't know where the remedies are shelved. So you approach a clerk and ask,

"Where can I find Contract cold medicine?" The clerk will no doubt direct you to the proper aisle.

This seems like a successful transaction. But what would happen if you changed the question a bit? For instance, you might ask, "What is the best remedy for a cold?" Given this question, the clerk might take interest in your problem and escort you to a cold medicine that is not only effective but on sale! The second question, being more open ended, encourages the respondent to become involved in the question and perhaps provide a more complete answer. And the more thorough the answer, the more the interviewer learns.

In essence, the quality of a news-gathering interview depends on the quality of the person being interviewed and the quality of the questions asked. If you ask the right person the right questions, your interview will be fruitful.

## COUNSELING INTERVIEW

During your lifetime, you might have occasion to formally counsel someone or to be counseled yourself. Ministers frequently counsel the prospective bride and groom before the wedding ceremony. Perhaps you received some career counseling at school. In counseling interviews, the interviewee goes to the counselor for advice. Thus, the counselor is perceived as the expert. The quality of the counseling depends on the quality of the counselor. You should, therefore, seek advice from qualified people. Go to a lawyer for legal advice, a physician for medical advice. Too often people go to unqualified friends for legal or medical advice. For such technical matters, this approach is seldom successful.

There will be times, however, when a friend or an associate will call upon you, asking for advice about a personal problem. Once you overcome your initial feelings of inadequacy ("I'm not a trained counselor"), you should recognize that your friend simply needs someone to talk to. Perhaps your friend needs to ventilate feelings with someone who can be trusted not to get angry or to spread gossip. People sometimes need to review their thoughts with others to discover that they are not alone in their thinking and that their thoughts are not abnormal.

Given such needs, then, your job as a counselor is more one of listening than of talking. You should help the person talk through the problem, and help evaluate possible solutions. Sometimes just talking helps people sort out their feelings and gain control of the situation. If this doesn't help, encourage your friend to seek professional assistance.

Effective counseling is a special skill that demands special training. For those of you interested in such a career, excellent counseling programs are available at most universities and colleges. For those of you who do not wish a counseling career but realize that you often counsel people, practice being a compassionate listener, and be willing to help your friends find professional help when needed.

## Advantages of Interviews

In many ways, a face-to-face interview is a very expensive way to communicate. A letter, a phone call, or even a questionnaire would be cheaper. Given the cost in time and money for interviews, why bother? There are three advantages to interviews that make them worthwhile.

### EFFICIENT FEEDBACK

Face-to-face interviews provide unrestricted feedback. That is, the people can observe each other's reactions during the interview. With letters and questionnaires, feedback is only as fast as the return mail. Phone interviews provide auditory feedback, but not visual feedback. It is to the advantage of both the interviewer and the interviewee to have access to free feedback occurring at all levels of communication (language, paralanguage, and kinesics). And this is possible in a face-to-face interview.

### TOPIC DEVELOPMENT

Interviews foster topic development through the use of probing questions. In other words, when a topic comes up, it can be pursued with additional questions, or it can be dropped by changing the topic with another question. Thus, interviews provide topic control so that the interview participants may decide how much time to devote to any topic. This kind of flexibility is needed to learn more about the topic under consideration. For instance, an interviewer might ask you what you remember about your parents as disciplinarians. After you respond, the interviewer might follow up the question with another that asks for your feelings about discipline in the home. Such follow-up questions are possible in an interview, whereas they are more difficult to design into a letter or a questionnaire. The spontaneity of the interview allows for topic development.

### IMPROMPTU TOPICS

The third advantage of interviews is impromptu topics. An impromptu topic is one that neither the interviewer nor the interviewee planned to talk about. Sometimes one person says something that reminds the other person of something else. Thus, an impromptu topic surfaces. This helps provide variety in the interview. Impromptu topics may also tell you more about the other person than do planned topics. Obviously, impromptu topics are impossible in a letter or a questionnaire. But during the course of a good interview at least one impromptu topic will arise.

The advantages of interviews can be summed up in one word: flexibility. The flexibility of the interview provides for spontaneous interaction, which helps make each interview unique. Interviews are costly, but their flexibility makes them worthwhile.

# Questions

By now, it should be evident that the gist of interviewing is asking and answering questions. In order to understand the interviewing process, you need to learn about the ways questions can be asked and answered. Let's start with the questions.

## OPEN-ENDED VERSUS CLOSED-ENDED QUESTIONS

In an interview, you will encounter both open-ended and closed-ended questions. The open-ended ones call for oral "essay" answers. They are general questions requiring more than a yes or no answer. For instance, you might be asked, "How would you deal with an irate customer?" Or, "What are your plans for the next ten years of your life?" Obviously, there are no correct or incorrect answers to such questions, but your reply should be thoughtful and in direct response to the question.

On the other side of the coin is the closed-ended question. These questions call for brief answers. Sometimes a simple yes or no will suffice. For instance, you might be asked, "Did you move to the state immediately after college?" Or, "What is your favorite hobby?" You might even be asked a closed-ended question that gives you a choice of answers, such as, "Would you be happier working in the front office or in the computer center?" If the interviewer wishes to follow up on your responses to such questions, you will be asked to explain your answers. But that is the choice of the person asking the questions.

Knowing the difference between an open-ended and a closed-ended question will help you determine how long your answers should be. If your answers are too short or too long, the interviewer will probe for more information or go on to another topic. Interviewers often ask more open-ended questions than closed-ended ones. Why? Because they learn more about you if you talk more.

When things get hectic, efficient interviewing skills are needed. (Photo courtesy of David Powers/Stock, Boston, Inc.)

## INITIATING VERSUS PROBING QUESTIONS

Questions differ not only in kind but in function. Some questions serve an initiating function—they are asked to induce you to talk about a new topic. Such initiating questions can be either open ended or closed ended in form. For instance, you might be asked, "How would you maintain positive working relationships among the people you supervise?" This open-ended, initiating question may lead you to start talking about interpersonal trust. From your answer on interpersonal trust, the interviewer might probe your feelings with a closed-ended, probing question such as, "Are you confident that you could promote trust among your workers?"

Probing questions, then, allow the interviewer to follow up on your previous answers. They also permit you to express yourself in more detail. Almost any in-depth interview will have both initiating and probing questions. Without them, topic development could not occur. Just how many probing questions you experience is up to the interviewer. If the interviewer takes an interest in you, you might encounter many probing questions.

## FUNNELING

Regardless of which kind of question you are being asked, you should realize that questions in an interview tend to form a pattern. This pattern is called funneling. Funneling is a way of arranging initiating

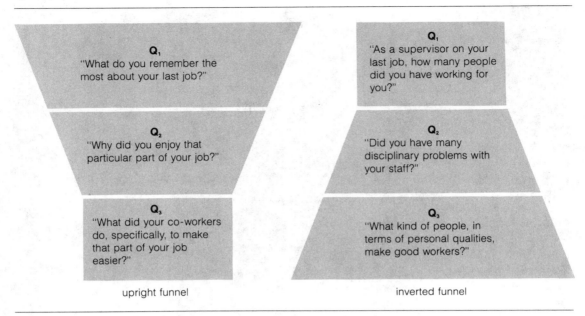

Figure 8.1 Funneling in Interviews

and probing questions so that the questions become either more specific or more general. If the questions begin as general and gradually become more specific, the upright funnel approach is being used. If the questions start as specific and become more general, the inverted funnel approach is being used. (See Figure 8.1.)

Regardless of which funnel approach is used, you must recognize that topic development is the goal. The interviewer is trying to understand more about you. So don't respond to each question with the same answer. Treat each question as though it is asking for new information.

## Answers

Giving advice on how to answer questions is tricky because the answer depends on the question. But there are some reasonable guidelines that you should follow as you attempt to answer questions.

### HONESTY

It is not a good idea to lie in an interview. If you are caught in a lie, your trustworthiness suffers, and you will not leave a favorable im-

Here are some possible questions that you might be asked in a job interview. Write a brief answer for each one.

*YOUR TURN...*

1. What courses in college did you like best?

   _____

   _____

2. What personal attributes are important for a person in your field?

   _____

   _____

3. How do you define *cooperation*?

   _____

   _____

4. What kind of material do you read most often?

   _____

   _____

5. Why would you want this job compared to others?

   _____

   _____

6. Tell me a story.

   _____

   _____

These are just a sample of possible questions. As you practice with these questions, think of others that may be asked and prepare answers for those as well.

pression with the interviewer. Professional interviewers are trained to detect inconsistencies in answers. So, avoid lying.

How do people lie in interviews? Some lies are outright fraudulent statements. For example, you might claim that you had a specific responsibility in your prior job when in fact you didn't. Perhaps you were fired from your last job, but you tell the interviewer that you decided to move on and look for better work. Maybe you didn't graduate from school, but you said that you did. All of these statements are deceptive and easy for the interviewer to check for accuracy.

Other forms of lying are more subtle, such as exaggeration. Stretching the truth to make it more attractive is too easy to do. Most interviewers know that exaggerations can occur, and they know how to trim back that kind of statement to get to the actual facts. Still another form of deception is withholding information. You certainly shouldn't volunteer "blemishes" in your past, but if asked about them, you should not try to hide them. Later in this chapter, you will learn how to handle negative information about yourself. For now, let's agree that honesty is better than lying. Interviewers realize that no one is perfect. How you cope with your weaknesses is more important to the interviewer than the fact that you made mistakes.

## COMPLETE ANSWERS

In order to make an accurate assessment, the interviewer needs enough information from you to know your competencies and personal qualities. If you give answers that are too brief or repetitive, the interviewer cannot make accurate judgments. This does not mean that each answer need be a speech. Quite the contrary. Your responses should directly answer the questions and clearly express your ideas.

In what ways can an answer be incomplete? It depends on the answer, but let's consider one example. Suppose you were asked what you did last summer and gave this answer: "Oh, I worked a bit, and then relaxed awhile." What is wrong with such an answer?

This answer suffers from two common problems: It is too short and too vague. Mentioning that you worked and relaxed says very little. There is simply not enough information in your response. Is that all you did last summer? Furthermore, words such as *working* and *relaxing* can mean many things. Did you work full time or part time? Did you work all summer or for only a month? When you were relaxing, what were you doing? Did you take a trip? Or did you lie around the house and watch television? How can the interviewer know what you did from such an answer? A better answer would say how long you worked, what job you held, and what you did for leisure. If you leave it up to the interviewer to figure out what you mean, he or she might draw some undesirable conclusions.

Complete answers are those that provide enough information so that the interviewer knows what you mean. Complete answers also are specific enough to leave the impression you want. Answers that are too short and too vague can lead to trouble for you.

Since resumes are an important part of job interviewing, here is a sample resume that contains the essentials needed to introduce the applicant.

Mary Wright
339 Poplar Lane
Durant, OK 25745

Born: May 13, 1958
Marital Status: Single
Phone: (475) 555-1009

**Career Objective:**  Public Relations

**Education:**  B.A., University of Oklahoma, 1980
Major: Journalism

M.A., Michigan State Univ., 1982
Major: Communication

**Experience:** Public Affairs Officer, U.S. Air Force, 1980—present

Public Relations Clerk, City National Bank, 1978—1980

Assistant Editor, City National Bank Magazine, 1980

**Activities:**  Yearbook editor as undergraduate at O.U., 1979—80

Scholarship selection committee for Arts and Science College, 1979

Sorority member (Delta, Delta, Delta) 1977—1980

**Honors:**  Graduated Magna Cum Laude (B.A.)

Outstanding Senior Woman at O.U., 1980

Rotary Fellowship, 1979

**Special Skills:**  Fluent in Spanish (reading, writing, and speaking)

Computer programming in FORTRAN, and PL1

**References:** Mr. Rodney Downey
President, City National Bank
Sunnyvale, OK 23069

Prof. Norma Yarrow
Dept. of Communication
Michigan State Univ.
North Linsang, MI 98822

Dean Alice Ice
University of Oklahoma
Elkhorn, OK 23069

## Employment Interview

It is time to get down to the business of interviewing for a job. This may be the most important interview you face in life. In many ways, the likelihood of your securing a good job depends on your employment interview skills.

### A PROPER PERSPECTIVE

How you approach the job interview is crucial to your success. Primarily, you should realize that you are probably as equally qualified as everyone else being interviewed for the job. The reason for this is that interviewing is costly, and companies usually screen applicants for basic qualifications before inviting them in for an interview. So unless you happen to be in a truly open-applicant interview in which anyone can talk to the interviewer, you should assume that you are in a tied race with the others being interviewed.

The implication of a tied race is that you must use the interview to demonstrate that you are better than the others. You do this by showing that you can think on the spot and that you are personable. In this way, you will appear competent and attractive.

How you conduct yourself in a job interview may determine whether you get the job. (Photo courtesy of Hazel Hankin/Stock, Boston, Inc.)

## THE THREE Ms

According to interviewing expert R. A. Fear (1958), employers are looking for people who manifest three qualities (the three *M*s): mental ability, motivation, and maturity. The interviewer will use the interview to evaluate you in these areas.

*Mental ability* refers to your intelligence, education, and mental quickness. Every position requires a certain level of mental competence. One of the things the interviewer must determine is whether or not you are mentally suited for the job. Your resume plays a large part in establishing your qualifications, but your face-to-face interview will indicate your articulateness and your ability to handle questions effectively. Mental ability, then, is more than training and prior experience; it includes your ability to answer intelligently the questions you are asked.

*Motivation* refers to your enthusiasm and commitment toward the job. Applicants who appear lazy or unconcerned about the job will be eliminated, even though their resumes indicate the proper training and experience. Don't assume, however, that the more energetic you are, the more likely you are to get the job. Not at all. In fact, you may be perceived as too pushy. The back-slapping, ever-smiling, fast talker rarely impresses people for very long. But the opposite, the dull, mumbling applicant, can put the interviewer to sleep. Strike a balance. Be alert but not slaphappy. If the interviewer feels that you are unmotivated or too pushy, you will not get the job.

*Maturity* is the most difficult of the three qualities to define. Maturity refers to the interviewer's perceptions of your ability to handle a number of different work and social situations in a careful and competent manner. One sign of maturity is being in control of your emotions. Being sympathetic to the shortcomings of others is another sign of maturity. A mature person is responsible. When given a job, the mature person will handle the job without a great deal of supervision. A mature person, then, is one who can move from situation to situation and handle himself or herself competently and confidently. If you show signs of serious immaturity, you may not get the job.

Whenever you are in a job interview, remember the three *M*s—mental ability, motivation, and maturity. Remember also that the interviewer often sees a dozen or more candidates in one day, many of whom are basically quite similar to each other. As Keenan (1979) points out, interviewers are likely to remember little about each individual candidate. Therefore, you need to do all you can to stand out from the other applicants, to present yourself favorably.

Research shows that there is a relationship between the amount of apprehension that an applicant shows when being interviewed and the likelihood of being hired for the job. Daly et al., (1979) found that high-anxiety applicants were less likely to be hired in a job interview than low-anxiety applicants.

Thus, if you manifest too much tension in a job interview, it may work against you. Interviewers expect you to be nervous, but they hope that you can handle your apprehension as well. So avoid as many nervous gestures as possible.

J. Daly et al., "Social Communicative Anxiety and the Personnel Selection Process: Testing the Similarity Effect in Selection Decisions," *Human Communication Research* 6(1979):18–32.

## PRESENTING YOURSELF FAVORABLY

To appear as the best person for the job, you have to communicate a favorable impression so that the interviewer will remember you. Your resume will attest to your qualifications, but your performance in the interview will be a key factor in the interviewer's decision. Clowers and Fraser (1977) found that the impression left during the interview is more important in hiring decisions than are academic background and work experience. If you approach the interview as though you are running a tied race with the other applicants, you can use the interview as your tie breaker.

Keeping in mind that your main objective is to appear competent and attractive so that your three M s stand out, what communication behaviors can you use to lead the interviewer to judge you favorably? Based on a study conducted in 1979, Brandt found five characteristics that led people to view others as competent and attractive. Because each of these characteristics is important in interviewing, they are discussed separately here.

**UNIQUE IMPRESSION** According to Brandt's research, the most important thing you can do in an interview is leave a unique impression. Saying something unusual (not bizarre) or doing something different helps people remember you. By noting something unusual about you during the interview, the interviewer will have a "handle" by which to remember you. I remember once serving on a homecoming queen selection commitee. Six of us interviewed 48 candidates. We started at 7:00 P.M. and didn't finish the interviews until 12:30 A.M. After a while, I simply couldn't remember one candidate from another. I generally lost track of who said what. But to this day, I remember that one of the finalists mentioned that she enjoyed hang gliding. So when I cast my ballot, her remark stuck in my mind. The other judges remembered this as well. Her comment about hang gliding helped us remember her. Isn't there something about you that is unusual or unique? If you share this unique feature with the interviewer, you might increase the chances of being remembered.

**OPENNESS** The second most important aspect to leaving a good impression is openness. People differ in how much they share with others. Those who are willing to share personal experiences reveal things about themselves that may make them more memorable. Being frank, sincere, and willing to talk about yourself will help you seem more attractive to the interviewer. If the interviewer feels that every answer needs to be forcefully pried out of you, your name may be scratched off the list after the interview. By being open with the interviewer, you will communicate a general willingness to cooperate that is important in many jobs.

**ATTENTIVENESS** This is one characteristic that looks easier than it is. Have you ever been in a conversation wherein two people are talking, but not to each other? In other words, they are not interacting, just giving speeches to one another. In your personal life, this kind of conversation may be common; but in an interview, it can be disastrous. When you are being interviewed, pay close attention to the interviewer. Be sure that your remarks are directly related to the immediate conversation. If your remarks appear unrelated to the conversation, you might leave the impression that you have an attention problem. And that can cost you the job.

**ANIMATION** During an interview enthusiasm counts. A person who is animated is one who uses hand gestures, varies facial expression, and does not avoid eye contact. A job interview is no place for a poker face. When you talk, you should do so with enough enthusiasm to indicate interest in the topic. If you seem deadpan, with a dull, monotonous voice coming out of an immovable body, you may leave the impression that you are aloof and unable to relate well to others. You may be extremely nervous, as many people are in interviews, but this is no time to turn into a frozen statue. Smile. Laugh once in a while. Don't lock your arms around your torso and hold that position throughout the interview. Feel free to shift positions in your chair. As long as your movements fit what's happening, they will not appear unnatural. What will appear unnatural is a fixed positioning of the body, never moving throughout the interview.

**RELAXEDNESS** This characteristic is related to animation. During an interview you should try to relax. Lean back in your chair. Don't sit on the edge of the chair with your legs properly crossed at the ankles or feet permanently planted on the floor. If you appear too stiff, the interviewer may be distracted. Interviewers expect nervousness, but they don't want it to interfere with your ability to handle the interview. When asked a question, speak in your normal tone of voice at your normal rate. Avoid things that will advertise your nervousness. For instance, if you are handed a single piece of paper, rest it on your lap or on a table so that it doesn't jiggle as you read it. Likewise, don't smoke or handle a cup of coffee that may give you an opportunity for an accident. You probably will not be able to eliminate your nervousness, but you can control it.

Let's review. There are five characteristics you can cultivate to communicate that you are competent and attractive in an interview. They are:

1. Unique impression

2. Openness

3. Attentiveness

4. Animation

5. Relaxedness

If you exhibit these qualities successfully, you might gain an advantage over the others who are being interviewed. And hopefully, you will land the job.

## PROBLEMS YOU MIGHT ENCOUNTER

During the job interview, problems may arise that you have trouble handling. If you are forewarned of some of the potential problems, you might be able to manage them better. Here are three common problems.

**NEGATIVE INFORMATION** What should you do when the interviewer asks a question that hits on a sensitive subject for you? For instance, if you are asked why you left school for two years, what should you say? If you flunked out of school, say so, but turn that event into a positive experience for you. Explain precisely what you did during your absence from school and what specifically you learned from the experience. Be ready with a specific answer, one that goes beyond "I learned from my mistakes." What did you learn, specifically? The key is to plan a specific and honest answer that does not excuse your mistake but turns it into a valuable experience for you. If you know your weaknesses, you can prepare a credible answer beforehand. If you don't know your shortcomings, you'll have to "wing it" when asked about them.

**FORGETTING** What do you do when you forget something during an interview? It depends on what you forget. If you forget your mother's name, you've got problems. But if you forget some dates, you can write them down on a card and keep it readily available to refer to. The interviewer will not mind if you have notes. But suppose you leave the interview and realize you forgot to mention something important. Can it cost you the job? Not likely. There will be no interview that you leave feeling you said it all. So, don't go back to the interviewer with your forgotten piece of information. It probably won't make any difference anyway.

**BEING CAUGHT OFF GUARD** Have you ever been asked a question that you never expected? If you haven't yet, you will in a job interview. The spontaneity of an interview invariably produces surprise questions—ones you aren't ready for. When you get one, don't be afraid to show your surprise. Smile, show your sense of humor, and give an honest answer to the question. If the question is really strange, the interviewer will allow more latitude in your answer. So don't feel bad if you get a surprising question.

## Summary Propositions

In this chapter on interviewing, you discovered that interviews are planned dyadic interactions that use questions and answers as the main vehicles for interaction. There are many kinds of interviews (counseling, news-gathering, and so forth), but one of the most important ones is the employment interview. No matter which kind of interview you are involved in, it is a good idea to know the difference between open-ended and closed-ended questions, and to realize that questions are not necessarily independent of one another. Often, a series of questions will be funneled, going from general to specific, or vice versa. Many qualities of the interviewee are important in a job interview. But being prepared and being honest and willing to talk about oneself are good prerequisites. If you present yourself in ways that make you more attractive than the other candidates, you might win the "tied race" of job interviewing.

1. An interview is a planned dyadic interaction designed to accomplish specific goals.

2. There are many different types of interviews. Among them are the counseling interview, the news-gathering interview, and the employment interview.

3. The main advantages of the interview over other methods of gathering information are:

      a. Immediate feedback

      b. Topic development

      c. Impromptu topics

4. Questions may be open ended or closed ended. They may also be initiating or probing.

5. Questions are often arranged in a funnel pattern.

6. When answering questions you should be honest and complete with your answers.

7. The employment interview should be approached pragmatically. You are in an even race with the other applicants.

8. Job interviewers will be looking for mental ability, motivation, and maturity in the applicants.

9. There are five characteristics you can cultivate to appear competent and attractive to an interviewer:

      a. Unique impression

      b. Openness

      c. Attentiveness

      d. Animation

      e. Relaxedness

10. The key to a successful interview is to remain in control of yourself.

# References

**Brandt, D.** "On Linking Social Performance with Social Competence: Some Relations between Communicative Style and Attributions of Interpersonal Attractiveness and Effectiveness." *Human Communication Research* 5(1979):223–237.

**Clowers, M., and Fraser, R.** "Employment Interview Literature: A Perspective for the Counselor." *Vocational Guidance Quarterly* 19(1977):13–26.

**Daly, J.; Richmond, V.; and Leth, S.** "Social Communicative Anxiety and the Personnel Selection Process: Testing the Similarity Effect in Selection Decisions." *Human Communication Research* 6(1979):18–32.

**Fear, R.** *The Evaluation Interview.* New York: McGraw-Hill, 1958.

**Keenan, T.** "Interviewing for Graduate Recruitment." In *Readings and Cases in Personnel Management,* edited by L. Byars, L. Rue, and N. Harbaugh. Philadelphia: W. B. Saunders, 1979.

# PERSONAL AND PROFESSIONAL SMALL GROUP COMMUNICATION

A well-worn cliche reminds us that people are social animals—we like to be together in groups. Although it is difficult to prove, we humans seem to have a need for grouping. We are, by nature, gregarious. Furthermore, when it is time to solve problems, work cooperatively on projects, or defend ourselves against foreign enemies, we band together to increase our chances of success. And we do this in both our personal and our professional lives.

In this part of the book, you will learn how small group communication functions, how people make decisions in small groups, and how you can improve your leadership skills. Although this section focuses on groups, you will soon realize that many of the principles covered apply to other communication settings as well.

# 9

# ELEMENTS OF
# SMALL GROUP
# COMMUNICATION

**Importance of Groups**

■

**Defining Groups**
A Definition
Interdependence and Interaction

■

**Group Interdependence**
Task and Social Needs
Productivity and Cohesiveness
Roles and Norms
Conformity
Review

■

**Group Interaction**
Proana 5
Bales's IPA

■

**Summary Propositions**

■

**References**

■

As I sit at my typewriter this afternoon, I hear outside a group of men resurfacing the roof of a nearby building on campus. There are a half dozen or so people working on the job. Their apparent goal is to repair the roof in a specific period of time. They work together in a coordinated fashion. One person works the conveyer pulley system that lifts the tar to the roof from the ground where the tar mixer is running, while another spreads the hot, steamy tar on the rooftop. Other men are performing other tasks. The point is that these men are a group. They have a goal and they are working to meet it. And the quality of their final product will be a function of the quality of their group.

## Importance of Groups

Without question, groups are a significant part of your everyday life. You are a member of a number of personal and professional groups. Both at work and in your home life and leisure time, your activities are governed by groups. Human nature is gregarious; people seem to like being part of groups. Unless you are a hermit, you seek other people to affiliate with.

Groups are important not only for the sake of people getting together, but also for what they can do. When people come together to interact or to deal with problems, they can produce what is called an "assembly effect bonus." That is, groups often produce better decisions, more total output, and higher quality products than would the individuals if they were working independently. It seems that the collective wisdom and effort of many people gathered together help us make better choices. Examples of this are juries and scholarship selection committees. In our society we believe that for making decisions about the guilt or innocence of the accused, or for selecting the best students to receive scholarships, it is better to have a group work on the problem than to have individuals work alone. Because the group members get together and interact, they will supposedly think better, evaluate better, and perhaps be more creative than will individuals alone. Even script writers for TV shows work in teams because they realize that, as a group, they can create more ideas for a show than each of them would individually.

Before reading the next section, take this test.

Not all aggregates of people make up a small group. Look at the following list and check those that constitute a small group.

_____ A store full of shoppers

_____ Your class

_____ Your family at dinner

_____ Four strangers in an elevator

_____ A concert audience

_____ People waiting in line at the bank

Certainly, there may be groups in all of the above, but if you were conservative in your judgments, you should have checked only the family at dinner. At face value, the others are either too large or gathered together by chance.

As you read on, you will discover that there are a number of criteria that must be met before we call a collection of people a group.

## Defining Groups

What makes a group a group? Why is it that you can call a committee a group, whereas a collectivity such as all the college sophomores in the United States is not called a group? Is it a matter of size, or number of members? Is it a matter of whether or not the group meets regularly? What are the essential elements needed before an aggregate of people can be called a group? Perhaps a definition would help.

### A DEFINITION

*A group is a collectivity of three or more people who join together to accomplish common goals through communication.* Notice that there are three key parts to this definition. The first part refers to the size of a group. Although there is no upper limit to how large a group can be, most researchers believe that groups need at least three members. The number *three* is chosen to distinguish a group from a dyad (two people). Communication scholars believe that the dyad and the group are sufficiently different in nature to be treated separately. By definition, then, groups need at least three members.

Although the definition establishes no upper limit for group size, we must set some practical limits when discussing *small* groups. The larger a group becomes, the more difficult it is for all members to interact with each other. For small groups—such as committees, problem-solving groups, and the like—a realistic upper limit is about ten members. More can be added, but the interaction then becomes considerably more cumbersome. Small groups typically number three to ten.

The second important part of this definition is "to accomplish common goals." A group works together to reach an agreed-upon objective. All members know the goal and work toward it. If there is no common goal that everyone is trying to reach, there is no group. Thus, a crowd of people at a shopping center are not a group. Different clusters of people are headed in different directions. Some are just arriving. Others are going home. Still others are just sitting there to pass the time. Some of the people are buying, but they are not necessarily buying the same items. At best, shopping centers have groups of shoppers, but not all the people are part of one group.

Finally, this definition of groups focuses on communication. In order for a group to function, some form of communication is required, although it is not necessarily verbal. I remember watching a group of bricklayers install the brick siding on a neighbor's house. What called my attention to the group was that they worked without saying a word to each other. They communicated through sign language. They were all deaf. In spite of their deafness, they had a competently functioning group. As long as there is a dependable system for communication among the members, a collectivity of people can form a group.

A group, then, requires three or more people, a common goal, and a system of communication. When these three requirements are met, there are the makings of a group.

## INTERDEPENDENCE AND INTERACTION

Interdependence and interaction are widely believed by communication scholars to be the cornerstones of all groups (Fisher, 1980). These two processes provide the "glue" that binds together the group members to give them a feeling of "groupness." Interdependence and interaction, then, are fundamental to a group, making the accomplishment of common goals more likely.

When groups develop interdependence, the members recognize

Interdependence and cooperation are often needed to perform the task. (Photo courtesy of the Norman Transcript.)

one another as legitimate members of the group who are important to sustaining the life of the group. Interdependent group members share mutual influence, in that each person's opinion is considered valuable, and the success of the group depends on the contributions of all members. The moment one person feels left out or unwanted, the total group's interdependence suffers. Thus, again, a horde of people at a shopping mall cannot be a group. The shoppers do not need each other to make their purchases. A person can run into a store, buy something, and leave without taking account of the other patrons. The feeling of interdependence in a group keeps the group alive. As soon as the members feel that they don't need each other, the need for a group disappears.

As group members communicate, they develop a system of interaction. The system of interaction represents the channels or lines of communication among the members. When all the channels are established, a communication network forms. Certain members talk to some people more than others. Some lines of communication are in constant use; others are periodically silent. But all the lines of communication are needed to weave the fabric of interaction that ties together the members of the group. Whenever interaction ceases

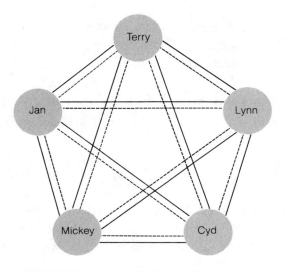

**Figure 9.1** Interdependence and Interaction in a Group

permanently, so does the group. Without interaction, there is no group.

A good way to visualize interdependence and interaction in a small group is to think of, say, five members who form a working group. Let's assume that the group is a surgical team in the operating room of a hospital. Figure 9.1 shows how the group is woven together by interdependency (solid lines) and interaction (dashed lines). Lynn and Cyd are physicians, Terry is the anesthetist, and Mickey and Jan are nurses. These five people form a working group, linked together through open communication channels and interdependent functions. In order for this group to be successful, the members must communicate and depend on one another to do their jobs. In many ways, the outcome of the surgery and the health of the patient will depend on how smoothly this team works.

So far, we have been considering interdependence and interaction in a general way. Because of the importance of these two components, the next sections explore them in more detail.

## Group Interdependence

Group interdependence is not something that happens automatically. Certain key variables work together to help the group develop its interdependence. These variables are the task and social needs of the group, the productivity and cohesiveness levels in the group, the

Burgoon et al. (1974) suggest that there are seven characteristics of groups that make them unique social units:

1.  Frequent interaction (unlike public speakers, group members talk spontaneously)

2.  Group personality (every group takes on an identity of its own)

3.  Group norms (groups produce rules of conduct, often unknowingly)

4.  Coping behavior (groups act to preserve the group, for example, establish officers, develop a special jargon, and so forth)

5.  Role differentiation (everyone finds a role or two to play; division of labor)

6.  Interdependent goals (members share goals and recognize the purpose of the group)

7.  Assembly effect bonus (extra productivity through dealing with tasks as a group rather than as separate individuals)

As you proceed through this chapter, you will see how some of these characteristics operate in small group communication.

M. Burgoon et al., *Small Group Communication: A Functional Approach* (New York: Holt, Rinehart & Winston, 1974).

roles and norms that emerge in the group, and the degree of conformity that operates in the group.

## TASK AND SOCIAL NEEDS

All groups have two needs that the members must be responsive to: task needs and social needs. Successful groups attend to both needs. . In essence, the task needs refer to the business of the group, the work to be done. Tasks vary according to the purpose of the group. For example, some groups are decision-making groups (juries, planning boards, and selection panels). Others are service groups (paramedic teams, adoption agencies, book review clubs, and so on).

Groups also have social needs, related to the morale of the group members. Social needs refer to the maintenance of interpersonal relationships among the group members. Successful groups will work not only to meet task needs, but also to keep up the morale of the members and to promote satisfaction among the members. It is quite possible for a group to be strong in fulfilling the task needs, but weak in meeting the social needs of the group. Such groups get the work done, but the members may not like working in the group because of dissension among the members.

## PRODUCTIVITY AND COHESIVENESS

How well a group attends to its task and social needs can be determined by its productivity and cohesiveness. Productivity refers to the total output of the group—how much they complete the task. It is often measured by the number and/or quality of the decisions or by the number and/or quality of the units of work accomplished.

Cohesiveness is related to the morale of the group. It refers to the perceived "togetherness" that the members feel. Highly cohesive groups have members who are strongly attracted to one another and enjoy working together. They get along well and are supportive of one another. A highly cohesive group feels a "oneness" that makes the whole group a tightly knit unit.

Marvin Shaw (1971) argues that, most of the time, highly cohesive groups will be more productive than groups that are low in cohesion. That is, cohesiveness and productivity are interrelated. This relationship, however, may not always be linear. Fisher (1980) points out that productivity and cohesiveness may be curvilinearly related. That is, as Figure 9.2 illustrates, as cohesiveness rises, so does productivity. But there is a point of diminishing returns when the group becomes so cohesive that they spend too much time enjoying one another's fellowship and not enough time getting the job done. The optimum condition, then, appears to be one of relatively high cohesion rather than maximally high cohesion.

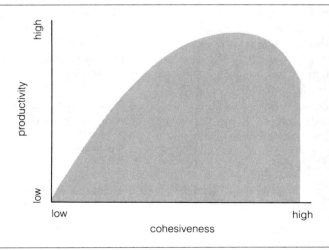

**Figure 9.2** Curvilinear Relationship between Productivity and Cohesiveness

One of the ways you can measure the productivity of a group is to count the number of different ideas that the members generate. In terms of numbers, one of the most prolific methods of producing ideas is brainstorming. But sometimes groups agree to brainstorm and then fall back into a critical group discussion mode without realizing it.

If your group needs to brainstorm to generate ideas, you should first establish some ground rules for brainstorming. Here are some suggestions:

1. Stay on the topic.

2. No idea is to be rejected, no matter how strange or unworkable it sounds.

3. Go for quantity, not quality.

4. Listen to each other, and let previous ideas stimulate your own creative thinking.

5. Resist the temptation to discuss and evaluate someone else's idea.

After the group has brainstormed, the members may wish to evaluate the ideas generated. But this should never be done during the brainstorming session. Effective brainstorming can produce ideas that would never surface if the group evaluated at the same time.

## ROLES AND NORMS

During the development of a group, roles and norms begin to surface. Roles are sets of behaviors that members perform. Some roles are officially designated, such as that of chairperson, secretary, or parliamentarian. Other roles are created more informally. These are the roles that emerge out of the personalities of the members and the task and social needs of the group.

Benne and Sheats (1948) divided these group roles into three types: group task roles, group maintenance roles, and self-centered roles. Some examples of each are:

### Group Task Roles

*Information Giver:* offers facts and information during the discussion

*Coordinator:* summarizes and shows how the ideas discussed can be interrelated

### Group Maintenance Roles

*Harmonizer:* helps members reconcile differences of opinions

*Tension Reliever:* tells jokes, is funny, puts others at ease

### Self-Centered Roles

*Blocker:* refuses to cooperate with the group

*Deserter:* is not interested in the task, remains detached from the group

As you can see, the first two sets of roles are supportive of the group, while the self-centered roles are not. If the group members enact too many self-centered roles, the group's level of interdependence and cohesion may fall.

Roles are also associated with role expectations. Whenever you perform a role, others expect you to meet certain standards for performance. Such role expectations apply not only to groups but to everyday life. You expect a dentist to know about dental care. You expect a car mechanic to do reliable repair work. You expect your spouse or your friend to provide affection when needed. Likewise, group members have role expectations of one another. A chairperson is supposed to exhibit some procedural leadership. A secretary is supposed to take notes. Committee members are expected to participate in the discussions. How well these roles are performed is a function of both the performer and the opinions of those who judge the performance, that is, the norms applied to the performer.

Norms are standards of appropriate behavior that apply to the group members. Most norms surface informally. They are not specified in a manual or code of conduct. Yet these norms have a powerful effect on the members. Almost any group will have norms that the members are aware of and attempt to adhere to. Such norms may be related to proper communication behavior (not swearing in public, taking turns when talking, and not talking too much), or they may be related to one's general conduct (being punctual, attending meetings, volunteering for assignments, and observing certain dress codes). If you behave ab*norm*ally, you might find your fellow members applying pressure to you to get back in line, to conform.

## CONFORMITY

Closely related to roles and norms is the concept of conformity. By definition, conformity is adherence to the norms of the group. It is a willingness to be influenced by the standards of the group. Its opposite is deviancy. The degree to which a member conforms to the group's norms can vary from total conformity to total deviancy.

Conformity can even affect our dress. Notice that both men are wearing caps. (Photo courtesy of D. Casonhua.)

Whenever a group applies pressure to its members to conform, it is elevating the interest of the whole group above the interest of the individual. Many times the interest of the group and the interest of the individual member coincide, and when that occurs, conformity is easy for the member. When there is a discrepancy between the interest of the group and the interest of the individual, then conformity is more difficult to attain. But if the individual wishes to remain in the group, he or she will have to conform to the important norms of the group, or face possible expulsion. If nothing else, a deviant member will experience a degree of group pressure to behave *norm*ally.

What are some of the factors that increase the likelihood that members will conform to the norms of the group? The answer lies in the nature of the group and in the natures of the individuals. In terms of the group, a person will conform to its norms if the group is attractive. That is, you will be well behaved if the group is prestigious or has high status or some other source of attractiveness for you. Country club groups often place great demands on their members, knowing that the members want the prestige associated with belonging to the club. Another source of power for the group is its ability to reward and punish its members. For instance, work groups that include people who are your supervisors are likely to have considerable control over your behavior. You will behave appropriately because your employment may depend on it. Finally, a group can influence its members to conform because, by comparison, the current group is better than the other available groups. People who are reluctant to make job changes often fear that the group they enter will be worse than the one they leave behind.

Conformity also varies with the natures of the individuals involved. For instance, if you have a high need to belong to a particular group and you fear being left out of the group, you will be more willing to conform than someone who would rather be home alone reading a good book. Your need for belonging, then, affects your susceptibility to conformity. Also, the importance of the group task to you will enter your decision to conform or not. If you are not very committed to the task, you may not be persuaded to conform to the group norms. In fact, if you are serving on a committee involuntarily, your lack of commitment could become a problem for the group.

In essence, then, a member's willingness to conform to the norms of the group will be affected by the attractiveness of the group, its ability to reward and punish its members, the comparative quality of the group, the member's need to belong, and the member's commitment to the task.

Look at the lines shown in this box.

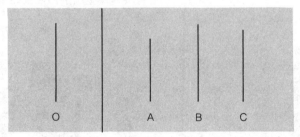

Which line on the right is the same in length as the line on the left? If you chose B, you are correct.

In 1952, Asch reported a study in which students were asked to judge the lengths of such lines. But instead of doing it alone, they judged the lines in small groups. What the subjects didn't know was that Asch hired the other members in the group to lie about the correct answer. So instead of saying B for the above set of lines, the group members would say C. Obviously, the unsuspecting person who was not part of the conspiracy was placed in an uncomfortable position. Should he or she agree with the group (answer C) or answer truthfully (answer B)? If the naive person agreed and said C, then he or she was yielding to conformity pressures.

The results showed that about one-third of the time, the subjects would give in to the group pressure and conform to the wrong answer.

S. Asch, *Social Psychology* (Englewood Cliffs, N.J.: Prentice-Hall, 1952).

## REVIEW

In this section, you have seen how four sets of variables affect group dynamics. These variables, though discussed separately, are not independent processes. They are intricately interrelated. Attendance to task and social needs leads to productivity and cohesiveness. Likewise, roles and norms lead to group pressure for conformity. And the interdependence of any group depends on the joint functioning of all of these processes simultaneously.

## Group Interaction

A thorough understanding of small group communication requires some familiarity with group interaction and how it can be described. As mentioned earlier, interaction is the essence of group communication. In fact, in order for individuals to develop into a group, they must interact with one another. Group interaction, then, is fundamental to small group communication.

How do people talk in groups? What is group interaction like? There are at least two ways to describe small group interaction. One

Don't forget—groups interact nonverbally as well as verbally. (Photo courtesy of D. Casonhua.)

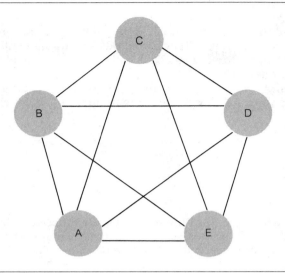

**Figure 9.3** A Proana 5 Network

approach is to keep track of who talks to whom. In doing so, you observe the communication network of the group. Another approach is to tabulate the different kinds of contributions that each member makes when he or she talks. That is, observe *how* people talk when they interact in groups. A complete analysis of group interaction includes both approaches.

## PROANA 5

Have you ever observed a group in which one person seemed to dominate the discussion? Or a group in which two people form a clique and refuse to talk with the others? One of the ways you can document such observations is to do a network analysis of the group discussion. Proana 5 is a tool for such analysis (Lashbrook and Lashbrook, 1972).* Using Proana 5, you can check who talks to whom, how often. With a network chart such as the one in Figure 9.3, you can mark on the communication lines the frequency with which each line is used in a group. For a five-member group (as in Figure 9.4), there would be ten lines of communication (A–B, A–C, A–D, A–E, B–C, B–D, and so on).

---

* Proana 5 was originally developed as a computer program to analyze small group interaction. The name, Proana 5, is simply an abbreviation for "process analysis of a 5-person group."

The quality and the quantity of small group interaction are functions of the kind of people assembled. If everyone talks a lot, there will be a lot of interaction. But if everyone sits back and does not get involved, there won't be much interaction.

As you think about your own small group communication style, how do you see yourself? Circle the appropriate numbers for each of the scales below.

| | | | | | | |
|---|---|---|---|---|---|---|
| Talker | 5 | 4 | 3 | 2 | 1 | Listener |
| Task-oriented | 5 | 4 | 3 | 2 | 1 | Socioemotionally oriented |
| Fighting | 5 | 4 | 3 | 2 | 1 | Acquiescent |

Everyone who takes this little test will score differently, but such personality differences are necessary for successful groups. Consider what it would be like if everyone in your group scored exactly the same as you.

Later on, you might want to check with others who took this test and compare answers.

By tallying how often each person speaks to another in the group, you can specify the amount of communication line usage when the discussion ends. Typically, all lines will be used, but they won't be used equally. Some lines will have much activity, others little. By inspecting all the tallies at the end of a discussion, you should learn a number of things about the group. For instance, if two people spend too much time talking exclusively to each other, your analysis will show them to be a clique. If someone has little activity (marks) on his or her lines of communication, that person may be an isolate (someone excluded from the main flow of discussion). Likewise, dominance can be noted if one person talks more than any two others combined. All of these things are observable using a scoring system such as Proana 5.

The main advantage of Proana 5 or any other method of scoring group interaction is that it gives you a record of the group activity. Such records are useful later when you wish to assess the effectiveness of the group. Without such a record, your observations and evaluations would be subjective based on your memory, rather than based on actual statistical data. Now let's consider another way to record group interaction.

## BALES'S IPA

Network models of group interaction (such as Proana 5) are particularly useful for measuring the frequency of talk in a group, but they don't measure the content of the talk. When recording group interaction, you often need to know the kind of contribution that each person makes every time he or she speaks up in a group. To meet this need, Robert Bales (1950) developed the IPA (Interaction Process Analysis).

The IPA is based on the notion that group members make contributions to the group in accord with the task and social needs of the group. Thus some remarks are made to facilitate the task; others are made for their socioemotional value. Every time someone says some-

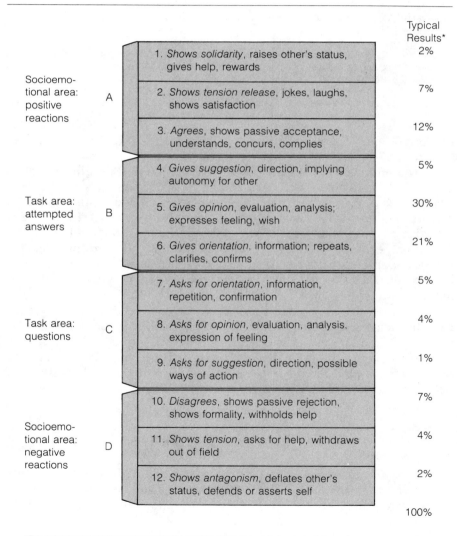

| | | | Typical Results* |
|---|---|---|---|
| Socioemotional area: positive reactions | A | 1. *Shows solidarity*, raises other's status, gives help, rewards | 2% |
| | | 2. *Shows tension release*, jokes, laughs, shows satisfaction | 7% |
| | | 3. *Agrees*, shows passive acceptance, understands, concurs, complies | 12% |
| Task area: attempted answers | B | 4. *Gives suggestion*, direction, implying autonomy for other | 5% |
| | | 5. *Gives opinion*, evaluation, analysis; expresses feeling, wish | 30% |
| | | 6. *Gives orientation*, information; repeats, clarifies, confirms | 21% |
| Task area: questions | C | 7. *Asks for orientation*, information, repetition, confirmation | 5% |
| | | 8. *Asks for opinion*, evaluation, analysis, expression of feeling | 4% |
| | | 9. *Asks for suggestion*, direction, possible ways of action | 1% |
| Socioemotional area: negative reactions | D | 10. *Disagrees*, shows passive rejection, shows formality, withholds help | 7% |
| | | 11. *Shows tension*, asks for help, withdraws out of field | 4% |
| | | 12. *Shows antagonism*, deflates other's status, defends or asserts self | 2% |
| | | | 100% |

*This column represents percentage of total number of remarks made in a typical discussion.

**Figure 9.4** IPA Categories

Your satisfaction with the personal and professional groups to which you belong may be a function of how much you feel a part of the daily communication activity of each group. For instance, Albrecht (1979) found that people who are in the center of interaction at work, and have frequent contact with many different people, tend to view the work climate as favorable. Those who are not so much "in the know" do not feel as satisfied with the group.

Apparently, people need communication to keep them happy on the job. If you feel that you are isolated from much of the communication in your groups, this may make you dissatisfied. Ultimately, you may leave the group, finding more suitable company elsewhere.

T. Albrecht, "The Role of Communication in Perceptions of Organizational Climate," in *Communication Yearbook 3*, ed. D. Nimmo (New Brunswick, N.J.: Transaction Books, 1979).

thing, you can classify the statement into one of 12 categories (see Figure 9.4).

You will notice from the percentages listed to the right in Figure 9.4 that the categories are not used equally by most groups. In fact, these percentages show that in typical group discussions members are often giving opinions and orientations (information). In the average group, more than half of the talk will be opinions and information. Furthermore, giving suggestions, opinions, and orientation (total of 56 percent of the remarks) greatly exceeds asking for the same (10 percent). I guess we simply prefer telling others what we think to asking what they think!

As with Proana 5, Bales's IPA can be used to discover the leaders, the isolates, and the dominant members. But if you combine the results of Proana 5 with the outcomes of the IPA, you will have a very powerful and complete analysis of a group discussion. With access to both records, you should be able to specify not only who talked to whom, but also how they talked to each other.*

## Summary Propositions

It is difficult to overstate the importance of small groups in your personal and professional lives. Modern decision making often depends on groups. Whether you are in a group to plan a fund drive or to

---

* For those of you who wish to use these techniques, check the references at the end of the chapter for the original sources (Lashbrook and Lashbrook, 1972; Bales, 1950).

select a bid for a new recreation center in your city, you need small group communication skills.

In this chapter, you have learned some basics of small group communication theory. In order to function properly, all groups need interdependence and interaction. The group's interdependence is a function of how well the group attends to the task and social needs, develops satisfactory levels of productivity and cohesiveness, forms roles and norms, and manages the pressures to conform. The interaction in a group can be measured through at least two methods—Proana 5 and Bales's IPA. The success of any group is closely tied to the group members' abilities to promote interdependence and effective interaction. The next chapter will help you acquire such skills.

1. As a social unit, groups play important roles in your personal and professional lives.

2. A group is a collectivity of three or more people who join together to accomplish common goals through communication.

3. Interdependence and interaction provide the "glue" that keeps the group intact.

4. Groups have task needs and social needs.

5. As a group strives to meet its needs, it becomes productive and promotes cohesion among the members.

6. There is a curvilinear relationship between cohesion and productivity.

7. Over time, groups produce roles and norms.

8. Roles and norms are enforced through pressure for conformity.

9. If a deviant strays too far from the norms, the group will exert pressure to conform on the deviant.

10. A member's willingness to conform is determined by the nature of the group and the nature of the individual.

11. There are two effective methods for quantifying and observing group interaction (Proana 5 and Bales's IPA).

## References

**Albrecht, T.** "The Role of Communication in Perceptions of Organizational Climate." In *Communication Yearbook 3,* edited by D. Nimmo. New Brunswick, N.J.: Transaction Books, 1979.

**Asch, S.** *Social Psychology.* Englewood Cliffs, N.J.: Prentice-Hall, 1952.

**Bales, R.** *Interaction Process Analysis.* Cambridge, Mass.: Addison-Wesley, 1950.

**Benne, K., and Sheats, P.** "Functional Roles of Group Members." *Journal of Social Issues* 4(1948):41–49.

**Burgoon, M.; Heston, J.; and McCroskey, J.** *Small Group Communication.* New York: Holt, Rinehart & Winston, 1974.

**Fisher, B. A.** *Small Group Decision Making.* New York: McGraw-Hill, 1980.

**Lashbrook, W., and Lashbrook, V.** *Proana 5: A Computer Analysis of Small Group Discussion.* Minneapolis: Burgess Publishing, 1975.

**Shaw, M.** *Group Dynamics.* New York: McGraw-Hill, 1971.

# 10

# GROUP
# DECISION MAKING

**Committees as Decision-making Groups**
Usefulness of Committees
When Not to Have a Committee

■

**Phases of Group Decision Making**
Phase One: Orientation
Phase Two: Conflict
Phase Three: Emergence
Phase Four: Reinforcement

■

**Dewey's Reflective Thinking Pattern**
Step One: Define the Problem
Step Two: Define the Causes
Step Three: Specify the Criteria for Solutions
Step Four: Consider More Than One Solution
Step Five: Choose the Best Solution

■

**Supportive Group Behaviors**

■

**Evaluating Group Performance**

■

**Summary Propositions**

■

**References**

■

175

Groups form for various reasons, but one of the most predominant reasons is to make decisions. Our society seems to be run by decision-making groups. Hardly a day goes by that your life is not affected by some committee's decisions. For instance, the city council makes decisions that determine how your drinking water is purified and delivered, where fire stations are located, how many parks you have in your part of town, and even which streets you may drive on to visit friends and relatives.

## Committees as Decision-making Groups

Decision-making groups are sometimes called committees. And committees are called many names, some not so nice. But even if you dislike committee work, you cannot deny the pervasive role committees play in our democratic society.

### USEFULNESS OF COMMITTEES

A committee is a group of people charged with fulfilling some task. The success of a committee often depends on the clarity of the committee's goals and on the members' feelings that they are empowered to make worthwhile decisions. If the members feel that their decisions will not be respected or if they are uncertain about their goals, then the committee work can be unsatisfying.

Although serving on committees can be, at times, exasperating, there are a number of benefits in committee work. First of all, because committees are comprised of a number of different people, many different kinds of information are available for the decision-making task. Each committee member brings a personal point of view, and if everyone is allowed to talk, the group benefits from such multiple sources of input.

Second, committees can collectively share the burden of decision making. In other words, if a number of people decide together to solve a problem a certain way, they all share the responsibility for the success or failure of the chosen solution. In a committee, no one person can be blamed for a poor decision. The whole committee is responsible.

Third, the time spent in committee work often benefits other tasks. People make friends on committees, and relationships form. These relationships formed during committee work may come in handy at a later time. It's amazing how often you know a helpful person simply because you both once served on the same committee.

Although committees can be beneficial, there are times when a committee is simply not needed. The decision to form a committee should not be haphazard. Certain considerations are required.

*Best of all worlds?* Is it possible to assemble a group of people that will work together optimally? Shaw (1971) suggests that such a group would have people that:

1. Are cohesive (attracted to one another)

2. Have compatible needs (individual needs that do not conflict)

3. Have heterogeneous skills (each person contributes personal talents to the work)

At times, it is difficult to form such a group. But when it is possible, the group will be very effective.

If you ever have to form a committee to work on an important project, you might want to keep these three qualities in mind.

M. Shaw, *Group Dynamics: The Psychology of Small Group Behavior* (New York: McGraw-Hill, 1971).

## WHEN NOT TO HAVE A COMMITTEE

Because we tend to favor democracy, we often view committees as cure-alls for our problems. Sometimes, the committee is indeed the best vehicle for dealing with a problem. Other times, however, a committee is unnecessary. Knowing when a committee is *not* needed is just as important as knowing the benefits of one. The decision to form a committee depends on three factors: time, difficulty of the problem, and the extent of the problem.

Forming a committee takes time, and if, for example, you are facing an emergency situation, you cannot plan a full-scale meeting. But you can talk to each person who would be a commitee member to get advice before you decide what to do. Too often, people allow pressing deadlines to inhibit their search for input from group members, and in the process, they may make a poor decision.

The second factor in considering whether to form a committee is the difficulty of the problem. Some problems are technical and depend on a particular skill. Others are not so clearly defined, thus requiring the collective wisdom and creativity of several people. For instance, if you need to arrange a concert group for a rally, forming a committee would be a good idea for choosing the group to invite. But a committee would be useless for the actual booking of the group. The mechanics of signing contracts and arranging facilities can be handled by an appointed person.

The third concern is the extent of the problem. Some problems are large and affect many people; others are smaller and affect only a few people. Minor problems that involve only a few people should be solved by those people, without a formal committee. In contrast, problems and solutions that will affect an entire office or organization deserve committee-level consideration. The key is to know the extent of the problem and its potential solution. Too often, people are called into meetings to discuss problems that don't concern them.

The decision to form or not to form a committee is often in the hands of one person. If you find that your position requires that you

In some organizations, the committee system is so popular that members of committees who have a long history of working together often become more efficient in decision making but less critical. This causes groupthink.

*Groupthink* is a term created by Janis (1972) to describe how a group can become so cohesive and conforming that the members do not study the issues very carefully. To avoid rocking the boat, the members may agree to solutions prematurely, without careful analysis of the problem itself.

When a group is suffering from groupthink, they are no longer thinking as individuals but as one agreeable body. Such like-mindedness can lead to poor solutions. Groupthink, therefore, can be detrimental to critical decision making.

Thus, it is a good idea to periodically shift the members of committees, so that "new blood" can stimulate the critical thinking of the committee.

I. Janis, *Victims of Groupthink* (Boston: Houghton Mifflin, 1972).

make this kind of decision, you need to know when to delegate a problem to one person, or perhaps two people, as opposed to forming an official committee. If you keep in mind the time considerations and the difficulty and extent of the problem, you should make effective decisions about forming a committee.

## Phases of Group Decision Making

Whenever group members meet to discuss problems and solutions, the group discussion will pass through a number of phases characteristic of problem-solving discussions. These different stages of development in the group discussion are marked by changes in the communication behavior of the members. Fisher (1980) claims that small group decision making is characterized by four successive phases.

### PHASE ONE: ORIENTATION

The first phase, orientation, occurs at the beginning of the discussion and is the time when the members get acquainted with the problem and with each other. During the orientation phase, the members communicate in cautious ways, as though they are "feeling out" one another. Whenever attitudes are asserted, they are done so with qualification (for example, "Perhaps we should . . ." rather than "We should . . ."). There will also be some problem clarification remarks during this stage as the members begin to focus more narrowly on the task. The orientation phase, then, is necessary for the group to home in on the task at hand. If a group does not spend enough time in the orientation stage, they may jump to solutions without adequately familiarizing themselves with the problem.

### PHASE TWO: CONFLICT

In the conflict phase of the decision-making discussion, the members are directly assertive. Their attitudes will not be as tentative as they were in the orientation phase. The conflict phase is the time when debate occurs, when the members disagree with each other and discover who's on whose side. In the conflict phase, the hard data emerge— the participants provide evidence for their assertions. The conflict phase is crucial for small group decision making. In this stage important issues and ideas surface that affect the quality of the decisions. If a group does not experience a conflict phase, they may turn into a yea-saying coalition that fails to evaluate ideas critically. The conflict phase is necessary for a fair evaluation of ideas. It is the time when conflicting ideas are weighed for their respective merit.

## PHASE THREE: EMERGENCE

The third phase develops from the conflict phase. In the emergence phase, decisions begin to surface or emerge. The differences of opinion that were so obvious in the conflict phase are now obscured by attempts to reconcile ideas. The coalitions among people start to break down as the group moves to act as a whole to produce a final decision. Talk of compromise and fair solutions develops. In many ways, the original charge or mission of the committee starts to take precedence over the differences of opinion. Convergence toward a group decision is the ultimate objective of the emergence phase.

## PHASE FOUR: REINFORCEMENT

Finally, group decision making is characterized by a reinforcement phase. In this phase, the members show an air of agreement. The discussion develops into consensus and centers on the chosen solution. As the members talk about the solution, they express positive attitudes. And as they reflect on their work, they may express positive feelings about one another as well. In any event, the group finishes the decision-making process with a spirit of unity.

It is important to realize that although these four phases or stages are listed as steps, the phases can overlap as a group moves from one to another. The discussion may also get out of sequence. For

During the latter stages of decision making, group members begin to adopt a solution and assume responsibility, as a group, for the consequences of the solution.

Solutions produced by groups are often superior to solutions produced by individuals. But solutions produced by groups are also more risky than solutions generated by individuals alone.

Wallach et al. (1962) found that people were more willing to choose risky solutions to problems when they were deciding the matter as a group than they were when dealing with the problem alone. Researchers reason that group deliberation gives the members more confidence in the solution, thus making them more willing to try risky solutions. Also, if the solution fails, the whole group is responsible, not just one member.

If you think about this, you will probably realize you take more chances when others around you are doing the same thing. The presence of others, along with the group interaction, may stimulate less conservative solutions to problems.

M. Wallach et al., "Group Influence on Individual Risk Taking," *Journal of Abnormal and Social Psychology* 65(1962):75–86.

instance, a group may begin with conflict, only to have to go back to an orientation phase before they can continue. Or a group may experience more than one conflict phase. But in general, groups will follow the four-step process of orientation, conflict, emergence, and reinforcement.

## Dewey's Reflective Thinking Pattern

The four phases of group decision making described earlier are natural phases—they seem to happen without specific planning. Sometimes, however, it is a good idea to plan a discussion with a more formal system of steps. Such a system is Dewey's reflective thinking pattern.

A number of years ago, John Dewey (1910) proposed a five-step problem-solving agenda that would be useful in small group decision making. This plan, when adapted to group discussions, encourages an orderly and thorough discussion of all parts of problem solving. The five steps are:

1. Define the problem.

2. Define the causes.

3. Specify the criteria for solutions.

4. Consider more than one solution.

5. Choose the best solution.

Let's consider each step separately.

### STEP ONE: DEFINE THE PROBLEM

The first thing that the group must do is define the problem. The members should agree on what the problem is, so that everyone talks about the same thing. Some people may not realize that a problem exists. Others may not feel that there is a problem at all. Thus, it is important to define the problem so that everyone will focus on the same situation or issue.

Defining the problem includes indicating what aspects of the problem are to be considered. For example, if your group is meeting to deal with parking problems on campus, you may want to define parking problems pertaining only to automobiles, not motorcycles; campus personnel, not visitors; available spaces, not ticketing procedures; and so on. By narrowing the focus of the topic the group avoids irrelevant remarks later. Too often, groups fail to adequately define the problem.

**F.Y.I.**

Many times a group discussion is cramped by the discussion question itself. In other words, the topic of discussion is phrased in a way that limits effective discussion. Consider, for example, this question:

"Should the grading policies be changed at the college?"

This question could be answered quickly by yes or no. As soon as the group decides on a yes or a no answer, the discussion ceases. Now if that is all the group wants to decide, then the question is fine. But if the group is attempting to establish policy, the question needs revision. To deal with this problem, the question could be restated:

"What changes should be made in the grading policies?"

This question calls for solutions, but it also calls for change. In other words, it is biased against the status quo. It assumes change is needed. A better way to phrase the question would be:

"What, if anything, should be done about the grading policies at the college?"

This final question neither assumes a yes or no answer, nor is it biased. It would, therefore, allow a free-flowing discussion, without limiting the choices of the group members.

## STEP TWO: DEFINE THE CAUSES

Next the group should discuss what caused the problem. The group members should look back in time and trace the emergence of the problem. In doing so, the members will understand why they have a problem. Knowing why a problem exists is often half the battle of solving it.

In order to define the causes, the group needs to do some research. The members need evidence to support their claims about the causes. For instance, if the campus has parking problems, is it because of increasing enrollment, or is it because some parking spaces have been removed recently? No matter what the reason, you need to research the causes and be ready to present actual facts and figures to back up your findings.

## STEP THREE: SPECIFY THE CRITERIA FOR SOLUTIONS

This is the step most often neglected by problem-solving groups. Some groups, in an effort to solve the problem as soon as possible, start offering solutions before they have decided what a good solution will look like. It is not a good idea to take the first solution that comes along. Yet groups often do this.

Groups need a basis for which one solution can be chosen over another. That is, groups need criteria for choosing solutions. In the parking problem mentioned earlier, an acceptable set of criteria for a good solution might be that the solution:

1. Increases the number of parking spaces

2. Is relatively low in cost

3. Does not increase student fees

4. Provides for future needs in parking

With these four criteria, the group could then go on to discuss a number of solutions, ultimately choosing the one that best fits the criteria. By specifying the criteria beforehand, the group's later work is made much easier.

## STEP FOUR: CONSIDER MORE THAN ONE SOLUTION

Step four calls for hearing a number of solutions. Too many groups, in need of a solution, take the first decent idea that pops up. Many better solutions do not surface, then, because the members failed to take time to consider alternatives. This commonly happens when one person in the group is particularly influential and is the author of the first solution expressed. Under such influence, many members are tempted to nod their agreement and adopt the solution.

To consider only one solution is not sensible, especially after taking time to develop criteria. Yet, to have multiple solutions, the group needs multiple sources of input. This requires that each member do some creative thinking (and research) and be willing to express his or her plans. If a group does not have a number of solutions from which to choose, the members may never know how good the chosen solution is. Concerned group members will seek other opinions before deciding on the first solution brought forward.

## STEP FIVE: CHOOSE THE BEST SOLUTION

If the group has done its work well, this step can be easy. For instance, if the group has established a good set of criteria and discussed a number of solutions, then choosing one over another is a matter of matching each solution to the criteria. In this way, some solutions can be eliminated quickly. However, other solutions may be equally good, that is, they equally meet the criteria. Choosing one over the others then becomes a matter of critically evaluating the solutions and seeking agreement on one.

For the most part, it is a good idea not to vote on the final solution. The group will experience more reinforcement (phase four) if they can choose a solution unanimously. Solidarity of feelings about the solution is important in group decision making (though not always possible).

The greatest benefits of using the five-step plan for solving problems occur after the group has completed its work. First, with such a systematic plan of attack, the group members should feel greater satisfaction with their efforts, knowing that they took the time to thoroughly explore the problem and its possible solutions. The second benefit is one of producing higher quality solutions. If the group considered more than one solution, and tested each against the criteria, the chosen solution should be the best one. So increased satisfaction and higher quality solutions are the main reasons for using a systematic plan of discussion.

Let's see if you remember the five steps of reflective thinking. They are listed below, out of order. In the spaces provided, number them in their correct order.

_____ Specify the criteria.

_____ Define the causes.

_____ Choose the best solution.

_____ Consider more than one solution.

_____ Define the problem.

Now go back and circle the step that is most often neglected by groups (according to the text).

There is nothing magical about these five steps for decision making. But if all the group members have these steps memorized, they might follow them more naturally in problem-solving discussions.

(Answers: 3, 2, 5, 4, 1; circle the criteria step.)

## Supportive Group Behaviors

An agenda such as Dewey's reflective thinking pattern is helpful in structuring group decision making. But such an agenda does not remove the members' interpersonal obligations to help the group function well. Every group member should see himself or herself as a contributing member of the group. This does not mean that everyone must talk a lot. Rather, it means that each group member will take on some of the responsibility to see that issues are introduced and prop-

Through communication we can share and carefully consider ideas. (Photo courtesy of B. Goss.)

erly considered before a decision is made. More specifically, each group member should keep in mind the following supportive communication behaviors (adapted from Benne and Sheats, 1948).

The first supportive behavior is called *initiating,* that is, making comments that stimulate the group to think about an idea. In order for ideas to surface, someone has to bring them up. Each member, then, has an obligation to raise issues that the group needs to deal with. People who do not initiate ideas, because they want to avoid conflict, often do a disservice to the group. Initiating is fundamental to group discussion. If no one brings up ideas, there will be nothing to talk about.

Second, groups need people who both *seek and give* information and opinions. Each member is responsible not only for sharing ideas but for seeking them from other members as well. Too often, we become so engrossed in our own opinions we forget to elicit ideas from our colleagues. When this occurs, many good ideas are never brought out, thus leading to poorer solutions to the problems.

Third, the problem-solving task can be handled more efficiently if someone remembers to *clarify and summarize* periodically. Restating some of the issues discussed helps the group members recognize their points of agreement and the stages of topic development. Periodic clarifying and summarizing also helps the group organize the discussion. At these times, the members can evaluate what has been said before proceeding further.

Initiating, seeking and giving, and clarifying and summarizing are supportive behaviors that facilitate the task needs of the group. Such behaviors help the group get its work done in an orderly fashion. But the group also has social needs that can be met through supportive behaviors. There are many ways to be socially supportive in your communication behavior. Two are discussed here.

The first socially supportive behavior is *harmonizing*. This occurs when members assist one another in resolving conflicts. Interpersonal conflicts in a group will not be damaging to the morale of the group if they are handled effectively. I was reminded of this recently on an airline flight when I witnessed a conflict among the crew. They were having difficulty serving the in-flight meal, and there was a notable amount of confusion and disunity among the crew members. One of the flight attendants was perceptive enough to detect an interpersonal conflict between two of the other attendants which was causing the poor service to the passengers. She met with the two troubled attendants (in the galley) and helped them resolve their conflict. From that point on, the attendants seemed more amicable toward one another, and the service improved significantly. If the sensitive attendant had not tried to harmonize the conflict, the crew would have had problems throughout the flight. Through harmonizing, you can help mitigate the morale-eroding effects of conflicts, and create an environment where people enjoy working together.

Earlier you learned that people have needs for inclusion. Being part of a group is one way that people meet their needs to belong. But some groups meet this need more than do other groups. You can differentiate these groups by how the members talk to one another.

Think about the five kinds of supporting behavior. Which one contributes the most to other people's needs for inclusion? Rank-order them according to how much they help others feel that they belong.

_____ Initiating

_____ Seeking and giving

_____ Clarifying and summarizing

_____ Harmonizing

_____ Encouraging

If everyone in your group were more attentive to these forms of supportive behavior, would your group be more cohesive? Would all members feel that they belong?

The second way you can be socially supportive is by *encouraging* your colleagues. This can be done by cheering up someone who seems dejected. Or you can encourage other group members by gently urging them to talk. In the everyday routine of committees and meetings, it is easy to forget that your cohorts may need to be encouraged to speak up. And if these people don't talk, they may feel left out of the discussion and become unwilling later to endorse the group's decisions.

Being a supportive group member means that you will do all you can to satisfy the task and social needs of the group. Not every member needs to adopt the five types of supportive behavior, but the group as a whole should show evidence of each of these as it conducts its business. In many ways, the quality of the group will depend on the quality of the communication behaviors of the members.

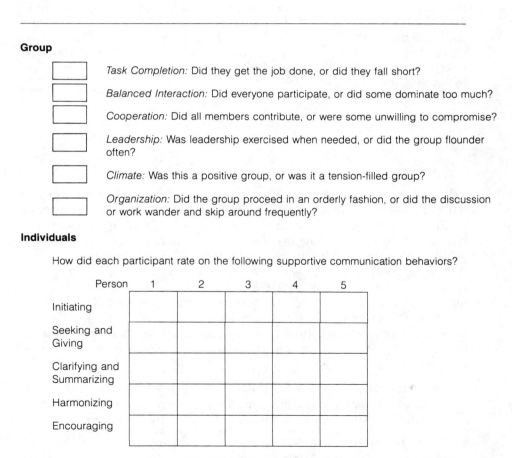

**Group**

☐ *Task Completion:* Did they get the job done, or did they fall short?

☐ *Balanced Interaction:* Did everyone participate, or did some dominate too much?

☐ *Cooperation:* Did all members contribute, or were some unwilling to compromise?

☐ *Leadership:* Was leadership exercised when needed, or did the group flounder often?

☐ *Climate:* Was this a positive group, or was it a tension-filled group?

☐ *Organization:* Did the group proceed in an orderly fashion, or did the discussion or work wander and skip around frequently?

**Individuals**

How did each participant rate on the following supportive communication behaviors?

| Person | 1 | 2 | 3 | 4 | 5 |
|---|---|---|---|---|---|
| Initiating | | | | | |
| Seeking and Giving | | | | | |
| Clarifying and Summarizing | | | | | |
| Harmonizing | | | | | |
| Encouraging | | | | | |

**Figure 10.1** Critique Form for Evaluating Group Performance

## Evaluating Group Performance

Sometime after the group discussion, it is a good idea to evaluate the group and its members. In Chapter 9, I discussed how Proana 5 and Bales's interaction process analysis (IPA) can be used to analyze a group. But now, I want to share with you a method that will help identify the strengths and weaknesses of both the group as a whole and each member. A thorough evaluation of the group would include an interaction analysis such as Proana 5 and/or Bales's IPA, plus a critique such as the one proposed here. In all cases, though, evaluation is designed to help improve group communication. Thus, careful evaluation can provide valuable feedback to the group and its members.

Using the concepts and ideas suggested in this chapter, you can assess the quality of a group using the critique form shown in Figure 10.1. This critique has two levels of analysis—of the group and of the individuals. With a 1 to 5 scale (5, highest score; 1, lowest score) you can score the group as a whole on six items, and each individual on five items. Hopefully, this kind of feedback will encourage improvement and reward good work.

## Summary Propositions

Effective group decision making is no accident. It depends on the willingness of the members to communicate in ways that facilitate action. Sometimes this requires a planned agenda such as the reflective thinking pattern suggested by Dewey. Other times, the discussion simply follows the four natural phases of group decision making. Whatever method of decision making the group employs, the members must practice the task-related and socially supportive communication behaviors. Each person in the group has an obligation to see that the group discusses openly the issues that need to be addressed. If your group follows the suggestions described in this chapter and in Chapter 9, you should notice a marked improvement in your group discussions.

1. The decision to form a committee to solve a problem should depend on whether multiple sources of input will produce better solutions than will one person working on the problem.

2. Problem-solving discussion groups pass through four phases of interaction (Fisher, 1980):

  a. Orientation

  b. Conflict

  c. Emergence

  d. Reinforcement

3. An effective problem-solving agenda proposed by Dewey (1910) is:

  a. Define the problem.

  b. Define the causes.

  c. Specify the criteria for solutions.

  d. Consider more than one solution.

  e. Choose the best solution.

4. Supportive group behaviors are helpful in group decision making. There are five kinds:

  a. Initiating

  b. Seeking and giving

  c. Clarifying and summarizing

  d. Harmonizing

  e. Encouraging

5. For evaluating a group discussion, it is useful to have a critique form that assesses both the whole group and each individual.

# References

**Benne, K., and Sheats, P.** "Functional Roles of Group Members." *Journal of Social Issues* 4(1948):41–49.

**Dewey, J.** *How We Think.* New York: Heath, 1910.

**Fisher, B. A.** *Small Group Decision Making.* New York: McGraw-Hill, 1980.

**Janis, I.** *Victims of Groupthink.* Boston: Houghton Mifflin, 1972.

**Shaw, M.** *Group Dynamics.* New York: McGraw-Hill, 1971.

**Wallach, M.; Kogan, N.; and Bem, D.** "Group Influence on Individual Risk Taking." *Journal of Abnormal and Social Psychology* 65(1962):75–86.

# 11

# LEADERSHIP

**What Is Leadership?**

■

**Sources of Influence**
Interpersonal Attraction
Source Credibility
Social Power

■

**A Brief Review**

■

**Deciding How to Lead**
Leadership Styles
Criteria for Leadership Choice
Specific Communication Strategies

■

**Sounding Like a Leader**
Speech Content
Speech Style
A Speech Profile

■

**Summary Propositions**

■

**References**

■

Why do some people really like their bosses, while others hate their bosses? Why do some groups outperform others, even if they all started as equals? What makes some people leaders and others not? These are difficult questions, but how you answer them may make a big difference in your life.

In 1979, three college professors published an exciting book on group discussion (Phillips et al., 1979). In their chapter on leadership, the authors begin by saying, "This may be the most important chapter in the entire book. It is about leadership, and it is addressed to all of you because we believe that virtually everyone can learn to lead" (p. 69). I agree. And if what I hear from employers is accurate, then developing your leadership skills through developing your communication skills should make you more attractive to potential employers. You have already looked at the job interview in an earlier chapter. There you saw how others' perceptions of you determine your future. In this chapter, you will learn how to enhance your perceived leadership, that is, how others see you as a leader. If you work with the suggestions presented here, you will be more successful as an employee, spouse, parent, and friend. Leadership extends beyond the job; it applies to all facets of your personal and professional lives.

## What Is Leadership?

Leadership is a strange phenomenon. Most people know it when they see it, but have difficulty specifying exactly what it is. It is not simply being the boss. Nor is it simply the person assigned to chair a group. Leadership is something dynamic, part of a person's communication skills, and something that everyone has the potential for. Each of you, at some time, has or will have the leadership skills that a group of people will need.

The term *leadership* can be used in many ways, thus causing confusion about the actual nature of leadership. For instance, you may say that a person is in a "position of leadership." Or, a person has "leadership potential." Or, that person is a "*real* leader." In all these examples, the term *leadership* is used somewhat differently. Yet somehow it refers to the same quality.

Given that there is no one true definition of leadership, we can still define it to accommodate its most common uses. Thus, *leadership is the process of influence that a person can have on others to mobilize them toward specific objectives*. In essence, leadership is influence.

There are three key terms in this definition of leadership: *influence, others*, and *objectives*. Taken together, these three concepts imply that (1) someone influences, (2) someone follows, and (3) there is somewhere to go, some place to reach. Thus, a leader is one who has a goal in mind and is influential. But more importantly, a leader needs followers. In fact, it is the followers who determine the extent to which someone can lead. Followers grant you leadership when they recognize your influence. You cannot reach out to take leadership, unless the others are willing to let you do so. And in spite of what cosmetic firms and cereal companies would like you to believe, you cannot find leadership on the grocery store shelves.

Most of what we know about leadership has come from literature dealing with leadership in small groups and on the job. But leadership is exercised in your personal life as well. For instance, a group of people trying to decide what to do on Saturday night needs leadership. You even lead others by the clothes you wear, the music you listen to, and the games you like to play. Anytime people look to you for direction, you are in a leadership role.

## Sources of Influence

If leadership is centered on your ability to influence others, where do you get influence from? There are three sources from which you can draw influence: interpersonal attraction, source credibility, and social power. All three are in the minds of your followers, in that they must perceive you to be sufficiently high in these variables to warrant following you.

### INTERPERSONAL ATTRACTION

Interpersonal attraction refers to the number of people who find you desirable to be with. People who are high in interpersonal attraction have many friends and have contacts with many different people. There are three forms of attraction: physical, task, and social.

**PHYSICAL ATTRACTION** This refers to your outward appearance. Physical attraction is what cosmetic firms want you to worry about. Your physical attraction is noted by your clothing, posture, relative beauty, and body shape. But there is another side to physical attraction—how well you "fit" certain expectations. For instance, if you are being interviewed for a job, one of the things that the interviewer might look for is how well you will look the part if you are hired. If you are applying for an engineer's job, you should look and sound like an engineer. Likewise, a potential dietician should look and sound like one. All of these qualities matter when people judge your physical attraction.

**TASK ATTRACTION** This second kind of attraction is based on how much people desire to work with you because of your "track record." If you are known for your competence and for successfully completing your work, you will be highly valued in task attraction. You need, then, to be concerned about your reputation, so that others will see you as attractive.

**SOCIAL ATTRACTION** This is the counterpart to task attraction. It is based on your perceived sociableness, and is not dependent on your job performance. People who are high in social attraction are fun to be with. They have many friends because they are pleasant and provide good companionship. In most groups, one person is perceived as the highest in task attraction, while another is seen as the highest in social attraction. But in every group, there must be an adequate amount of both task and social attraction among the members so that they can function as a group and be willing to be influenced by one another.

**LIKELIHOOD OF INTERPERSONAL ATTRACTION** As you think about the groups of people that you affiliate with, you will discover that there are three variables that determine the likelihood of a group of people being attracted to one another. One is *proximity*, the geographical distance among people. The closer people are in physical proximity, the more opportunities they will have to interact and form relationships. Thus, friendships, marriages, business partnerships, and committees are often established by people who have convenient access to one another.

Another important variable is *similarity*. You tend to be attracted to people who are similar to you in thoughts and actions. You choose such people because they will reinforce you, and not be antagonistic. Apparently, most of us are more comfortable with people like ourselves. So, unless we don't have much choice in the matter, we spend most of our time with such people.

Finally, there is the impact of the *situation*. Sometimes people develop high levels of attraction for one another because they are on

YOUR TURN...

As you consider yourself in terms of attraction, which one are you best in? Check one of the following:

_____ Physical attraction

_____ Task attraction

_____ Social attraction

Now go back and place an X next to the one you need to improve on.

What, specifically, will you do to enhance the one that needs improvement?

_____

_____

_____

_____

_____

No matter how you evaluated yourself, you can be sure that everyone has a certain amount of attraction in all three categories. Only a terribly ugly, lazy oaf with offensive social skills is devoid of attractiveness. Fortunately, such a person is not likely to be reading this book.

the same team, trying to win for a common cause. This effect is evident in team members in sports, or in military combat, or in a project team at work. Because the group members are drawn together by the situation, they find ways to be attracted to one another. This is especially true under conditions of threat, when the welfare of the group is jeopardized by some external force.

## SOURCE CREDIBILITY

Closely allied to leadership is your personal source credibility. Source credibility is how other people evaluate you in terms of your believability. It is an attitude that others hold about you; thus you do not simply *have* credibility, it is given to you by others.

Like so many attitudes, your receivers' attitudes about you as a source are multifaceted. Most people judge credibility on at least two dimensions: competence and trustworthiness. Your perceived competence is based on how expert and how reliable you seem to be. Your perceived trustworthiness will be based on the receivers' judgments of your honesty, fairness, and compassion.

Obviously, it is desirable to be high in both competence and trustworthiness, but this is not always the case. For instance, a fast-talking salesperson may seem competent to you, but not very trustworthy. Likewise, when you ask your friends for advice on topics they are not trained to comment on, you might view them as trustworthy, but not very competent in that area.

Of the two dimensions of credibility, losing trust may be more disastrous than losing competence. Let me explain. People are more tolerant of ineptitude (because "all people make mistakes") than they are of deceit. If you betray people by a deceitful act, they will not trust you, and your ability to influence them will disappear— especially if you try to cover up your deception. Many politicians are removed from office not because they are incompetent, but because they are perceived as untrustworthy. Apparently, people find it hard to follow a leader that they cannot believe. Thus, credibility is an important part of leadership.

Using the scales below, circle the appropriate number indicating your feelings about your instructor's source credibility.

Qualified    5   4   3   2   1    Unqualified

Intelligent  5   4   3   2   1    Unintelligent

Honest       5   4   3   2   1    Dishonest

Pleasant     5   4   3   2   1    Unpleasant

The first two scales refer to the teacher's competence, while the third and fourth ones measure the instructor's trustworthiness.

Now that you have judged your instructor, ask yourself why you feel this way. What has the instructor done, if anything, to deserve the marks given? You might discover that your feelings about your instructor are mostly intuitive and not firmly grounded in specific observations.

## SOCIAL POWER

Social power is the third source of influence. Social power is often related to status, but status is only part of it. Actually, your social power is determined by how much others value your assets that make you an important person to please. Sometimes these assets are related to personal wealth, or to the number of personal contacts a person may have in a community. But just because a person is wealthy or socially influential in a community does not mean that he or she will be a leader. For instance, socialites may be looked to for trends in fashion in the clothes they wear in public, but they may not have much influence in other aspects of life.

According to French and Raven (1968), there are five kinds of social power: reward, coercive, expert, referent, and legitimate.

**REWARD POWER** This refers to your ability to positively reinforce people through rewards. The reward is not necessarily money. It may be a compliment, a new job, a paid vacation, or an appointment to an important commission. Even your instructors have reward power through the grades they give.

**COERCIVE POWER** This second kind of social power is the opposite of reward power. The main source of coercive power is through punishments. To the degree that someone can administer punishments to you (withhold rewards, introduce either physical or social pain, and so forth), that person has coercive power over you. Your parents, teachers, police, and friends sometimes use this form of power. People even exercise coercive power in their communication activities. For instance, withholding a secret from someone who knows you know the secret is a way of using power coercively. Children apply this kind of coercive power more obviously than adults do, but adults use it too.

**EXPERT POWER** The third kind of power is based on your reputation for knowing a lot about the topic at hand. Your physician has expert power when it is time to diagnose your illnesses. Expert power is similar to the competence dimension of source credibility, except that it focuses more on one's training and education than does the competence dimension.

**REFERENT POWER** This fourth form of social power is one of the hardest to define. It refers to the power that people have over each other because of friendships or obligations. "Do it for me" is the sales pitch that uses referent power. Groups often pressure their members to behave according to the group norms because the group is important. In order for this kind of power to work, the listeners or receivers must feel that their relationship with the source is important to preserve.

**LEGITIMATE POWER** This is the fifth, and final, form of social power. You acquire legitimate power when you are assigned to rule over others. This kind of power comes from your position in the office, club, organization, or institution. Thus, supervisors have legitimate power over their workers, union leaders over the union members, and college deans over their faculty members. In essence, your legitimate power is assigned to you by those in authority above you.

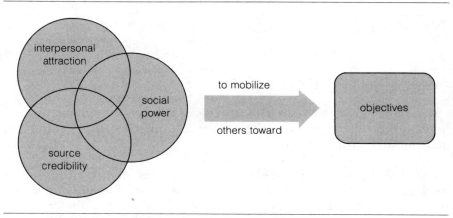

**Figure 11.1** Leadership Diagram

## A Brief Review

Before continuing on to consider how to lead, let's review what has been said so far. Leadership is defined as a process of influence that a person can have on others to mobilize them toward specific objectives. People must be willing to be led. Leadership, therefore, is given to a person by the followers. Three sources of influence have been identified: interpersonal attraction, source credibility, and social power. Leaders can draw upon these three sources of influence as they lead their groups. Figure 11.1 provides a good way to remember all this.

## Deciding How to Lead

There are many ways to lead a group, and effective leaders carefully choose methods that fit their personalities and their groups' needs. When deciding how to lead, however, the leader must consider two factors: (1) overall style and (2) the specific communication strategies that can be used to solve problems.

### LEADERSHIP STYLES

Rensis Likert (1967), an expert on leadership styles, tells us that there are essentially four kinds of leadership, in a continuum ranging from totally authoritarian to totally democratic. Figure 11.2 illustrates the four styles on the continuum. As you will see, the choice of

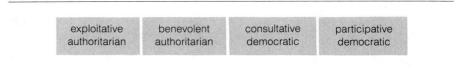

**Figure 11.2** Continuum of Leadership Styles

leadership style depends on the person leading, the people being led, and the task at hand.

**EXPLOITATIVE AUTHORITARIAN** At one end of the continuum is exploitative authoritarian leadership. This style of leadership is the most dictatorial. It assumes that those being led are incapable of making decisions, and that following orders is their way of life. This kind of leader makes decisions, then passes them down to the followers for compliance. The followers do not participate in the decision making. As Likert points out, this type of leadership can lead to distrust of the leader among the followers. And if the followers form a clique, they can move in opposition to the leader.

You can recognize the exploitative authoritarian leaders by how they talk. Instead of suggesting, they order. Instead of offering constructive comments on workers' performances, they criticize. This kind of leader often has a definite, firm speaking style. Such a leader has little doubt of the correctness of his or her views.

**BENEVOLENT AUTHORITARIAN** The more moderate authoritarian style is that of the benevolent authoritarian leader. This style is somewhat more people oriented. The benevolent authoritarian still controls the group with a firm grip, but does so with the welfare of the group foremost. When decision making is necessary, this kind of leader permits input from the group members but within restricted guidelines. The difference between this kind of leader and the exploitative authoritarian is really a matter of degree. The more benevolent the leader is, the more he or she allows group participation in decision making. But the benevolent authoritarian still runs the show.

A benevolent authoritarian leader might announce that the company is going to change its vacation policies and ask for suggestions to be submitted by a certain date. Usually, under this style, no open meeting is conducted. If one is, however, it will have a strict agenda and a clearly designated format for speaking in the meeting.

**CONSULTATIVE DEMOCRATIC** This third style of leadership assumes that the group members can be trusted to come up with good ideas for solving problems. The consultative democratic leader has confidence in the group members. Under this pattern of leadership, the group decides how to deal with most of the problems. Only a few of the major issues are reserved for top-level decision making. The leader using this style might actually consult with the group before making a decision (even a major one). Thus, the group is seen as a resource of ideas rather than just a bunch of people who need careful supervision.

**PARTICIPATIVE DEMOCRATIC** This is the most democratic leadership style. Under participative democratic leadership, no decisions are reserved for the executives or withheld from the group. The leaders and the members work side by side and have complete trust in one another. They tackle problems in an unrestricted manner, without previously determined guidelines. In such a group, it may be impossible to determine who the leader is, since that person simply blends in with the others in dealing with the problem.

The participative democratic style assumes that there will be much discussion, and that everyone will feel free to participate. The participative democratic leader must be careful not to impose his or her structure on the group. Thus, such a leader phrases questions carefully and tries not to impose one value system on all the others.

**A CONTINUUM** None of these four leadership styles is fixed. In other words, these styles are simply points on a continuum. The differences among them are a matter of degree. As you become more democratic, you move toward the democratic styles, and vice versa. At any time, your style may be somewhere between two of the four styles mentioned. But whatever style you choose as a leader, it will be more or less authoritarian or democratic.

## CRITERIA FOR LEADERSHIP CHOICE

How do you determine which style of leadership is best for you? Your decision depends primarily on three factors: you and your position in the group, the clarity of the task, and group harmony (how well your group members get along and work together).

**YOU AND YOUR POSITION** Have you ever heard the expression, "The right person, at the right place, at the right time"? Well, this notion applies to group leadership. Certain styles of leadership are better suited to some people than to others. For instance, some people may want to be participative democratic leaders, yet their personalities make it difficult for them to keep quiet and let the group do most of the talking. Others may want to be more authoritarian but discover that they cannot delegate authority without feeling guilty about asking people to do things. Whenever your personality does not fit your attempted leadership style, you will fail as a leader. If you are not a

There is another kind of leadership called laissez-faire leadership. In this style, the leader does not participate in the problem-solving discussion.

Research into the laissez-faire style of leadership has demonstrated that it is an undesirable form of leadership. It is almost like having no leadership at all.

Groups working under laissez-faire leadership are not very productive, and their work is poor in quality. Since the groups experience little direction under such conditions, they work less and play more. Laissez-faire leadership is, then, nonproductive leadership.

This raises the issue of the need for leadership in groups. Is it possible that some groups do not need any leadership? Can you think of instances wherein there is no need for directive leadership? Can any group survive without leadership? If so, under what circumstances?

D. Cartwright and A. Zander, *Group Dynamics: Research and Theory,* 3rd ed. (New York: Harper & Row, 1968).

disciplinarian in your own personal life, don't expect to be an efficient authoritarian leader. Likewise, if you are highly task oriented in your own personal life, you may not be a very good democratic leader.

Even if your personality is conducive to the leadership style you prefer, you must still face the question of your relationship with the group. Do your group members look to you for guidance? Do they like and respect you? The answers to these questions will tell you whether you are in a position to lead. Knowing how you are perceived by your colleagues is important to your decision to lead or not to lead.

**TASK CLARITY** Next, you should evaluate how clear-cut and unambiguous the task will seem to the group. If the group is experienced in dealing with similar tasks, there may be little uncertainty among the members. Consequently, they will need little supervision. For instance, a group of workers that are erecting the sixth floor of a building that has had five previous, identical floor plans, wiring, window locations, and plumbing patterns needs minimal leadership. In contrast, a community action group meeting for the first time to establish ways to deal with neighborhood vandalism will need a lot of leadership. The question is, what kind of leadership?

The answer depends on the nature of the task. If it is fairly routine, such as constructing a building, then an inexperienced group of people need training more than they need group leadership. However, if the task is more open ended, such as the community action task mentioned before, then the leadership should be democratically based. Whenever the task has a degree of uncertainty about it, the democratic styles of leadership are best because they allow the group to discover their own goals, norms, and directions.

Rosenfeld (1973) argues that when a group of people do not know "where they are going"—that is, they lack task clarity—they are likely to rebel or simply avoid tackling the problem to be solved. Some may even get up and leave the group.

Have you ever been involved in such a group? Did it frustrate you?

In such a group, leadership is needed. To avoid unproductive fighting or mutual disinterest in the group, someone needs to step forward and offer direction for the group. If no one takes the responsibility to provide direction, the group will dissolve.

L. Rosenfeld, *Human Interaction in the Small Group Setting* (Columbus, Ohio: Charles E. Merrill, 1973).

**GROUP HARMONY** Often the desirability of a particular leadership style depends on the interpersonal relations within the group. If the group members are highly attracted to one another and enjoy working in the group, you can exert authoritarian leadership without much resistance from the group. However, if the group members dislike and mistrust one another, authoritarian leadership tactics will be rejected. Under such conditions of dislike and distrust, you will have to be more democratic as the leader.

If your group is just forming and has not had time to establish positive working relationships, then you need to allow time for the members to become acquainted with each other and with the task. This typically calls for democratic leadership, encouraging the members to do most of the talking. Too often a leader is tempted to step in and take control of a new group without letting them go through the important phase of getting oriented to one another. Getting acquainted first may temporarily postpone work on the task, but the time thus spent will prove worthwhile later when the group needs positive relationships to complete the task.

As you can see, your leadership choice depends on many factors. Sometimes an authoritarian style is just what the group needs. Other times, a more democratic style is required. No matter which you choose, though, there is a price. For instance, if you choose an authoritarian style, you may be rejected by the group because they don't want to be "bossed around." Yet, if you never use an authoritarian style, you may not get enough work done. Knowing when to be more authoritarian and when to be more democratic really depends on the answers to these questions:

1. Am I liked by my group?

2. Do they understand the task and know how to handle it?

3. Do they work well together?

4. Do I have the authority to give them orders?

If you can answer yes to these questions, then an authoritarian style can be safely used. If you cannot answer yes to at least three of them, try a more democratic style.

## SPECIFIC COMMUNICATION STRATEGIES

Part of being a good leader is knowing how to dispense with daily problems. If you try to solve every problem democratically, you will be swamped with committees and reports. If you make all the decisions yourself, you will overload yourself.

Effective leaders not only make choices about their personal leadership styles, they also use a number of different communication strategies in solving problems. Let me illustrate. Suppose you are the head of a group that has been experiencing a decline of attendance at the weekly meetings. You believe that the meetings are important, so you exercise a bit of authoritarian leadership and create a mandatory

Effective leaders not only command attention from others; they are influential as well. (Photo © Abigail Heyman/Archive Pictures, Inc.)

**Table 11.1** Communication Strategies for Leaders

| Communication Strategy | Conditions |
| --- | --- |
| 1. Announce decision. | Emergency situations that call for fast action |
| 2. Announce decision with reasons. | When the group members agree with you and when you have credibility |
| 3. Group discussion with guidelines. | When the group members have a stake in the outcome and are competent to deal with the matter |
| 4. Group discussion without guidelines. | When the problem concerns the group members but does not involve many other people |

attendance policy for the group. Now, how do you communicate this new policy to your group? This is when you need a communication strategy.

A communication strategy is nothing more than a plan for disseminating and sharing information within a group. In the situation of the new mandatory attendance policy, you can post the policy notice on a bulletin board and hope that everyone reads it. Or you can distribute a written memo announcing the policy. Or you can call a meeting to discuss the problem, hoping that the group will agree that a mandatory policy is needed.

You have many options in choosing how to communicate with your group members. For our purposes here, these options can be summarized into four major strategies. Table 11.1 illustrates the choices.

Let's distinguish among the four strategies. The first two are authoritarian strategies, while the latter two are democratic. The first strategy is the quickest, but not always the most desirable. The difference between strategy 1 and strategy 2 is whether or not you publicly justify your decision. If you don't want to defend your position, you will choose the first one. If you feel that the group deserves an explanation, you will use the second. Strategies 3 and 4 differ primarily in how the group discussion will be conducted. With strategy 3, you give the group some guidelines, limitations, deadlines, or perhaps a set of solutions from which they should choose. With strategy 4, you offer no set of solutions or guidelines. Rather, you give the members total freedom to work out a solution. This last strategy is particularly useful for dyadic (two-people) or triadic (three-people) conflicts, in which the parties are secluded together to settle their differences.

Of the four strategies listed, no single strategy is better than the others. They are all mentioned here because effective leaders should use more than one strategy for dealing with problems. Like other behaviors, our communication behaviors can become habitual, leading us to use only one favorite strategy to solve every problem. When we fail to see that we have options in dealing with problems, we fail to be good leaders.

# Sounding Like a Leader

Earlier you learned that leadership is something that others give you. Observing your behavior, people judge you in terms of leadership skills, and a significant part of your behavior is how you speak. Recent research makes it possible to determine which speech characteristics are seen as most attractive in leaders. Thus, both what you say (speech content) and how you say it (speech style) serve as reference points for your leadership potential.

## SPEECH CONTENT

As people listen to you talk in conversations, they learn about you as a person. They discover what you like to talk about, how you view the world, and what kinds of attitudes you display. All of these things contribute to the listeners' feelings about your interpersonal attractiveness and credibility.

Given this, what can you do to enhance your leadership image? There are five ways to improve the content of your talk. First of all, speak in a personal way, referring to real experiences that you've had. If you talk of abstractions and use the infamous *they* instead of *you, me,* or *I,* people will tend to perceive you as less personable. Obviously, you can overdo the first-person style to the point where you appear egotistical, but you can control that.

Second, speak positively. Don't be a grouch, or a person who sees the negative side of every topic. People who make others feel better by talking about good things instead of bad things are more attractive. Third, talk about things that the other person is interested in. You don't have to patronize others, but you can be sensitive to topics that interest your listeners.

Fourth, speak in a way that communicates a willingness to cooperate. Let people know that you are truly interested in them and willing to help them. Offer your time to others, and you'll have more friends. Finally, speak in a supportive manner. In other words, help others meet their needs for affiliation (friendships), affection (love), and self-esteem.

These five methods of improving your speech content are not just commandments for winning friends and influencing people. They are actual patterns of communication behavior that others find attractive. If applied sincerely, they can enhance your perceived leadership.

## SPEECH STYLE

Here are some suggestions for improving your speaking style. The first concerns your talkativeness. No one likes an incessant talker, but the silent type rarely emerges as a leader in groups. You must talk and appear outgoing if you want people to be attracted to you.

You should also appear relaxed as you speak, not displaying too much speech fright. This does not mean, however, that you should be a smooth talker. As indicated in Chapter 2, the perfectly fluent speaker is not the one awarded the highest amount of credibility by listeners. Your speech style should be relatively free of nonfluencies, but not devoid of them. For normal speech, nonfluencies occur about once in every 16 words, or about one every five seconds or so (Mahl, 1956).

Next, you should avoid speaking styles that are associated with emotional extremes. For instance, depressed people often mumble and have monotonic voices. Hyperactive speakers talk too fast with nervous gestures. So regulate your rate of speech and the variety in your voice.

Finally, be sure that your verbal messages agree with your non-verbal messages. Don't contradict yourself because whenever what you say doesn't match how you say it, your leadership suffers.

## A SPEECH PROFILE

Now let's put together speech content and speech style to build a profile of the preferred patterns that make you sound like a leader. In terms of speech content, try to be personal, positive, interested, cooperative, and supportive. In terms of speech style, speak up, relax, speak naturally without talking too fast or in a monotone, and be sure that your verbal and nonverbal messages coincide.

## Summary Propositions

Our society is dependent on the leadership skills of its people. Yet some people believe that they can never be leaders. After reading this chapter, you should realize that you have leadership potential, and that if you simply know how it works and what you can do to enhance your leadership, you can be a leader. If you understand your own levels of interpersonal attraction, source credibility, and social power, you can more accurately judge your ability to influence others. Likewise, if you understand the various leadership styles available to you, and know how to project yourself so that you sound like a leader, you can become the leader your group may need at any given time. If everyone works to improve his or her leadership skills, we can make some important improvements in the quality of our personal and professional lives.

1. Leadership is the process of influence that a person can have on others to mobilize them toward specific objectives.

2. You exercise leadership in both your personal and your professional life.

3. You have three sources of influence to help you lead:

   a. Interpersonal attraction

   b. Source credibility

   c. Social power

4. There are three kinds of interpersonal attraction: physical, task, and social.

5. Three factors increase the likelihood that people will be attracted to each other: proximity, similarity, and the situation.

6. Your source credibility is dependent on how people perceive you in terms of competence and trustworthiness.

7. There are five kinds of social power: reward, coercive, expert, referent, and legitimate.

8. When deciding how to lead, you choose from four general styles of leadership:

   a. Exploitative authoritarian

   b. Benevolent authoritarian

   c. Consultative democratic

   d. Participative democratic

9. Which style you choose depends on you and your position, the clarity of the task, and the relationships among the group members.

10. The specific communication strategies that you choose for solving problems depends on the conditions in which the problem occurs.

11. You can control your everyday communication behavior to sound more like a leader.

   a. In terms of speech content, you should be personal, positive, interested, cooperative, and supportive.

   b. In terms of speech style, you should speak up enough to be noticed, try to relax, speak as naturally as you can without mumbling or chattering, and be sure that your nonverbal messages do not contradict your verbal messages.

## References

**Cartwright, D., and Zander, A.** *Group Dynamics: Research and Theory.* New York: Harper & Row, 1968.

**French, J., and Raven, B.** "The Bases of Social Power." In *Group Dynamics,* edited by D. Cartwright and A. Zander. New York: Harper & Row, 1968.

**Likert, R.** *The Human Organization.* New York: McGraw-Hill, 1967.

**Mahl, G.** "Disturbances and Silences in Patients' Speech in Psychotherapy." *Journal of Abnormal and Social Psychology* 33(1956):1–15.

**Phillips, G.; Pederson, D.; and Wood, J.** *Group Discussion: A Practical Guide to Participation and Leadership.* Boston: Houghton Mifflin, 1979.

**Rosenfeld, L.** *Human Interaction in the Small Group Setting.* Columbus, Ohio: Charles E. Merrill, 1973.

# PERSONAL AND PROFESSIONAL PUBLIC SPEAKING

What do the following instances have in common?

**1.** A deacon or an elder reporting to the congregation about the progress of a pastoral call

**2.** A lawyer talking about her ceramics hobby to a group of international visitors in an art center

**3.** You warning a class of high school students about the hazards of drugs

**4.** A materials executive explaining to the board of directors recent changes in dealing with vendors

**5.** A training instructor teaching employees how to use a newly acquired computer system

The one common factor in all of these instances is that each is an instance of public speaking. We use public speaking skills more than we realize. And public speaking is not confined to our professional lives. In fact, of the five examples just listed, only the last two represent public speaking in professional life. The first three are examples of public speaking in personal life.

This part of the book is devoted to teaching you how to plan, build, and present an effective speech. The speech can be for either personal or professional purposes. Common principles of public speaking apply to both.

# 12

# PLANNING THE
# SPEECH

**Audience Analysis**
What Is an Audience?
Adapting to the Audience
Audience Effects on the Speaker

■

**Choosing a Topic**
Discovering a Topic
Refining the Topic

■

**Summary Propositions**

■

**References**

■

In your everyday life, you may not have too many opportunities to present a formal speech. But many jobs require public speaking skills, even if only to present a clear report at a board meeting. Not all of us want to be dynamic public speakers, but each of us needs a firm foundation in preparing and presenting speeches if we are to be effective communicators in our personal and professional lives. So, even though you may not need these particular skills as often as you need the more interpersonal skills covered in earlier chapters, you would be unwise to overlook training in public speaking.

In the next few chapters you will learn how to prepare and present an effective speech. But before you dive into writing the speech, you need to take time to evaluate two important aspects of public speaking: the audience and your topic. The quality of any speech will ultimately be determined by your audience. The more you understand your audience, the better your speech can be. Likewise, an effective speech is one that fits both the speaker and the audience. It is impossible to write one speech for all audiences. No matter how well your arguments are thought out, or how cleverly worded your narrative is, the speech is not likely to fit every audience that you face. So effective speech planning calls for analyzing your audience and adjusting your speech to fit your audience.

## Audience Analysis

### WHAT IS AN AUDIENCE?

In Chapter 9, I discussed a number of variables that make a collection of people a group. In many ways, an audience is a group. Audiences can have many of the social and psychological features found in small groups. Though usually larger than small groups, audiences have aspects of cohesion, common goals, norms, roles, and so forth.

Some audiences will have more "groupness" than others, but even an audience assembled for the first time will have some of the dynamics of a group. Thus, as you plan your speech, it is useful to think of your audience as a group.

By definition, *an audience is a nonrandom group of reactors who are assembled to hear a speech.* Two parts of this definition deserve closer consideration.

First, the definition assumes *nonrandomness.* In your personal and professional lives you are not likely to face an accidental audience, one assembled by chance. Most audiences are made up of people who either have been together before, or have come together for a specific purpose. In either case, the members of the audience are assembled for a reason and have some commonalities that link together their interests, values, or concerns. The shared commonalities are what make an audience nonrandom. If there were no commonalities among the audience members, the speaker would have a difficult time adapting the message to fit the audience. For purposes of audience analysis, then, you need to assume that your audience is nonrandom. Later we will look at the commonalities that need to be considered as you plan your speech.

The second important aspect of the definition of audience is the term *reactors*. In the communication model presented in Chapter 1, I talked about sources and receivers. In public speaking, these can be identified as speakers and reactors. You see, the members of your audience are not passive sponges just waiting to soak up your insights. Instead they are active listeners who provide feedback for you and for the others in the audience. They will evaluate your ideas, and

Audience feedback is noticed not only by the speaker but by the audience members themselves. And sometimes, the reaction of the audience can be just as persuasive as the message of the speaker.

In fact, Hylton (1971) found that when the members of the audience observe that others are reacting favorably to the speaker, this influences their feelings about the speaker and the message. Likewise, negative feedback can inhibit the extent to which the audience is persuaded.

Thus, as a member of an audience, you should realize there are many sources of persuasion operating on you. You will be influenced both by the speaker and by others in the audience.

C. Hylton, "Intra-audience Effects: Observable Audience Response," *Journal of Communication* 21(1971):253–265.

they may even produce counter ideas during your speech. In any event, they will be active. So you should think of your audience members as reactors as well as receivers.

## ADAPTING TO THE AUDIENCE

Just as no two speeches are exactly alike, no two audiences are identical. Thus, it is important to know some specifics about your particular audience. By knowing important information about your audience, you can adjust your speech to fit the specific group you are addressing. For instance, you wouldn't give the same informative speech on dental care at a country club luncheon that you would give to a third-grade class in elementary school. Knowing your audience is almost as important as knowing your subject matter.

As you plan your speech, you need to adjust your presentation to reflect four characteristics: purpose of the gathering, demographics of the members, the audience's knowledge of the topic, and the attitudes of the members toward you and your topic.

**PURPOSE** This is the easiest audience feature to uncover. It doesn't take much time or energy to find out why the audience is assembled. Before you plan your speech you need to inquire about the reason for the meeting. If you don't know, or haven't been told, ask someone who should know. Don't blindly prepare your speech for an audience without knowing why they are gathered.

An understanding of the purpose for gathering can help you assess the importance and seriousness of the meeting. For instance, if you are speaking at a monthly meeting of an organization, then you are probably one of a series of speakers invited to every monthly meeting. However, if you are invited to speak at an annual convention for which you will be the keynote speaker, this engagement is more serious and more important than the monthly meeting. Likewise, if the purpose of the meeting is to tactfully poke fun at a guest of honor, your speech should reflect the levity of the event. In contrast, if you joke too much at a serious event, you will be labeled insensitive and never invited back. The first thing you should do, then, is find out the purpose of the meeting.

**DEMOGRAPHICS** As you size up the audience, look for specific personal characteristics such as average age, sex, social status, employment, marital status, political party preferences, religious preferences, and so on. Such items of information—demographics—can be useful in discovering the common denominators of the group. For instance, most service clubs, such as Rotary and Kiwanis, are comprised of men (more than women) who work in the local community and have an interest in the welfare of the community. If you were to give a speech on the U.S. space program to such a group, you should adapt your material to include the benefits that the space program offers to local communities. If you were giving a speech on the same topic to a class of elementary school children, mentioning local benefits would be a waste of time. The kids just wouldn't care as much as the Rotarians or the Kiwanians.

The value of demographic data lies in using them. If you prepare your speech without reference to the specific audience, you may miss a real opportunity to speak directly to your audience. In fact, if you prepare your speech without knowing about the audience, or with an inaccurate idea of the audience, you could end up in trouble. I nearly experienced this once when I prepared a speech to be given to a group of supervisors (management-oriented people). When I arrived the night before, I visited with my host who told me that the audience was made up of fire-line laborers for the U.S. Forest Service. Needless to say, I had to change a number of things in my speech to fit this newly discovered audience. If I had given my originally planned presentation, it would have been a failure because my actual audience was younger, more politically conservative, and less educated than the one I was expecting. Luckily, I found out about the actual demographics before I spoke, and I took advantage of the information to adjust my speech.

**KNOWLEDGE** Have you ever listened to a speaker who "talked over your head" or one who addressed the group as "children"? If so, then you realize how important it is for a speaker to know the knowledge level of the audience. This kind of information about your audience is crucial when you are deciding how much background material to include, what language to use, and which perspective to take. You can lose your audience if you do not aim your speech at the listeners' average level of comprehension. This is especially a problem for speakers trained in highly technical areas. I remember once touring a U.S. naval base with a group of educators who were being shown the modern training facilities on base. The speakers were naval personnel who frequently forgot that lay people are unfamiliar with military jargon, particularly acronyms. Eventually, we became tired, of asking for explanations of the terms that were understandable to the speakers but not to the audience. Knowing what your audience knows will help you plan effectively.

**ATTITUDES** The purpose of the meeting, the demographics of the members, and the knowledge level of the listeners are relatively easy data to gather. But audience attitudes are more difficult to determine. Yet the audience attitudes are often the deciding factor in your success as a speaker.

Audience attitudes vary in two ways: direction and commitment. Direction refers to a person's feelings of favor or disfavor for the attitude object. Commitment refers to the intensity with which people maintain their attitudes. It is quite possible for two people to agree in their attitudes (both favoring, or both disfavoring) but differ in their respective levels of commitment to those attitudes. For instance, you and I might agree that a college education is worthwhile (both of us favor college education). But because I make my living teaching college, I might be more committed to my favorable attitude than you are to yours. This is often the case between the speaker and the audience. That is, the speaker frequently tries to increase the commitment of the audience, rather than change a negative attitude to a positive attitude or vice versa.

Whatever the direction and commitment, the attitudes of the audience will affect their receptiveness as listeners. An effective speaker recognizes the importance of the listeners' feelings and adapts the message to accommodate the audience.

There are a number of ways to determine the audience's attitudes. You can administer questionnaires that ask for their opinions on the issues you plan to talk about. Or you can interview someone who is familiar with the group that you will be addressing and get advice about their attitudes. Either of these methods can be effective if managed carefully.

A third method uses the homogeneity-of-attitudes approach. This approach assumes that most members of an established audience hold similar attitudes about a number of issues. Thus, there is homogeneity in the audience's attitudes. This similarity in attitudes is caused by the fact that most members of established audiences have chosen to belong to a group because that group holds attitudes that are congruent with the member's attitudes. Thus, people who belong to charitable organizations are perceived as people who hold favorable attitudes toward charities. Those who belong to sailing clubs must like to sail. Those who play bridge must have positive attitudes about it. Membership in a group (and audience) carries with it an endorsement of the group's attitudes toward different issues. By knowing either the attitudes of the typical group member, or the general attitudes of the group as a whole, you can estimate the reaction the audience members will have to you and your speech.

Let me illustrate how two different audiences might be perceived in terms of their respective attitudes. Suppose you are planning a speech on recreational improvements for urban cities, to be given to a group of experienced city planners. The demographic data on the audience indicate that the average age is 38. Most are men, married, with children. There are more Democrats than Republicans, and the members are primarily Protestant in faith. You also realize that these people are attending a small but important convention on city planning.

Given this situation, what attitudes can you predict of this audience? Obviously, you cannot predict each person's attitude, but if you understand the audience as a group, you can estimate general attitudes. In this case, you might expect that a group of committed city planners would hold favorable attitudes toward recreational improvements. But because the group contains veteran city planners, they would probably have firmly fixed attitudes. As long as your speech does not advocate changes that will interfere with their pet projects, your speech should be acceptable to such a group.

Now let's consider an audience that is not so homogeneous in their attitudes—college students. With a group of college students as your audience for the same speech topic, you might expect a lot of interest in the topic but not much knowledge or commitment to one particular attitude. Most college students (such as those in a speech class) gather to hear speeches for educational purposes, not for city planning goals. Consequently, the college students would be more diverse in their attitudes than experienced city planners would be. The students' attitudes would not necessarily be firmly built on per-

Whether your audience is a group of new recruits or a room full of city officials, you have to adjust your presentation to fit the audience. (Photo © Michael O'Brien/Archive Pictures, Inc.)

sonal experience with recreational problems. Although an audience of college students would be receptive to a speech on recreational problems of cities, this group would require more education about the topic than would city planners.

Whether you are projecting attitudes of city planners or of college students, you need information about the audience (purpose, demographics, their knowledge) from which you can estimate the probable attitudes. If you assume that most audiences are composed of people who choose to be together, then you can base your evaluation of their attitudes on what you know about a typical member or about the group as a whole. Whatever you do, you need to take time to analyze your audience, so that you don't just "shoot in the dark," hoping to convince enough people to be effective. Good speech planning calls for good audience analysis.

It is certainly difficult to know exactly how an audience feels about an issue, but you can speculate about their general attitudes. Different audiences are likely to have different attitudes toward the same topic. For instance, how would you rate the following audiences on the issue of increasing the defense budget? (Rating: 5, strongly in favor; 1, strongly against.)

_____ U.S. Naval Academy members

_____ Rotary International members

_____ American Civil Liberties Union members

_____ Class of college sophomores

As you estimate the probable attitudes of such audiences, you need to think about how you would adapt your speech to fit each one. You cannot give the same speech to all four audiences without losing some effectiveness with each one.

## AUDIENCE EFFECTS ON THE SPEAKER

When you take an audience-centered approach to public speaking, you learn things about your audience that influence your choices in planning and presenting your speech—affecting what you say and how you say it. Ellingsworth and Clevenger (1967) identify four ways in which knowing your audience affects your speech: restraints, constraints, alternative messages, and special effects.

**RESTRAINTS** These are things that are not allowed, given your audience. For instance, ethnic jokes are usually not acceptable in a public speech. Certain kinds of stories may be inappropriate for your particular audience. Even your vocabulary or tone of voice may need restraint with certain audiences. In essence, your audience can set limits on what you can say and do; and if you fail to adhere to these limitations, you might offend your listeners.

**CONSTRAINTS** These are the "must do" things. For instance, an engineer speaking to a group of people who are unfamiliar with engineering terms is obligated to explain the language that is confusing to the audience. Certain occasions, such as speeches of acceptance or funeral orations, call for specific references to people who are at the ceremony or are known to the audience. In the business world, visual aids are often mandatory as you present your material to your colleagues in a meeting. Knowing your audience and its demands on the speaker can help you prepare your presentation correctly.

**ALTERNATIVE MESSAGES** As mentioned before, rarely will one message fit every audience. Consequently, a speaker who is to speak to many different audiences on the same topic needs more than one form of the message from which to choose. Since each different audience can have different values, interests, and so forth, the effective speaker emphasizes those parts of the speech that match the values of the particular audience. A speech on wearing seat belts in automobiles might emphasize child safety to an audience of parents, but emphasize personal safety to a group of college students. Rather than try to cover everything, the effective speaker accents the most salient points that would convince the audience more than would thoroughness of coverage.

**SPECIAL EFFECTS** By knowing about a recent event or a specific concern of an audience, the speaker can relate the gist of the message to that event or concern to produce a special effect. For instance, suppose you are speaking about ways to persuade people, and you know that many of the audience members were part of a fund-raising drive for a new wing of a community hospital. You can use their experience in fund raising as an example of persuasion in action. Exactly how you incorporate information such as this into your speech for a special effect depends, of course, on your speech and the information at hand.

In a nutshell, audience analysis is a necessary prerequisite to effective public speaking. The more you understand your audience, and the more you adjust your message to fit your particular audience, the greater are your chances for success. Now let's see how your topic choice is part of effective speech planning.

## Choosing a Topic

One of the hardest questions to answer when preparing a speech is, "How do I choose a topic?" People often lament that they don't know what to talk about. Or they declare that they don't have anything to say. Although I can appreciate such feelings, I cannot endorse them. Certainly, choosing a topic can be awkward, but with the proper approach, you will find a topic that you can talk about competently.

Sometimes, choosing the topic is no problem because one has been assigned to you. For instance, your boss may ask you to explain to others the budgeting procedures in your office. Or you might be asked to give a speech on the historical origins of a club you belong to. Perhaps, because of your reputation, you have been asked to address a Kiwanis club or a church group on a subject that you are an expert in. If you know your topic already, and if you feel that it is sufficiently narrowed in scope, you may want to skip this section of the chapter and go on to the next chapter. However, some of the material coming up may be valuable in helping you refine and adjust your topic to suit you and your audience.

### DISCOVERING A TOPIC

Your main goal in seeking a topic for a speech is to find one that meets both your needs and your audience's needs. In other words, you need a topic that fits you and your audience.

To fit your needs as a speaker, you should first look for a topic that is in line with your interests. The topic should be relevant to your life. It should be a part of your hobbies, your major in school, your career, a group or club that you belong to. The reason for this is that you need to be interested in your topic. If you find the topic uninteresting, you're going to have trouble stimulating your audience to feel interest. So find a topic that interests you.

Second, you should look for a topic that is related to your personal credibility. In other words, your topic choice should be governed by this question: "Why should *I* be the one who speaks on this topic?" If you choose a topic in which you have some expertise or past experience, the audience will find you more believable than if you pick a topic you know nothing about. For instance, if you work for the local food store chain, you would be in a good position to talk about rising food costs. If you are a Big Brother or a Big Sister (in the Big Brothers-Big Sisters organization), you might talk about that program. With a little reflection on your own personal and professional lives, you should discover one area wherein you have some expertise. When you find that area, prepare a speech on it. Most audiences would rather hear you talk about something you have hands-on experience with than on a topic you just read about.

Sometimes you find a good topic when you are reminded of a pet peeve or some kind of annoyance in your life.

To help you think about topics that come from your personal and professional lives, try completing these sentences:

1. One thing that bothers me about the parks in this town is _____

_____

2. One thing I dislike about cars is _____

_____

3. One thing that annoys me about the library is _____

_____

4. One thing that frustrates me about the post office is _____

_____

5. I get irritated by store management that _____

_____

These are just a few. Can you think of more? Good luck.

You also must fit the topic to the audience, that is, try to meet their needs and interests. You should say to yourself, "Does my topic deal with a subject that the audience needs to know about?" Or you might ask, "Can my audience benefit from hearing my speech on this topic?" If the answer is no to these questions, then your topic is not meeting the needs of your audience. If the members of the audience have nothing to gain by listening to your speech, they won't bother to listen. In fact, it is a good idea early in the speech to remind the audience how important the topic is to them.

In addition to speaking on topics your listeners need to hear about, you should choose topics that are relevant to their interests. For example, if you are speaking to a group of young people, you should find a topic that is relevant to this age group. Speeches on recent changes in the retirement laws might not be very relevant to an audience under 25 years of age. But a speech on the parking problems around campus might get a more interested response. It's all a matter of relevance. If the topic fits the needs and interests of the audience, your speech is more likely to be successful.

In summary, a good topic is one that fits both you (your interests and credibility) and your audience (their needs and interests). The better the topic fits you and your audience, the greater your chances for success.

Sometimes it is helpful to thumb through magazines and reference books to discover interesting and relevant topics. Here is a list of some that you might find useful:

**Magazines:** *Time, Newsweek, U.S. News & World Report, National Review, Congressional Digest, Scientific American, Consumer Reports, Facts on File,* and *Saturday Review.*

**References and Indices:** *Information Please Almanac, Encyclopaedia Britannica, Reader's Guide to Periodical Literature, International Index to Periodicals, Education Index, Index Medicus, Psychological Abstracts,* and *Social Sciences Index.*

## REFINING THE TOPIC

The most common single problem in public speeches is that the speaker tries to cover too much territory in too little time. In reality, no topic can be covered completely in any speech. So no matter how long you plan to speak, you need to refine your topic by narrowing its scope. If you have been given a very short time limit such as 5 to 8 minutes, then narrowing the topic is imperative. But even if you have 30 to 45 minutes for your speech, you still need to refine your topic so that it has a clear and specific focus. Let's consider how you should refine your topic.

Suppose that you have an interest in photography. Since it is a hobby of yours, you can speak about it with some authority—you have credibility. Suddenly you realize that the topic of photography deals with a broad range of topics—picture-taking techniques, equipment, the right film to use, how to use lighting, developing, printing, and so on. In a brief speech, you could not cover this vast range of topics.

How do you refine your topic? First of all, you need to know enough about your topic. If you haven't done enough research on the subject, you won't have the foggiest idea how to narrow your topic. So read first, then refine, and then read a lot more. Next, make a list of all the topics that can be refined from your original, larger topic. Then look at each topic on the list and determine your level of interest and what you perceive to be your audience's level of interest in that topic. Choose the topic that you like best and think the audience will find interesting. For instance, regarding photography, the audience may not be too interested in how to develop film, but they might appreciate information and advice on how to buy a good camera. By choosing the latter topic, you can take advantage of your hobby and your credibility in photography and help your listeners make good choices in cameras.

At this point in your topic refinement, you might have to narrow your topic further. If you have only five minutes to present your talk, you may have to limit your topic to something such as the advantages and disadvantages of fixed-focus cameras compared to single-lens reflex cameras. Now you have narrowed your topic twice. Don't be surprised that you have to narrow your topic more than once. Most good speeches are on topics that have been narrowed several times.

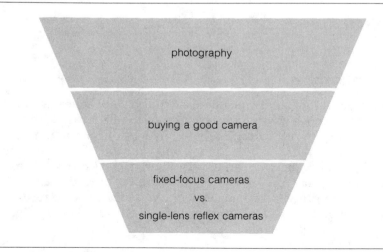

**Figure 12.1**  Narrowing the Topic

Figure 12.1 shows how a broad topic is made more manageable through narrowing the topic.

## Summary Propositions

Effective speech planning requires preliminary evaluation of both your audience and your topic. Before you sit down to construct your speech, you need to take time to discover the purpose of the gathering, some demographics about the members of the audience, how much they know about your topic, and what their attitudes toward you and your topic might be. By having a clear profile of your audience, you can adapt your message to fit your audience. The same is true of the topic you choose to speak about. It should be adapted to your interests and credibility and to the audience's needs and interests. Furthermore, to be of any real value, a good speech topic must be sufficiently refined so that the important details of the topic can be covered within the assigned time limit. Far too many speeches fail because the speaker tries to cover too much material in too little time. A carefully refined topic gives you a sharp focus on the topic and provides a manageable topic that you can cover and that the audience can learn.

1. An audience is a nonrandom group of reactors who are assembled to hear a speech.

2. Adapting to the audience requires that you take into account:

    a. Purpose of the gathering

    b. Demographics of the listeners

    c. Knowledge level of the listeners

    d. Attitudes of the listeners

3. The audience affects the speaker in terms of the restraints and constraints on the speech, and in terms of alternate messages and special effects.

4. A good topic is one that fits you (your interests and credibility) and your audience (their needs and interests).

5. In order to produce a manageable topic, you need to refine it by narrowing the scope of the topic.

6. An effective speech is one that is clearly refined and adapted to the audience.

# References

**Ellingsworth, H., and Clevenger, T.** *Speech and Social Action*. Englewood Cliffs, N.J.: Prentice-Hall, 1967.

**Hylton, C.** "Intra-audience Effects: Observable Audience Response." *Journal of Communication* 21(1971):253–265.

# 13

# BUILDING THE SPEECH

**E**ffective public speaking not only requires careful planning in terms of audience analysis and topic selection, it demands thoughtful preparation of the message itself. If listeners are going to take the time to listen to your speech, you need to take the time necessary to construct a good speech. The more time you devote to gathering information and building the various parts of the speech, the better your chances for success.

In essence, speech preparation calls for research and organization. As you will see, research means more than library research—you have many sources of information that you can tap. Likewise, there are many ways to organize a speech, but all speeches have a common underlying structure that you will learn about in this chapter. If you approach speech building using the guidelines set forth in this chapter, you will be well on your way to producing an effective public speech.

## Gathering Information

Now that you have narrowed your topic and have begun to gather information about it, you need to consider your information-gathering strategies in more detail. Most importantly, you need to assess whether or not your current sources of information are adequate. You also must decide what information you are actually looking for.

### SOURCES OF INFORMATION

Many people mistakenly think that the library is the only place where they can get information. They often search the card catalogue or the periodical index, looking for the perfect source from which they can write their speeches. This approach or strategy is too limited. A good speech will be composed from many different sources. And not all of those sources will be written ones. Let me explain.

Suppose that you are going to compare fixed-focus cameras to single-lens reflex cameras for an audience of potential camera buyers. To prepare your speech, you can get a good book on photography and base your talk on the chapter in the book that makes this comparison of cameras. If you do so, you will provide a service to your audience, but it will be a limited service. In fact, you may as well photocopy the chapter and distribute it to your audience so they can read it instead of listening to your speech. You see, a good speech is more than a paraphrase of a good book chapter or article. It is a compilation of ideas based on research that audiences may not have time to conduct on their own. If you truly want to advise the audience, you should go beyond one or two sources of information to get the best perspective available on your topic.

When investigating a topic, not only read all you can about it, but also interview experts on the topic. For instance, for the photography topic, you should interview professional photographers (such as owners of a photography store, or people who own and run studios). As you talk with your experts, ask them questions that your reading has not answered. Let your interviewees do most of the talking. Ask them for personal experiences that might be useful to you in your speech. Think of questions that your audience might ask about the topic, and then ask your experts for answers to such questions.

Another source of information is the public, through informal public polling. You can conduct surveys to discover how the average person feels about your topic. In such surveys you look not so much for expert information as for feelings about the topic. By knowing how other people feel about the topic, you might be able to predict your audience's feelings as well. Furthermore, you can use the results of your survey to demonstrate how the general population views the topic.

## TYPES OF EVIDENCE

Centuries ago, Aristotle argued that if you assert, you must prove. That is, you need evidence in a speech. It is considered inappropriate to present a speech that consists of a series of opinions and assertions without documentation in the form of examples, statistics, quotations, and/or analogies. An audience of critical listeners, especially, will not believe you unless you support your points. A speech without evidence is like a bridge without girders—it won't hold up.

**EXAMPLES** An example is a reference to a person, place, idea, or incident that the speaker uses to prove or embellish a point. You use examples when you want to support or clarify what you have said. The example can be real or hypothetical. In persuasive speaking, however, the examples should be real if the speaker is using them for proof.

As you accumulate evidence, it is a good idea to have a filing system to keep track of your information.

Many people use research cards to note data that will be used in a speech. Below is an example:

---

**Trends in Spending**

"Americans are currently spending 3–5 times more money for food, clothing, and other essentials than they did 20 years ago. Thus, today's dollar buys less than a third of what it would buy before."


Wilson, M. "The High Cost of Living" *Home Economic Digest*, April 11, 1983, p. 34.

---

Notice that the research card includes a title, the material to be used or quoted, and a complete reference.

Having your evidence on cards not only provides order for you, it also allows you to arrange your cards to determine which order of presentation would be best in your speech.

Examples, according to Barrett (1977), can be used in two ways—as illustrations and as instances. When you use an example as an *illustration,* you formulate a narrative or a story that is detailed and describes what you are talking about. Illustrations are best used when the audience is unfamiliar with the topic at hand. Here is an illustration:

> Our highly technical society has come to the point where a homemaker can do business with the bank while drinking coffee in the kitchen. Inexpensive home computers make it possible for a person to contact the bank, check the current balances in both checking and savings accounts, and at the same time pay bills. All transactions are displayed on a television screen. Every time a transaction is made, the new balance flashes on the screen. After completing all transactions, the homemaker knows the final status of each account.

An *instance,* in contrast, is very brief. You refer to instances by reminding the audience of a particular person, event, or idea. In doing so, you simply mention the instance, without details or elaborate descriptions. Instances work best when the audience is familiar with the topic. Here is an example of using instances:

> Because of the upcoming "changing of the guard" in the White House, the lame duck congress will drag its feet on a number of bills. For instance, we will not see action on: the tax cut measure, the budget for next year, job training programs, specific energy projects, and federal aid to cities for mass transit.

Notice that the speaker simply recites a number of instances, and does not elaborate on any of them.

Whether you choose to support your point with an instance or with an illustration is a matter of personal choice. There are advantages to each, however, that you should consider. The illustration, if explained well, can be inherently more interesting than the instance. But illustrations are time consuming, whereas instances can be rattled off rather quickly. So you must choose which form to use. It is probably best to have at least one illustration in every speech, so that the audience is not barraged by one instance after another. In this way, you can take advantage of the strengths of both kinds of examples.

**STATISTICS** Statistics are helpful when you want to talk about the *size* of a problem. Thus, you can refer to the population of a city, the square footage of a building, the distance in miles between two places, and so on. Be careful, however, when using numbers. Large ones can be numbing to the mind. It is a good idea to relate your numbers to something that the audience can immediately deal with. For example, in a recent article on Liberia, the author reported that the area of the country is approximately 43,000 square miles. To make this figure more meaningful, the writer noted that Liberia is about the same size as the state of Tennessee. Such comparisons make large numbers more relevant to the listeners.

You can also use statistics in rapid succession, such as reciting the percentage increases in the different categories of crime in your state. A rapid succession of many statistics can give the impression of extensive research on your part. But be careful, too many, too fast may be overwhelming.

**QUOTATIONS** A good way to document your points is to quote experts on the subject. By quoting an expert, you give your listeners a reason to believe you. But you must be careful to quote people that the audience views as experts. For instance, you wouldn't be wise to quote Senator William Proxmire on issues of defense spending when

There is one time when evidence *must* be included for the speech to be effective. This is when the speaker is trying to prove that there will be negative consequences to the audience if they do not heed the warning of the speaker. For example, if you are warning the listeners about the health hazards of cigarette smoking, you need to provide concrete evidence that shows the negative consequences of smoking cigarettes. According to the research on fear appeals (messages designed to scare the audience), if the speaker does not demonstrate that the negative effect will occur *in fact,* the audience may dismiss the warning as a simple scare tactic.

G. Cronkhite, *Persuasion: Speech and Behavioral Change* (New York: Bobbs-Merrill, 1969).

speaking to a group of military personnel. Proxmire's history of criticizing the military does not make him a credible source to a military audience.

You should keep two things in mind when including quotations in your speech. First, keep them short. Listeners have short attention spans when faced with a lengthy quotation. If necessary, read only a portion of the quotation if you think it might be too long. Second, whenever you quote someone, identify the individual, mentioning the person's relevant credentials. In this way, you can add credibility to your speech, while showing that you are quoting an expert.

**ANALOGIES**  As supporting material, analogies are different from examples, statistics, and quotations, in that they don't really prove anything. Analogies are comparisons that are intended to provide interest and clarity to your point. You use an analogy when you want your audience to see the similarities between your topic and what it is being compared to. For instance, you might compare your job to that of a fly swatter (you go around stopping problems on the spot). Or you might see yourself as a gate keeper (one who controls the flow of messages in an organization). Whatever the analogy, it doesn't prove much of anything, but it can certainly add color to your speech. Through the creative use of analogies, you can make your speech fun to listen to.

Of the four types of evidence—examples, statistics, quotations, and analogies—no one is necessarily better than the other. The kind of evidence you use in your speech will be determined by the topic and by the extent of your research effort. Evidence is essential for making your speech believable. If you do not have enough evidence, your critical listeners will not believe you—and rightly so. All things considered, it is better to have too much evidence than too little. Only uncritical audiences will accept a speech that does not document its points.

According to research, there are times when including evidence in a speech is not necessary to make the speaker more believable. McCroskey (1969) found that if the speaker is a highly credible source talking about a familiar topic, the audience believes the points made by the speaker without requiring the speaker to prove the points with evidence. So, if you are highly credible to your audience and you are talking about things everyone is familiar with, you won't need evidence.

Before you conclude that evidence is useless, however, consider the other side of the McCroskey study. He also found that when the speaker is low in credibility or perhaps only moderately credible to the audience, and when the topic is an unfamiliar one, the speaker's believability depends on his or her inclusion of evidence.

All this means that if you are unsure of your own credibility and if you are unsure of how familiar your listeners are with the topic, you had better include evidence. Thus, you will be safe. In any event, the inclusion of evidence has never had a detrimental effect on the persuasiveness of a speech.

J. McCroskey, "A Summary of Experimental Research on the Effects of Evidence in Persuasive Communication," *Quarterly Journal of Speech* 55(1969):169–176.

## Organizing the Body

Now that you have gathered your materials, how do you organize your speech? To start, you must think of the speech as having three major parts: an introduction, a body, and a conclusion. When you begin writing your outline, though, you should *not* start at the beginning with the introduction. You should begin with the first point of the body of the speech. The introduction should be prepared last, not first.

In this section, you will learn how to prepare the body of the speech. To do so, we need to consider how to structure a point, how to develop a point, how to choose a format for arranging your major points, and finally, how to create your running theme.

### STRUCTURING A POINT

Have you ever heard a person say, "Oh, I just don't know how to begin my speech"? This kind of thinking assumes that a speech must be planned, starting with the first word. In such linear thinking a speech is seen as a series of words, beginning with word one and ending on the final word. Such a perspective places too much emphasis on the wording of the speech and not enough on the structure of the speech.

A better way to view a speech is to think about it structurally, not linearly. When you think about a speech in a structural fashion, you see the body of the speech as the main part, containing major points along with supporting evidence. Structural thinking focuses on the major points of the speech, not on the words. In order to think structurally, you must begin to see your speech as having three or four major points. For example:

Topic: Credit Card Abuses

I.   Ease of getting credit

II.  Preferential treatment for credit card customers

III. Interest rates and limits

IV.  Spending spiral

Seeing the body as containing a number of major points is only the beginning of structural thinking. You now need to consider the structure within each point. By doing so, you think of each major point as a package of information containing:

I. Major point

   A.  Subpoint

      1.  Evidence

For example, a speech on the qualities of an effective leader might have its third major point structured as follows:

III. Leaders should be visible.

   A.  They should be seen at work.

      1.  Management consultant, Q. E. Reemer, says that "supervisors who. . . ."

      2.  A nationwide survey of auto workers demonstrates that job satisfaction drops off significantly when the boss is unavailable to the workers.

   B.  They should socialize with the group.

      1.  I remember a fellow in Michigan who was good at socializing with his workers. He would. . . .

2. Statistics show that more than 60 percent of the people who work for a living see their bosses as unfriendly and unwilling to mix with them socially.

Notice that the major point (III) is supported by two subpoints (A and B). And the subpoints each have evidence underneath them (1 and 2). Whenever you have a major point supported by subpoints and evidence, you have a properly packaged main idea in the body of your speech.

## DEVELOPING A POINT

In order to help your listeners understand your points, you must develop each point through explanation and/or restatement. Such rhetorical devices reinforce your ideas in the minds of the listeners.

**EXPLANATION** Any point made in a speech needs to be explained to the listeners. This can be accomplished by showing the implications of a point or by showing how the parts of a major point go together. Consider this:

II. Many Americans have poor dietary habits.

    A. Fast-food lunches have little nutrition.

        1. For example, hot dogs can contain 50 percent water, with less than 25 percent meat.

        2. Soft drinks are mainly sugar and water.

        3. This means that every time you stop by Der Wondersnickel for lunch, you are paying for more water than food.

Notice that point 3, under A, is an explanation of how the evidence cited in 1 and 2 fits into the nutrition argument made in subpoint A. Point 3 ties together the evidence and relates it to the subpoint.

**RESTATEMENT** Another way to develop a point is through restatement. Restatement is simply saying your argument again before going on to the next point. It is not necessary to restate your point verbatim; in fact, it is better to paraphrase it. In the example just mentioned, a good restatement might be, "As you can see, fast-food lunches do little to rectify our poor dietary habits." Such a restatement could be inserted as point 4 in the foregoing example. As you can see, restatement helps you wrap up a point and reinforce the idea in the minds of the listeners.

When mistakes can be costly, it is important that the speaker and listener understand each other. (Photo courtesy of David Powers/Stock, Boston, Inc.)

In summary, then, a well-structured and well-developed point will have subpoints, evidence, explanations, and restatements. If you set up each major point this way, you can be sure that you have covered the important ideas.

## CHOICE OF FORMAT

At this stage of your speech building, you need to decide how to order your major points. You have essentially four choices: chronological order, spatial order, topical order, or causal order. Depending on the topic, one arrangement will be the most suitable to use.

Here's an example of *chronological* order:

I. European beginnings

II. Settling in the Ohio Valley

III. Moving to California

IV. Establishing a business here

When the sequence of events is important, the chronological order is clearly preferred.

The *spatial* pattern is used when you can "see" the layout of the topic in your mind. You would use a spatial order of major points when you want to refer to specific locations. An example of a spatial order would be:

I. Sex education programs in Cleveland County

II. Sex education programs in Orr County

III. Sex education programs in Ingham County

A *topical* order is determined by the natural categories of the subject under study. For example, if you were speaking about institutions of higher education, the topical order of your speech might be:

I. State-supported universities and colleges

II. Private universities and colleges

III. Junior colleges

Let's see if you can recognize which of the four orders of major points a speech uses. Which order is this?

**Topic: Going to Graduate School**
 I. Applying for admission
 II. Taking the GRE test
 III. Being accepted
 IV. Enrolling in classes

How about this one?

**Topic: Juvenile Crime**
 I. Increased violence on TV
 II. Decay of the family unit
 III. Increased leisure time for youth
 IV. Growing juvenile crime rate

You should recognize the first one as chronological and the second as causal. If you had trouble with these, go back and review before you decide which order to use in your speech.

Finally, a *causal* order is appropriate when there is a clear cause-and-effect relationship between the points. This is especially useful for problem-solution speeches. Here's an example:

I. Poor dental hygiene

II. Symptoms of gum disease

III. Treating gum diseases

IV. Preventive techniques

The choice of format for arranging your major points in the body depends on your topic. Choose the order that makes the most sense.

## RUNNING THEME

You are now ready to determine what your theme is. A theme is a one-sentence statement that summarizes your overall argument or philosophy. The theme is the one supramajor point, the ultimate idea around which all of your major points revolve.

One way to think about the running theme is to envision it as the one statement you would make to your audience if you were somehow restricted to a one-sentence speech. To discover your running theme, review your main points and see what ties them together. This is your running theme. When you give your speech, it is a good idea to mention your running theme near the beginning of your speech and again toward the end of your speech. All speeches should have running themes. So determine your running theme before you work on the next steps in preparing your speech.

YOUR TURN...

What would be a good running theme for the following major points?

**Topic: ERA Amendment**

I.  Women have not had equal rights with men in many aspects of life.

II. We have made little progress in the 20th century to solve the problem.

III. The amendment needs to be ratified before the deadline set by law.

Obviously, the speaker is advocating the passage of the ERA amendment. Thus, the running theme might be: We need to ratify the ERA amendment so that women can have equal rights.

This running theme ties together each of the major points and gives the speech a unified direction. That is the purpose of a running theme.

## Ending the Speech

Every good speech needs a conclusion. In the conclusion you want to review your major points and reiterate your running theme. You should also plan a direct appeal to the audience so that they will take what you say and apply it to their lives. Thus, a good conclusion not only summarizes the speech, it instructs the audience how to respond to your speech. *Summarize* and *appeal* are the key ideas in producing an effective conclusion. Here's an example:

> As I have tried to demonstrate, there are many advantages to a military career. The pay is improved. The personal and family benefits are good. And, the opportunities for travel are good. If you are looking for a career with an organization that is not likely to go bankrupt or suffer interminable layoffs, then the military life is for you. A high-quality organization needs high-quality people. Are you one of those people?

In this conclusion, the speaker restated the main points of the speech and made an appeal for action. Depending on how well developed the body of the speech was, this would be a persuasive conclusion to the speech.

---

Conclusions that are unclear or not explicit enough can hinder the audience's understanding of the message. Thus, Applbaum and Anatol (1974) suggest that conclusions should be stated explicitly when (1) you have been covering difficult material, and (2) you are talking to an uneducated audience. However, if you are talking about simple matters to a well-educated audience, explicit conclusions may not be so necessary since your listeners can come to the proper conclusion by themselves.

Pragmatically speaking, it's probably a good idea to clearly conclude any speech. In this way, you can be sure that any audience will understand you on any topic.

R. L. Applbaum and K. W. E. Anatol, *Strategies for Persuasive Communication* (Columbus, Ohio: Charles E. Merrill, 1974).

---

## Beginning the Speech

Now you are ready to prepare your introduction. An introduction reveals the topic of the speech, reminds the audience how the topic is relevant to their lives, and then explains how you plan to cover the topic in the body of the speech. It is also a good idea to mention your running theme during the introduction.

Here's an introduction to a speech on improving safety standards for children's toys:

> Not long ago my nephew was playing with a plastic truck in the backyard of his home. The truck was one of those advertised on TV and is reported to be capable of carrying and dumping dirt. Well, this authentic-looking toy truck has a hinge on the tailgate that is fastened with a steel wire that can protrude out the side of the tailgate. I know this because my nephew Eric has a hole in the palm of his left hand from picking up the toy.

> As you might guess, I am concerned about the safety of children's toys that are being sold today. Even if you don't have your own children, you need to know what makes a toy safe or unsafe. After all, you might find yourself buying a toy for your nephew for his birthday. In essence, I want to demonstrate to you what you should look for in evaluating children's toys. I will consider such things as the kinds of materials in the toy, the strength of the construction, and the presence or absence of safety standards in the inspection of toys at the manufacturers.

Obviously, there is no single best way to write an introduction. But you need to keep in mind that you are trying to arouse interest in your topic and forecast what you are going to talk about. A good format for accomplishing this would be:

1. Begin with a brief story that illustrates what you are going to be talking about.

2. Announce your topic and your running theme.

3. Explain why the topic is important to the audience.

4. Tell the audience what your major points are going to be.

5. Then begin the body of your speech.

## Putting It All Together

By this point, you should have the three major parts of the speech prepared: the body, the conclusion, and the introduction. Now you can arrange the speech in the proper speaking order: introduction, body, and conclusion.

It may seem strange to you to work on the introduction last when it will be delivered first. But this is how the structured approach operates. By working on the introduction last, you know what you are going to say in the body before you try to forecast it. Also, working on the introduction last gives you the opportunity to sit back and create an interesting story or opening example that will add interest to your presentation. You are now ready to work on presenting your speech. The next chapter will help you with your presentation.

## Summary Propositions

Building a credible speech requires adequate research so that you can present enough information and evidence to make your points cogently. Each major point of the speech must be constructed as a unit, carefully organized and developed. Which format you use in your overall outline (chronological, spatial, topical, or causal) depends on your topic. But the major points of the speech should center on your running theme. Finally, it is a good idea to prepare your introduction after you have finished preparing the body and the conclusion. In this way, you know what your speech is going to say before you design a way to introduce it to your audience.

1. A good speech will be drawn from many sources, not just one or two.

2. There are four types of evidence:

    a. Examples (illustrations and instances)

    b. Statistics

    c. Quotations

    d. Analogies

3. The best way to organize a speech is to think about it structurally, not linearly.

4. Every point needs development by explanation and restatement.

5. The choice of format for arranging your major points depends on you and the topic. There are four possible formats:

    a. Chronological

    b. Spatial

    c. Topical

    d. Causal

6. The running theme is the one idea that your speech is designed to advance.

7. Conclusions should have at least a summary and an appeal for action.

8. Once you have written the body and the conclusion, you can prepare your introduction.

9. The introduction should be prepared last and written to arouse interest in your topic and to forecast your main ideas.

# References

**Applbaum, R., and Anatol, K.** *Strategies for Persuasive Communication.* Columbus, Ohio: Charles E. Merrill, 1974.

**Barrett, H.** *Practical Uses of Speech Communication.* New York: Holt, Rinehart & Winston, 1977.

**Cronkhite, G.** *Persuasion: Speech and Behavioral Change.* New York: Bobbs-Merrill, 1969.

**McCroskey, J.** "A Summary of Experimental Research on the Effects of Evidence in Persuasive Communication." *Quarterly Journal of Speech* 55(1969):169–176.

# 14

# PRESENTING
# THE SPEECH

**Decisions about Delivery**
Extemporaneous Style
Directness
Language Style
Dealing with the Podium

■

**Visual Aids**
Dual Coding
Types of Visual Aids

■

**Maintaining Audience Attention**
Movement
Uniqueness
Familiarity
Humor
Audience Involvement

■

**Practicing**

■

**Special Occasions**
Speech of Introduction or Welcome
Speech of Acceptance
Speech of Tribute

■

**Summary Propositions**

■

**References**

■

Now that you have constructed your speech, you need to think about delivering it. Depending on the circumstances, each speech calls for adaptations in delivery. Some occasions demand a more formal style of presenting the speech, while other occasions permit more freedom and informality. Thus, you should make some decisions about delivery before you give your speech.

But before you deal with such decisions, consider how you feel about public speaking. If you are like many people, preparing the speech is not as frightening as giving it. But don't be too concerned—even the professionals in the performing arts are tense before they speak. It's a natural feeling. For your own sake, complete the test in the next box. It will help you assess your own feelings about public speaking. After you have done this, continue reading. Perhaps you can learn things that will make presenting a public speech as enjoyable for you as preparing it.

## Decisions about Delivery

Teachers of public speaking generally agree that speech content is more important than speech delivery. Thus, a poorly researched and disorganized speech delivered in a flashy style is still a poor public speech. But delivery is important to your effectiveness as a speaker and is a necessary part of your preparation.

The style of delivery most often used is extemporaneous speaking. This section will investigate the different characteristics of the extemporaneous style and offer tips on directness, language style, and how to handle yourself around the podium. If you follow the suggestions in this section, you will have taken the first steps in developing an effective style of delivery.

Indicate the degree to which the statements apply to you by circling whether you strongly agree (SA), agree (A), are undecided (U), disagree (D), or strongly disagree (SD) with each statement. Work quickly; just record your first impression.

YOUR TURN...

1. I look forward to an opportunity to speak in public. SA A U D SD

2. My hands tremble when I try to handle objects on the platform. SA A U D SD

3. I dislike to use my body and voice expressively. SA A U D SD

4. My thoughts become confused and jumbled when I speak before an audience. SA A U D SD

5. I have no fear of facing an audience. SA A U D SD

6. Although I am nervous just before getting up, I soon forget my fears and enjoy the experience. SA A U D SD

7. I face the prospect of making a speech with complete confidence. SA A U D SD

8. Although I talk fluently with friends, I am at a loss for words on the platform. SA A U D SD

9. I feel relaxed and comfortable while speaking. SA A U D SD

10. I always avoid speaking in public if possible. SA A U D SD

11. I enjoy preparing a talk. SA A U D SD

12. My posture feels strained and unnatural. SA A U D SD

13. I am fearful and tense all the while I am speaking before a group of people. SA A U D SD

14. I find the prospect of speaking mildly pleasant. SA A U D SD

15. I look forward to expressing my opinion at meetings. SA A U D SD

16. While participating in a conversation with a new acquaintance, I feel very nervous. SA A U D SD

17. Conversing with people who hold positions of authority causes me to be fearful and tense. SA A U D SD

18. I would enjoy presenting a speech on a local television show. SA A U D SD

19. I feel that I am more fluent when talking to people than most other people are. SA A U D SD

20. I am tense and nervous while participating in group discussions. SA A U D SD

Test developed by James C. McCroskey, West Virginia University, and used with his permission.

Notice how the speaker's personality shows through her nonverbal expressions. (Photo courtesy of B. Goss.)

## EXTEMPORANEOUS STYLE

In most public speaking situations, you need an extemporaneous style of delivery. This kind of speaking lies somewhere between memorized speaking (as in a drama) and impromptu speaking (as in everyday conversation). By definition, extemporaneous speaking means planning your main points and supporting materials in advance but choosing your words at the time you are speaking. In essence, extemporaneous speaking combines the careful planning and outlining of materials with the spontaneity of everyday speech.

Two characteristics of extemporaneous speaking are important. Most notable is the outline you use as you talk. In order to speak extemporaneously, you need a speaking outline to remind you of your next point. This outline is not a full-sentence outline—that is, a manuscript simply turned into an outline. Instead, the speaking outline should be a key-word outline. It should be prepared so that when you look down at it, it reminds you of the next topic or idea, not the next words to be spoken. Too often, inexperienced speakers make their speaking outlines too detailed. That is, they write out what they want to say and then essentially read it. This practice turns an extemporaneous speech into a manuscript speech. And most people find the average manuscript speech quite boring.

Many instructors ask you to submit a speech outline on the day you speak—often a full-sentence outline. The full-sentence outline that you turn in to your instructor, however, should *not* be the same outline you use at the podium.

The outline that you use at the podium is for you, the speaker. It serves as your "cue cards" and may not be appropriate to submit as your speech outline.

In most cases, then, you should expect to prepare two outlines: the formal outline to submit to your instructor, and the speaking outline to have with you as you address the audience. Check with your instructor for specific directions for preparing these outlines.

The second important characteristic of extemporaneous speaking is its flexibility. When you speak extemporaneously, you know where you are headed, but you can make changes along the way. You can talk a little longer on a point that the audience appears confused about. You can eliminate a topic that you don't have time for. You can embellish an idea that the audience seems to be enjoying. You can inject a joke or a story that comes to mind as you are giving your speech. All of these are examples of how extemporaneous speaking can be flexible.

In order to take advantage of the flexibility in extemporaneous speaking, you must be able to read the feedback from the audience and adjust your speech accordingly. If you cannot see your audience because you look at your notes too often, you cannot assess your performance. Thus, it is a good idea to practice your speech so that you can look at your audience more than you look at your notes. Use your notes only as a reminder of what to say next, not as the complete text of your speech.

## DIRECTNESS

Have you ever listened to a speaker who wouldn't look at the audience? Such a person might as well be addressing an empty room, because the presence of the audience doesn't seem to matter. Speakers are indirect when they are not responsive to the presence of the audience. Such indirect speakers are mechanically detached from the audience. Their speech patterns may be dry and uninteresting. They show little animation in their faces, and they rarely, if ever, look at anyone.

Obviously, an indirect style of speaking is undesirable. But what can you do to be more direct? First of all, aim for a conversational style of speaking that is warm, pleasing to listen to, and that communicates *with* the audience rather than *at* the audience. If you opt for a grander style of speaking, using esoteric language and flamboyant gestures, your aloofness may alienate the audience. Said more directly, if you try to impress your audience with your speaking style, you may turn them off. Conversational speakers use a normal rate of speech and everyday language.

Second, you can be more direct if you look at your audience members individually. During your speech, talk to each member of the audience at least once. Seek eye contact with each member of the audience. By doing so, you will involve them in your presentation. The more directly you speak with your audience, the more they will pay attention to you, and the more effective you will be with them.

Third, to be a direct speaker, be a personal speaker. Talk about *you* and *me* rather than *they* and *them*. Speak of experiences that audiences can relate to easily. Look for and use everyday illustrations to drive home your points. Talk not about distant, abstract ideas but about immediately relevant, concrete ideas. The more you talk about life as your audience is experiencing it, the more direct you will be as a speaker.

Let's assume that you have been asked to give a speech to a group.

A good way to become familiar with the group on the day or the night of your speech is to arrive early enough to mingle informally with some of the audience members. In talking with them, you may learn of some recent event that you can refer to during your speech.

By referring to something that happened to the audience recently, you gain their respect as one who has done his or her homework.

## LANGUAGE STYLE

As mentioned earlier, your language style can affect others' impressions of you. In public speaking, you want your listeners to understand you and to be able to relate easily to your points. Thus, you need to develop a language style that will be appealing to the listeners' senses and imagination. You can accomplish this through specificity and vividness.

Specificity refers to choosing words that are concrete as opposed to abstract. As you talk about your topic, get down to the "nuts and bolts." Avoid abstractions and talk about actual events, actions, and behaviors. For example, in a speech on workers' rights, you can talk about your company's policy of requiring substantial donations to particular charities as "institutional pressures," or you can call it "forced giving." The first expression is so vague and abstract it says little. The second one gets down to specifics. If you go on to describe how this contribution policy is enforced, you have even more opportunity to be specific. The more specific your words, the more easily the audience can see what you are talking about.

You can also appeal to the senses and imaginations of your listeners through vivid language—words that paint verbal pictures in the minds of the receivers. For example, instead of talking about a "beautifully landscaped garden," describe it in terms of the "full, green, hanging ferns, the shaded white gazebo under the old oak tree, and the array of gold, yellow, red, and orange flowers that border the back fence." Such descriptions help the listeners see the scene in their minds. They can use their imaginations to understand what you are talking about.

The key to an effective language style, then, is appealing to the psychological abilities of the listeners. The more your language involves the listeners in your topic, the greater your chances for success. Thus, it is to your advantage to work on a more specific and vivid language style in your speech presentation.

Just how important is effective delivery? Thompson's (1967) review of the research on the effect of delivery in public speaking makes it very clear that how a message is presented makes a difference in listener comprehension and in the persuasiveness of the speech. As Thompson concludes, "Every study of delivery . . . arrives at the same conclusion: Good delivery does matter" (p. 83).

Listeners learn better and are persuaded more by good delivery skills, but good delivery does not ensure an effective speech. In other words, a poorly built speech, delivered in an exciting manner, is still a poor speech. Educated, critical listeners, especially, are not impressed by a well-delivered speech of little substance. Thus, good delivery is an addition to effective speaking, not a substitute for it.

W. Thompson, *Quantitative Research in Public Address and Communication* (New York: Random House, 1967).

## DEALING WITH THE PODIUM

In a number of public speaking situations you will speak from a podium. If you are not careful, the podium can hinder communication more than help it. Some podiums are large and immovable;

others are simple and quite portable. In either case, you should not feel constrained to give your speech from behind the podium. If you let the podium become a physical barrier between you and your audience, it may affect your speaking style, making it more formal than necessary.

If you want to develop a direct speaking style, you have to work around the podium. Don't drape your arms and body over it, as though it is designed to physically support you. The podium is a place to lay down your notes. It is not supposed to be a crutch. So step away from it once in a while and stand in full view of the audience. This will provide visual variety to your presentation. In fact, you can even consider giving your speech without a podium, if the situation permits. Whatever you do, don't let the furniture (podium) interfere with your direct speaking style.

# Visual Aids

A public speech is usually more than spoken words—it can have visual aspects as well. In fact, visual aids add interest to your speech and can also help you feel more confident about your presentation.

## DUAL CODING

*Dual coding* is a term used in research on human memory. It refers to the fact that you store certain learned information in more than one place in your brain—especially information about things that you have experienced through both hearing and sight. For instance, your recollections of your pet dog are probably stored in your brain by what the dog looks like and by what it sounds like. When something is stored in memory in two ways (such as by hearing and seeing an object), it is dual coded. Data that are dual coded in memory are easier to recall than data that are stored only one way in memory.

Dual coding is important to public speaking because it relates to visual aids. Whenever you use a visual aid to support your spoken word, you are giving your listeners a chance to dual-code the information and store it in memory. Such dual-coded information will be easier to recall later because the listeners have it stored both as what they heard and as what they saw. So if you want to make your speech more memorable, consider using visual aids.

## TYPES OF VISUAL AIDS

Ehninger et al. (1980) suggest 10 types of visual aids that you should consider using. They are:

1. *The object itself.* If you are talking about something that can be brought along with you, then bring it and show it to the audience as you discuss it.

2. *Yourself.* Sometimes you can demonstrate what you are talking about by doing it yourself in front of the audience.

3. *Models.* If you have access to a replica of what you are talking about, your audience would appreciate the opportunity to inspect a model of your topic.

4. *Slides.* If you have access to a projector and a screen, slides are a colorful way to bring life to your talk. Be careful not to have too many slides. Your purpose is to give a speech, not a slide show.

5. *Films.* If the film is brief enough, it can be used effectively to illustrate what you are talking about. Again, be sure that the film does not dominate your speech.

6. *Chalkboard.* In classroom speeches, you will often have access to the chalkboard. If you have an elaborate drawing, draw it on the board before it is your turn to speak. Erase it when your speech is over.

7. *Graphs.* These are very helpful but require prior planning. Hints: Draw your letters and figures large (very large) so that everyone can see them. Also, use different colors of ink for the different parts of the graph.

8. *Diagrams.* These are charts that are prepared beforehand to illustrate how something works, how various parts of a process fit together, and so forth. Diagrams are primarily devices for explanation.

9. *Organizational charts.* An organizational chart is an illustration of how a company is organized. It shows who works for whom, how work groups are organized, and so on. It can be useful to illustrate a social structure, such as a business or a fraternity.

10. *Printed information.* Commonly called handouts, these are distributed during the speech so that the listeners can see what the speaker is talking about. The only problem with handouts is persuading the listeners to set them aside after you are finished talking about them. Otherwise, they are very useful.

---

Whenever you prepare graphs and charts to use during your speech, it is a good idea to remember the following hints about graphics:

1.  Make the letters and numbers large enough to be seen from the back row.

2.  Keep it simple, using lots of white space so that your letters and art work stand out.

3.  Don't put too much information on one chart. If you have a lot of data to display, use several charts.

4.  Make sure that your printing and art work are neat. Sloppy graphs are distracting.

5.  Be sure that your visual aids are portable enough to be handled smoothly.

See Figure 14.1 for a graph that could be used as an effective visual aid.

**Profile of the 1980 Electorate**

among the estimated 160,491,000 Americans of voting age this November—

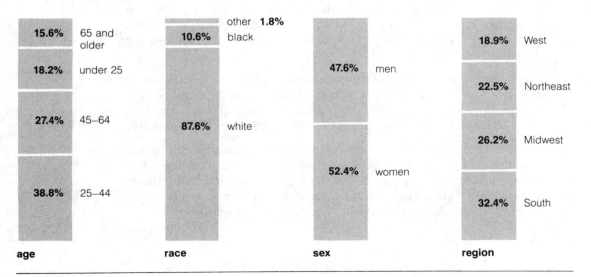

**Figure 14.1** Graphs as Visual Aids

Notice how the speaker is not blocking the listener's view of the visual aid. (Photo courtesy of B. Goss.)

Whenever you are planning a public speech, choose at least one visual aid. Too many potentially exciting speeches are dull because the speaker wasn't thoughtful enough to include visual aids. Visual aids increase the impact of your speech. They not only assist memory, they reinforce your points and add interest to your speech. You only sell yourself short when you do not consider using a visual aid or two.

Another benefit of visual aids is that they can help you remember what to say. In other words, the visual aid itself can become part of your speaking notes. By reviewing the details of a chart you prepared, you can cover a significant part of your speech. The visual aid itself reminds you of what to say. You can even pencil notes on charts and graphs to cue yourself as you handle the visual aid.

A word of caution: Whenever you use a visual aid in your presentation, be sure that it is out of sight and out of your way both before you use it and after you use it. If it remains in view of your audience when you are not talking about it, the audience may pay more attention to the visual aid than to you as the speaker. So remove the visual aid when you don't need it. It can be distracting.

# Maintaining Audience Attention

In many ways the quality of any speech depends on the ability of the speaker to keep the attention of the audience. Maintaining audience attention is one of your greatest challenges in public speaking. It is all too easy for a listener to mentally drift away from the speech and think about something else. An effective public speaker plans on doing things to keep the listeners focused on the speech.

What are some things you can do to increase audience attention? Using visual aids has already been suggested. Let's consider other ideas.

## MOVEMENT

A good speech goes somewhere. It doesn't get bogged down at one point. As an effective speaker, you also should show movement. Use gestures, step away from the podium, demonstrate the topic through sight and sound, and so on. In other words, your speech should have some animation, some action. You should vary your voice, both in volume and speed. Do whatever you can to show movement, and your audience will follow your moves.

## UNIQUENESS

Look for the unusual in your speech topic. Audiences enjoy strange features and new notions they haven't heard about before. You can also create some uniqueness in your preparation. Tell a story that has some suspense in it. Or arouse the curiosity of the listeners by asking them a sequence of questions pertaining to the topic of the speech. Whether you tell an interesting story or ask stimulating questions, you are trying to arouse your audience so that they remember your speech as unique.

## FAMILIARITY

This idea works well because you take advantage of what the audience knows. To use familiarity as an attention device, mention something that the members of the audience all know about and have clear memories of. This allows you and the listeners to share a common experience. Audiences enjoy being reminded of past events, especially when the speaker can take advantage of that memory to make a point. So hit your audience with examples and ideas that strike close to home for them. Don't use examples and illustrations that are so far removed from the audience's experiences that they cannot relate to them.

## HUMOR

Many people complain, "I can't tell a joke." If you think you can't, then don't. But everyone can tell an amusing story that helps humanize a point. Many times a story, particularly one that the audience can relate to immediately, comes out funnier than the speaker expected. So don't shy away from humor; at least, give it a try.

## AUDIENCE INVOLVEMENT

This idea is a certain winner. Take advantage of the audience members. Realize that you are talking with people and acknowledge various individuals in the audience, by name if possible. They love the recognition. Tell stories about them (tactfully, of course). Be willing to respond immediately to the feedback you see as you speak. If you stand up before an audience and act as though they don't exist, your listeners won't be very attentive. Nothing is more likely to turn off an audience than the feeling that they are not part of the event.

You may have other ideas for maintaining the attention of your audience. But those just mentioned—movement, uniqueness, familiarity, humor, audience involvement, plus visual aids—are devices that have been effective in the past. The key point to remember is that as a speaker, you are the one mainly responsible for keeping your audience's attention. The listeners have other things on their minds, and your presentation must compete with those distractions. Plan, then, to do things that will increase the attention the audience gives to your speech.

## Practicing

Just as you carefully prepare the contents of your speech, you need to carefully prepare the delivery of your speech. This means that you need to practice your speech, and that takes time. You cannot give an effective speech without some practice. If you approach the podium without having practiced your speech at all, you could be headed for trouble.

Most people, when they think of practicing a speech, only think of rehearsing how to say it. Actually, practice involves all aspects of the speech—verbal and nonverbal. You need to rehearse the introduction, body, and conclusion, but you also need to rehearse gestures, movements, how you will handle your visual aids, and so forth. In other words, you should practice each time as though you were actually presenting the speech in front of your audience. Here are some tips on practicing.

First of all, practice aloud. Don't silently rehearse your materials. Go somewhere and practice alone; then enlist the cooperation of your roommate, spouse, or friend to listen to your presentation. When you practice your speech, stand up. Don't lie on your bed and mumble the outline to yourself. The more actively you participate in practicing your speech, the more you will remember when the time comes to give it. So take an active approach, not a passive one.

If you know where you are going to give your speech, take a moment now to visualize the setting. If necessary, close your eyes and reconstruct the scene. Then answer the following questions:

1. Where will you be sitting before you rise to speak? _____

   _____

2. Where will you place your notes during your speech? _____

   _____

3. How about your visual aids? How will they be set up and where will you place them? _____

   _____

4. How close in distance will you be to the audience? _____

   _____

5. How do you plan to move about as you talk? _____

   _____

By reflecting on such questions, you can mentally rehearse some of the physical aspects of your speech and hopefully be more prepared to deal with the setting when it is your turn to talk.

Second, practice frequently. Don't wait to give it one good shot before class. Have your speech ready to go early so that you can rehearse it several times. It's even a good idea to carry it around with you, so that you can review it periodically.

Third, practice mentally as well as physically. In other words, as you rehearse your speech, imagine yourself in front of the audience. Imagine the faces of the audience members. Envision some of your hand gestures. Plan how you will move your body in order to provide variety in your presentation. Think about your visual aids. Where will you place them when you are not speaking about them?

The more you mentally rehearse what you are going to do, the easier it will be for you to speak when it is your turn.

In summary, then, practicing takes time. You must allow enough preparation time to rehearse your speech. Practice aloud several times. You will never give the speech the same way twice, so don't try to duplicate your prior trials. Finally, practice mentally, especially how you are going to coordinate the nonverbal parts of your speech with the verbal parts. If you are well prepared and have practiced your speech enough to be thoroughly familiar with it, you will have more confidence in yourself as you face the audience.

## Special Occasions

From time to time, you may be asked to make a short speech to introduce a speaker, welcome a speaker, pay tribute to a person, or even accept an award. Each one of these special occasions calls for specific speech strategies.

### SPEECH OF INTRODUCTION OR WELCOME

If asked to introduce a speaker at a formal gathering, you should do your homework before you attempt to introduce the speaker to the audience. Your goal is to create a climate of anticipation, to stimulate the listeners so that they will be anxious to hear the speaker. This means that you must briefly explain the speaker's credentials, indicating how he or she is especially qualified to speak on the topic. Learn enough about the speaker beforehand so that you can talk mostly about the speaker and his or her past. It is a good idea to introduce the topic as well, but limit your remarks about the topic. That is the speaker's job, not yours.

In essence, then, your goal in introducing or welcoming a speaker is to create a climate of anticipation in which you establish the credibility of the speaker and quickly introduce the topic of the speech.

### SPEECH OF ACCEPTANCE

This can be one of the most awkward speeches you ever give. For many people, saying thank you is difficult. Yet knowing how to do so gracefully is a valuable skill. In the speech of acceptance your goal is to create a climate of gratitude. You want the audience to be as thankful as you are. You want them to feel that you truly deserve the award and that you are truly grateful for it. To accomplish this, point out the importance of the award to you. Explain some of the past events that permitted you to accomplish your feat. And finally, thank those who were especially close to you in your accomplishment.

Accepting an award is sometimes awkward. But remember this—you earned it. Don't deny the group the opportunity to praise you. The audience wants to enjoy your delight with the award. So make them happy and gratified as well. If your remarks are sincere, you should be able to create the climate of gratitude.

## SPEECH OF TRIBUTE

Somewhere along the way in life you may be asked to pay tribute to someone. It may be at a funeral, or it may be at a meeting designed to honor one of the others present. In any case, you have certain responsibilities as you attempt to honor someone. Your goal in a speech of tribute is to create a climate of respect. In order to accomplish this, you must do your homework and then present a brief speech that covers three points. First, you should mention some of the person's key personal strengths. Talk about his or her strong, admirable personality characteristics. Next, mention some of the person's notable accomplishments in life. Make sure that these facts are relevant to the audience and to the occasion. Finally, explain why this person is important to the audience. After covering the personal strengths and accomplishments, you should find this last part fairly easy. Just knowing someone who deserves such a speech of tribute is important to the audience. Nonetheless, try to relate the person being honored to the audience listening to you. If you cover these three points, the audience should feel even greater respect for the person being honored than they did before you spoke. And that's exactly what you want.

## Summary Propositions

The purpose of this chapter has been to encourage you to develop a direct, extemporaneous speaking style that relates well to your audience. A well-planned speech requires some important decisions about delivery, visual aids, and techniques for maintaining audience attention. If you plan, build, and practice your speech in the manner suggested, you will increase your chances for an effective presentation.

1. An extemporaneous style of delivery is planning your main points and supporting evidence in advance, but choosing your words at the time you are speaking.

2. A speaking outline serves as a "cue card"; it should be a keyword outline, not a full-sentence outline.

3. A direct speaker looks directly at the audience and personally converses *with* them, rather than *at* them.

4. Your style of language should be specific and vivid.

5. Don't let the podium restrict your movements as you speak.

6. Visual aids help the audience remember your speech, allowing them to dual-code your verbal and nonverbal messages.

7. There are at least 10 types of visual aids that you can use.

8. You can maintain the attention of your audience through movement, uniqueness, familiarity, humor, and audience involvement.

9. It is important to prepare your speech early enough to practice it before you deliver it.

10. Special occasions call for specific speech strategies.

## References

**Ehninger, D.; Gronbeck, B.; and Monroe, A.** *Principles of Speech Communication.* Glenview, Ill.: Scott, Foresman, 1980.

**Thompson, W.** *Quantitative Research in Public Address and Communication.* New York: Random House, 1967.

# 15

# SPEAKING
# TO INFORM

**Learning: The Main Goal**
Knowing and Applying
Association and Reinforcement

■

**Message Strategies**
Clarity
Interest

■

**Enhancing Recall**
Primacy/Recency
Information Load
Memory Cues
Active Participation

■

**Sample Outline**

■

**Summary Propositions**

■

**References**

■

In your personal and professional lives, you will encounter speeches of various types (sales pitches, eulogies, after-dinner speeches, briefings, tour guide presentations, and so forth). Some will be serious, others more entertaining. Some informative, others persuasive. In reality, all speeches have some informative and persuasive aspects to them. But each speech has a guiding purpose that affects its intent and content. For instance, if your boss asks you to give an oral report on your office filing system, you will be giving an informative speech. In contrast, if you have been appointed to convince a school board not to close a local school, you will be giving a persuasive speech. The main difference between these two speeches is their respective purposes (informing versus persuading).

This chapter focuses on the informative speech. You will discover how learning is the main objective of the informative speech, and how listeners can vary in their learning needs. From that point, you will read about the learning process in general, and then turn to the specific strategies you should use when constructing a speech to inform.

## Learning: The Main Goal

A speech to inform is designed to do just that—inform. The process of informing has been described as illustrating, defining, explaining, demonstrating, and so on. All of these synonyms, however, refer to the same process: the act of giving information. When you are speaking to inform, you are imparting knowledge to your audience. Your audience is informed when they understand your speech and have learned from it. Learning, then, is the key objective.

### KNOWING AND APPLYING

The goals for an informative speaker are the same as the goals of a teacher. The teacher desires that the students learn the subject. Likewise, the informative speaker desires that the audience learn the

A clerk talking to a customer about a product may be giving a speech to inform. (Photo ©
Kent Reno/Jeroboam, Inc.)

material in the speech. Learning can take place on many levels. Two
are highlighted here.

Learning occurs when the respondents know the information
(level one) and/or can apply the information (level two). *Knowing*
assumes that the listeners are able to recite the information presented and, if needed, can explain it to someone else. Knowing, then,
implies recall and explanation. *Applying* goes deeper than knowing.
It assumes that the listeners can actually use their new knowledge in
a skillful manner. For example, a baseball coach may know baseball
backward and forward, but he or she may be unable to hit the ball
well or even throw the ball accurately. In this case, the coach knows
well but does not apply well. Yet as long as the coach explains the
skills effectively, it matters little how well he or she performs those
skills. The best baseball teacher is not always the best player.

As an informative speaker, you must decide which level of
learning you desire in the audience. Your choice of level should be
determined by the audience's needs. For example, a clerk in a
hardware store should know the customer's need when showing the
customer an electric drill. If the drill is a gift for someone else, then a
demonstration of how to use the drill (application) may be inappropriate. Or if the customer is a carpenter, then such a demonstration
could be insulting. The point is this: The informative speaker must
fit the goals of the speech to the needs of the learners. If your goals

are inappropriate, your speech can fail. So know your audience as well as your goals.

It has been said that there is nothing more useful than good knowledge, and if people understand something well, they will be able to apply this knowledge on their own. While this statement is probably true, speakers often overlook the application aspects of their chosen topics.

Just about any informative speech topic has potential for applications, although some topics have more obvious applications than others. As you plan your speech to inform, you may want to think in terms of both knowing and applying.

To see how applications can be derived from various topics, write down both a knowledge goal and an application goal for each of the topics listed here.

1. How the placement office works:

    Knowledge goal _____

    _____

    _____

    Application goal _____

    _____

    _____

2. Learning Morse code:

    Knowledge goal _____

    _____

    _____

    Application goal _____

    _____

    _____

3. What keeps marriages happy:

    Knowledge goal _____

    _____

    _____

    Application goal _____

    _____

    _____

## ASSOCIATION AND REINFORCEMENT

As you are probably aware, informing is more than just telling. Learning must take place. Learning occurs when your listeners acquire a new idea, attitude, or form of behavior after listening to your speech. More specifically, learning involves some psychological or behavioral change on the part of your audience. In other words, if your audience does not change in some way, you have failed to be an effective informative speaker.

The change does not have to be radical. In fact, change can occur when the listeners simply learn something new, that is, add to their mental storehouses of knowledge. But change can also occur when something is seen from a new perspective. For instance, you might look at the military differently after serving in the Army. Or you might feel differently about the tedium of college after you have been out of college for a couple of years. In essence, people change when they learn, and some changes are more drastic than others.

How do people learn so that it causes them to change? There are at least two methods of such learning: through association and through reinforcement. When your listeners learn through *association,* they relate your speech to ideas that they have already stored in memory. In other words, they associate your ideas with their ideas. Your ideas then become easier to remember because they are successfully stored with previously learned information in memory. Thus, the more easily your listeners can associate one of your ideas with ideas they already understand, the more likely they are to remember your idea later. Learning by association, then, is a kind of "meeting of the minds" between the speaker and the listeners.

Learning through *reinforcement* takes place when the listeners realize that rewards or punishments follow from thinking or behaving in certain ways. For instance, you may have learned the value of driving slowly in icy weather because your car nearly slid off a mountain cliff one frosty day. Or you may have learned to be more punctual in attending class when you discovered that assignments and exams were always announced at the beginning of the class hour. In either case, you learned from experience.

Learning through reinforcement is facilitated when the learners realize two facts about reinforcements. First, learning is made easier when people realize that their behaviors have consequences, consequences that can be rewards or punishments. People must see the cause-and-effect relationship between their actions and the results of those actions. Children, for instance, need to understand that certain behaviors are considered desirable and thus are rewarded, while other behaviors lead to uncomfortable punishments. If people do not recognize the consequences of their behaviors, they are not likely to change those behaviors—which means that they are not learning.

The second fact of reinforcement learning is that reinforcement serves as feedback to the learner. If rewards and punishments are to facilitate learning, the learners must not only recognize them, but also use them. Positive and negative reinforcements should be instructive, telling the learner what works and what needs to be avoided. The learners must use reinforcements to adjust their behaviors. Generally, people naturally repeat those things for which they are rewarded and avoid those things found punishing. But they need to go further, to use that feedback to analyze what needs to be changed or continued in order to maximize rewards and minimize punishments. For example, if you earn praise for a paper you wrote or a project you developed, you not only should celebrate the pat on the back you received, you should also reflect on those things that made your performance noteworthy. In this way, you can use the same strategies in the future. Too often we are rewarded or punished without realizing which aspect of our performance produced the positive or negative results.

In summary, people learn new ideas, attitudes, or actions through either association or reinforcement. As an informative speaker, you must recognize that learning takes place not because you talk, but because the listeners change and acquire new information, beliefs, and so on. Teaching, then, is the responsibility of the speaker, but learning is in the laps of the listeners. To be an effective informative speaker, you should do all you can to maximize the chances that your listeners will learn.

## Message Strategies

As an informative speaker, you can take advantage of association and reinforcement during your speech. To promote learning by association, you can be sure to speak the language of your receivers. You can refer to common experiences that you share with the listeners. To capitalize on reinforcement learning, you can restate your main points so that the listeners have more than one chance to learn them. You can elaborate on the positive benefits that are available to people who adopt your ideas.

Since you cannot force your audience to learn your ideas, you must center your speech strategies on the message itself. You must prepare your informative speech with care, keeping in mind those strategies that will make your presentation clear and interesting.

### CLARITY

Essential to the success of any informative speech is its clarity. When giving a speech to inform, you must be especially careful to present the material in a clearly understandable way. If the audience does not understand your speech, you have not informed them. The responsibility for clarity must rest with the speaker.

You can achieve clarity in your speech in two ways: through organization (structure) and through word choice (language).

**ORGANIZATION** Your speech should be well organized. That is, it should have a logical pattern that is easy to follow. You cannot throw together your speech at the last minute and expect it to be perfectly organized. Organizing a speech takes time, but it is time well spent. By carefully arranging your speech, you will understand it better and so will your audience.

Organization is primarily a matter of preparation. In Chapter 13, you learned of four patterns of organization: chronological, spatial, topical, and causal. No one pattern is better than the others; your choice depends on the topic. But you need a recognizable pattern of organization if you wish to help your audience learn from you. A disorganized speech is hard to follow, and thus, difficult to learn from. If the audience members recognize your organizational pattern, they can use it to assist their recall of your information. In fact, it is a good idea to identify your organization early in the speech so that your listeners know what your main points are before you discuss each one.

Generally the more structured the information to be learned is, the easier it will be to learn. Structure can be provided through clear organization, but it can also come from message devices such as advanced organizers.

An advanced organizer is simply a statement made by the speaker that forewarns the listener about upcoming information (Ausubel, 1968). For instance, the speaker might say, "After looking at the cell structure of these bacteria, we will consider the known patterns of mutation." By saying this, the speaker helps the listener organize, in advance, the upcoming information.

Any time you provide structure for your listeners, they can use it. And if your structural devices help learning and recall, they have served their purpose.

D. Ausubel, *Educational Psychology: A Cognitive View* (New York: Holt, Rinehart & Winston, 1968).

**WORD CHOICE** One of the factors that inhibit clarity in a speech is the ineffective use of words. Speakers often use jargon or words unfamiliar to the audience. Speakers can also be too abstract, using words that refer to nothing in particular.

It is important to adjust your message strategy to fit your receiver. (Photo courtesy of Jean-Claude Lejeune/Stock, Boston, Inc.)

The main problems to avoid in choosing your words are ambiguity and vagueness. Ambiguity refers to words that can have more than one meaning (such as *bark* for tree bark or dog bark). Vagueness occurs when you choose words that are so abstract they do not refer specifically to anything. When a speaker is being vague, the listeners aren't sure they know just what the speaker is talking about. For instance, suppose I claim, "Our educational institutions are in trouble." Such a statement says very little. You cannot know with certainty what I mean by *educational institutions* or by *trouble*. By itself, the statement is vague. Sometimes, vagueness is desirable in politics and in diplomatic settings, but in a speech to inform it can actually undermine the whole speech.

If your goal is to maximize understanding between you and your audience, you cannot afford ambiguity or vagueness. In most speeches, vagueness is a greater problem than is ambiguity. Speakers often talk about ideas without making any concrete references to illustrate those ideas. What is clear to you, because you have thought about it a lot, may not be clear to your listeners. You need to avoid vague statements in your speaking.

How can you make your wording clearer? Think operationally. That is, think in terms of what something does, what it looks like, how it moves, what it sounds like, and so forth. Think in terms of images that you can translate into words that get down to the "nitty gritty" of your topic. If you are talking about educational institutions, specify which ones. If you are talking about trouble, tell the audience what trouble looks like, sounds like, feels like, and so on. As I mentioned in the last chapter, you need to speak in a language style that deals in specifics and not in vague generalities. The more operational your speech is, the more easily your listeners can identify with and understand it.

Answer the following questions:

1. What percentage of votes is needed to "win by a resounding majority"?_____

_____

2. How many drinks per day does "a heavy drinker" drink?_____

_____

3. How soon should you start studying for a final exam if you want "an early start"? _____

_____

4. When is an ice hockey player "too old to play competitively"?___

_____

The answers to such questions will vary from person to person because of the judgmental nature of the questions. Such expressions are not uncommon in speeches to inform. To the speaker, the expressions are clear. But to the listeners, the issue may not be so clear.

Just for fun, ask someone nearby how he or she would answer the questions. You'll understand then that what is obvious to you may not be so to others.

Clarity, in summary, is a function of organization and word choice. If you have carefully arranged the parts of your informative speech and if you are striving for an operational style of wording, your speech should be quite understandable. Keep in mind, though, that your success depends on how much the audience understands you, not how much you understand your topic. Your success depends on how much your listeners learn from you. So pay close attention to clarity as you plan your speech.

## INTEREST

The absolute importance of clarity cannot be overlooked, but neither can the level of interest that the speech creates. It is easily possible for a very clear informative speech to be dull and uninteresting. And the dullness of the message is as undesirable as much as it is detrimental to the learning of the listeners. Developing an interesting message, then, is an important part of informative speaking. But how do you build interest into a speech?

In Chapter 14, I mentioned six specific devices for maintaining your audience's attention: visual aids, movement, uniqueness, familiarity, humor, and audience involvement. Obviously, those ideas apply here as well. But let me add a couple of new strategies and review one already mentioned, all of which may be useful as you try to add interest to your speech.

**NEW INFORMATION** In a speech to inform, information that the listener doesn't know yet will be seen as more interesting than a rehash of prior knowledge. The informative speaker is obligated, then, to provide new information for the listeners to learn. People typically do not find the same old information very interesting. In fact, the listeners are bored when they feel that there is nothing new in a speech.

New information can be in the form of new facts, new findings, new concepts, or even new relationships between old ideas. In your research for the informative speech, keep your eyes open for new and unusual bits of information that your audience may not know about.

**RHETORICAL QUESTIONS** You can create interest in your speech by asking questions of the audience that you do not intend for them to answer aloud. A rhetorical question is designed to cause the listeners to think about your topic. You may use these questions to remind them of a need that they may have. For instance, you might ask an audience, "When was the last time you went into a store to buy something on sale, only to find that it wasn't available?" Such a question causes the listeners to retrieve from memory the last time that happened to them. The question, when answered in the listeners' minds, prepares the audience for the point to be made in the speech. A good rhetorical question can put your audience into the proper frame of mind to respond to your speech.

The rhetorical question also adds interest because it involves the audience in your speech. In other words, by asking questions of your audience (rhetorical or otherwise), you encourage them to become involved in your topic. If they do not become involved, they may not learn much.

**VISUAL AIDS** This strategy was mentioned in Chapter 14, but it is so important to adding interest to an informative speech that it must be included here. Whenever you have something for the audience to look at as well as hear about, you not only arouse curiosity about your speech, you also provide the audience with another way to remember what you talked about. To this day, I can remember a speech given by a classmate (over 15 years ago!) in which he took a bowling ball that looked realistic (but was lightweight plastic) and threw it on the floor in front of the podium. We were expecting a floor-breaking crush when the ball hit the floor, but instead it made a hollow sound, telling us that it wasn't a real bowling ball. The speaker used this visual aid and demonstration to introduce his topic of deception in consumer products. I don't remember many other speeches given in that class, but I remember that one.

If you build interest into your speech—no matter what device you choose—you can expect your audience to learn and remember more about your speech than they would about a speech without interest-building materials. But including interesting information, ideas, examples, and visual aids is often easier than finding them in the first place. This is why careful research is necessary. You cannot expect items of interest to just fall into your lap. You must be alert and look for them. And when you find them, use them. They will make your speech not only more interesting, but more memorable as well.

# Enhancing Recall

Throughout this chapter, learning has been the primary focus of attention. But learning is most useful when people are able to recall at a later date what they have learned. Thus, the informative speaker needs to be concerned about facilitating not only learning, but retention as well. If the audience members forget your speech soon after you sit down, your effectiveness has been short-term, at best.

Recent research on the memory processes has revealed that there are a number of factors that enhance recall of information. Effectively put to use, the following principles will increase the likelihood that your listeners will remember your points.

## PRIMACY/RECENCY

A number of studies show that people tend to remember the first and the last ideas presented in a speech more than they remember the middle ideas (Rosnow and Robinson, 1967). This refers to a phenom-

Information recalled later is rarely in the same condition it was when it was originally learned. This is due to information distortion, which occurs over time as people receive, store, and later retrieve information.

One of the more interesting studies of distorted recall is Allport and Postman's (1945) study of rumors. They found that as a rumor was passed among people, it was changed in three ways:

1. It was made shorter and simpler with each telling.

2. Major items were forgotten, and minor ones were overemphasized.

3. People added "reasons" of their own interpretations to the story.

Obviously, information distortion is a hindrance to learning and recall. As a speaker, you may have to remind your listeners of the information you want them to remember so that they don't forget it or distort it.

G. Allport and L. Postman, "The Basic Psychology of Rumor," *Transactions of the New York Academy of Sciences,* 2d ser. 8(1945):61–81.

enon in human memory in which people recall more easily those things that occur first in a series of events (primacy), along with those things that occur last in the series (recency), while having the most difficulty remembering the in-between things. For example, you might recall the first and the last items on your shopping list more easily than the items in the middle of the list. Thus, it is a good idea to arrange your main points so that the most important ones occur early and/or late in your speech. If the most important idea is sandwiched in the middle, it may not be remembered later.

## INFORMATION LOAD

People have limits to the amount of information they can handle at one time (Smith, 1975). So be sure that you do not include too much information in your speech. Don't give the audience more than they can digest. For most speeches, three or four points are plenty. If you have seven or eight main points, you may overload your listeners. So choose selectively those few major ideas that you need to cover, and save the rest for another speech. You will be more effective if you cover a few points well, rather than many points poorly.

## MEMORY CUES

People have enormous capacities for storing information in their brains, but retrieving the information at a later date is another matter. How many times have you taken an exam or filled out a report only to discover later that you forgot to include some important information? The same problem exists for audiences. In any given speech, presented at 150 words per minute, over a period of 5 to 10 minutes, each listener must accommodate approximately 750 to 1,500 words into memory. Of course, your listeners need not remember your every word, but you can help them remember your key points by providing cues to help them organize your speech. These cues can be signposts ("My next point deals with the causes of the problem") or mnemonic devices ("A good way to remember this is to recall the word *homes,* which will remind you of the five great lakes in the United States"). Another strategy is to identify the key words in your point ("The important word in my definition is the term *interaction*"). Whatever method you choose, your listeners will be better able to recall your speech if you offer such memory cues.

## ACTIVE PARTICIPATION

Studies in human learning demonstrate that people learn more when they become personally involved (Manis, 1966). As an informative speaker, you can encourage your audience to respond actively to your speech by asking them questions, having them raise their hands to an informal poll, or by repeating aloud something you have taught them. The more they actively react to your speech, the more they should remember about your presentation later.

If you take advantage of these principles—primacy/recency, information load, memory cues, and active participation—you can make your speech more memorable. Too often speakers fail to provide ways for their listeners to recall the information being presented. Such speakers simply assume that the listeners will absorb the information and be able to pour it out later. But people are not like sponges. They need assistance not only in learning new information but in recalling it as well. The more you can do to make your speech memorable, the more effective you will be as an informative speaker.

## Sample Outline

Now that you have studied goals and strategies for the speech to inform, let's consider a sample outline. The following outline is a content outline of a speech, not an actual speaking outline. Even so, this outline is skeletal—that is, the speaker actually says much more than is written in the outline. The outline does, however, show the order of the points, running theme, goals, and so on.

## Buying Shoes

**Goals:** I want my listeners to know what to look for when they buy their next pairs of shoes.

**Running Theme:** A smart shopper knows how to get the best pair of shoes for the money.

### Introduction

When was the last time you bought a new pair of shoes? Do you remember why you bought the ones you did? What do you look for in shoes? A smart buyer knows how to get the most for his or her money when purchasing shoes.

### Body

  I. Consider the cost.

   A. For most people, cost is a major consideration.

   1. Know what you can afford to spend.

   2. Do not exceed it.

   B. Cost and quality go together.

   1. The more you pay for your shoes, the better quality they should be.

   2. If you pay a cheap price, expect poorer quality.

 II. Consider style.

   A. Fashion shoes are nice to own, but they go out of style quickly.

   1. If you want fashion shoes, don't buy expensive ones.

   2. By the time inexpensive fashion shoes wear out, they will probably be out of style.

   B. Traditional shoes rarely go out of style.

   1. These shoes will be used for a long time.

   2. So invest in a good pair.

III. Judge the quality.

   A. Obviously, the shoes should fit and be comfortable.

    B. Consider the construction.

        1. Is the inner lining made of leather or synthetic materials?

        2. Is the heel rubber or a synthetic product?

           a. Rubber heels last longer.

           b. Rubber heels are safer.

        3. Look at the outer leather.

           a. Check for the "break" in the vamp (top of shoe).

           b. A shoe made of good leather will not leave major crease marks across the vamp.

**Conclusion**

There is so much more that could be said about buying shoes. But if you know what to look for, you can get a good bargain. Remember: You get what you pay for, but sometimes you can get more. It depends on whether or not you are willing to spend enough to buy good shoes, willing to stay with traditional styles, and able to judge the quality of the shoe in terms of its lining, heel, and outer leather. The more you know about shoes, the better off you'll be when you go into the store.

## Summary Propositions

As mentioned early in this chapter, informing is more than just telling. A successful informative speaker knows that in order for the listeners to learn they need to be paying attention. The speech must be clear and interesting so that the audience will listen. So as you prepare your speech, think about some of the suggestions in this chapter. Don't be satisfied with finally getting your speech down in outline form. Be willing to adjust your speech to enhance learning.

1. Learning, the main goal of the informative speech, occurs when the listeners undergo a psychological or behavioral change.

2. Learning takes place on two levels: knowing and applying.

3. People learn through association and through reinforcement.

    a. Ideas that can be quickly associated with past experiences will be learned more readily.

    b. Reinforcement follows behavior and serves as feedback for the learner.

4. The informative message should be prepared to be clear and interesting.

   a. Clarity is a function of organization and wording.

   b. Interest can be created by new information, rhetorical questions, and visual aids.

5. In order to make the material more memorable, the speaker should take advantage of the factors that enhance recall:

   a. Primacy/recency

   b. Information load

   c. Memory cues

   d. Active participation

# References

**Allport, G., and Postman, L.** "The Basic Psychology of Rumor." *Transactions of the New York Academy of Sciences*, 2d ser. 8(1945):61–81.

**Ausubel, D.** *Educational Psychology: A Cognitive View.* New York: Holt, Rinehart & Winston, 1968.

**Manis, M.** *Cognitive Processes.* Belmont, Calif.: Brooks/Cole, 1966.

**Rosnow, R., and Robinson, E.** *Experiments in Persuasion.* New York: Academic Press, 1967.

**Smith, F.** *Comprehension and Learning.* New York: Holt, Rinehart & Winston, 1975.

# 16

# SPEAKING
# TO PERSUADE

**Attitude Change: The Main Goal**

■

**Reasoning**
Reasoning by Example
Reasoning by Sign
Reasoning by Cause
Reasoning by Analogy

■

**Arguments**

■

**Promoting Attitude Change**
Centrality
Reward
Threshold
Readiness
Consistency
Credibility

■

**Sample Outline**

■

**Summary Propositions**

■

**References**

■

Everyday life in democratic societies is filled with instances of persuasion. Democracies are built on people's persuasive skills. In fact, it is difficult to envision a democratic society that does not use persuasion to establish common values (norms, laws, and so forth), to settle conflicts without resorting to violence, or to institute change in an evolving society. Without question, persuasion is a major tool of communication that helps shape our personal and professional lives.

Even though persuasion is prevalent in our world, people are not equally skilled in using persuasion, either in public speaking or in other pursuits (selling, teaching, writing, advertising, music, and so on). Thus, most people need to work on their persuasive skills if they want to become effective members of society. To help you develop your persuasive skills, this chapter covers different aspects of persuasive speaking, offering several suggestions on how to create a persuasive speech. After establishing the main goal of persuasive speaking, the chapter reviews various reasoning patterns and some useful principles of persuasion that should help you plan your speech.

For many people, the speech to persuade is the most difficult to prepare. Much of the apprehension about persuasive speeches is due to the false notion that it is possible to create a perfectly persuasive speech, one that no one can resist! This is simply not possible. Even the best-laid persuasive strategies meet with some resistance.

Why is it impossible to create a speech that will persuade everyone? The reason lies in the nature of attitudes. Persuasive speeches are designed to change attitudes. The speaker uses logic and evidence to convince the audience of the merits of the proposal. But since attitudes have their foundations in emotions (as opposed to logic alone), some people will not agree no matter how well the speaker argues.

Your goal as a persuasive speaker, then, is to persuade most of the people in your audience. You will have presented an effective persuasive speech when you have convinced most of the listeners that your position is worthy of belief. So, try to put together the best message you can, realizing that you cannot create the perfectly persuasive speech.

Wayne Minnick (1968), an expert on persuasion, offers four conditions that should be met if society is going to effectively use persuasion for decision making. According to Minnick, a decision arrived at through persuasion is wise and expedient when:

1. All parties to a controversy are permitted free expression.

2. All views are presented by advocates of approximately equal skill.

3. All parties to a controversy are willing to admit and take into account whatever sound arguments exist in support of contrary views.

4. All parties to a controversy are willing to abide by majority decision.

As you think about these, which one seems the most important? Which seems the least important? And, finally, which one is most often violated in everyday life? Mark your answers next to the chosen items.

As a final exercise, consider items 2, 3, and 4 as they might operate in nondemocratic societies. How would each one fare in a country that does not permit free speech?

W. Minnick, *The Art of Persuasion*, 2nd ed. (Boston: Houghton Mifflin, 1968).

## Attitude Change: The Main Goal

In the informative speech the goal is learning, but in the persuasive speech the goal is attitude change. Through effective reasoning, you try to convince your listeners of the validity of your position. Simply informing them of the facts and figures surrounding your topic will not suffice. You need to activate the audience as well.

The purpose of the persuasive speech, then, is to change attitudes through effective reasoning. Theoretically, the sounder your reasoning, the more likely you are to be persuasive. But the theory doesn't always work in practice. The reason for this is that attitudes, the target of persuasion, are built on emotions and thus have unreasonable aspects to them. For the most part, you can depend on people holding attitudes that are consistent with one another. But you must remember that attitudes are organized by "psychologic" rather than by pure logic. Whereas logic is supposed to be objective and free of emotions, "psychologic" is not so objective. In fact, it is often quite subjective. Thus, as a persuasive speaker, you can use a number of reasoning strategies, but you should never lose sight of the emotional aspects of attitudes.

Caution: Public speaking may alter your attitudes. In a recent study of speaker attitudes after persuasive speeches, Jensen and Carter (1981) found that the speakers not only persuaded their audiences, they persuaded themselves as well. The act of public speaking, then, has some significant self-persuasion aspects to it. If you publicly advocate a position on a topic, you will become a more fervent champion of that position than you were before you gave the speech.

The implication of this finding is that you should choose speech topics that you are willing to be persuaded on yourself. If you choose a theme that you don't believe in, you might find that your beliefs will be changed by your own speech.

K. Jensen and D. Carter, "Self-Persuasion: The Effects of Public Speaking on Speakers," *Southern Speech Communication Journal* 46(1981):163–174.

## Reasoning

Reasoning refers to the way you come to conclusions. When you reason, you arrange your information and evidence to reach a conclusion that follows from the materials you have gathered. Any speech of persuasion should be an exercise in reasoning, wherein the speaker presents arguments and evidence to secure the audience's belief in the conclusions.

Reasoning comes in many forms or patterns. The most common patterns of reasoning are called:

1. Reasoning by example
2. Reasoning by sign
3. Reasoning by cause
4. Reasoning by analogy

### REASONING BY EXAMPLE

When you reason by *example,* you infer conclusions based on specific instances. Each of your instances is seen as an example of your point. Consider this:

> Students are receiving higher grades today than they received ten years ago. In our fraternity house, our grades have risen every year for the last five years. Other houses report the same trend.

This is a case of reasoning by example. The speaker makes an assertion that grades are higher and then proceeds to use his fraternity as an example. He also mentions other houses as additional evidence.

## REASONING BY SIGN

Reasoning by *sign* occurs when you infer that two or more phenomena are related to each other. You reason by sign when you see one phenomenon as a sign that another phenomenon exists. Clouds can be signs for rain. When you drive by your aunt's house and see her car parked in her driveway and then infer that your aunt is home, you are using sign reasoning. Here's a case of reasoning by sign:

> Morale must be down at work. People aren't talking to each
> other as they used to. It seems that absenteeism has increased as
> well.

The speaker's conclusion is that morale is down at work. The reasoning is derived from the signs the speaker has noticed (lack of communication and absenteeism).

## REASONING BY CAUSE

Reasoning by *cause* can be defined as concluding that one phenomenon produced another phenomenon. You have two ways to reason by cause: either from cause to effect or from effect to cause. For instance, you might reason that buying a new car (cause) will put a strain on your family budget (effect), or that the gas mileage on your car is down (effect) because the spark plugs in the engine are dirty (cause).

The difference between causal reasoning and sign reasoning lies in the underlying relationship between the two phenomena. In sign reasoning, the phenomena are simply associated together; one doesn't cause the other. In causal reasoning, one phenomenon causes the other. For instance, modern scientists believe that colds are caused by viruses—this is causal reasoning. Getting stuck out in the cold weather may make you shiver and wish to be inside, but feeling cold and catching a cold are not causally related. At best, they are correlated. Simply because two things occur together, you should not reason that one causes the other.

The important point of causal thinking is to be able to identify it when you encounter it. Here is an example of causal reasoning:

> Did I foul up: I flunked the exam because I didn't study enough.

The speaker concludes that she failed the exam because she didn't study enough. Whether or not that is the only cause is irrelevant. The speaker believes that it is true. It is, therefore, causal reasoning.

## REASONING BY ANALOGY

When you reason by *analogy*, you suggest that the features of one phenomenon are the same as the features of another phenomenon.

Reasoning by analogy is a comparison process. You infer that there are similarities in the two things you are comparing, and that your listeners should react to both things in similar ways. Here is a case of reasoning by analogy:

> If this class is as interesting as my 8:30 class, I'll be asleep in 10 minutes. Wake me when it's over.

The speaker reasons that the current situation is going to be similar to a past one. He argues that both classes are boring enough to put him to sleep. The 8:30 class is used as an analogy.

These four kinds of reasoning—by example, sign, cause, and analogy—represent the most common forms. Each leads to conclusions, derived from evidence. Each of the four is useful in persuasive speech preparation. So take advantage of as many different forms as you can in preparing your speech. By the way, a convenient way to remember these four kinds of reasoning is to think of the word *case* (*c*ause, *a*nalogy, *s*ign, *e*xample). If you reason well, you will develop a good case.

*The three reasons speech:* A good way to begin thinking about the structure of a speech to persuade is to evaluate why you believe in the proposition you wish to advocate. For instance, if you want people to go down to the Red Cross Center and donate a pint of blood, why? What are your reasons? What good will it do?

In the space below, list three reasons why giving blood is worthwhile:

1. _____

2. _____

3. _____

Now you have the beginning of a persuasive speech. Next you would need to find supporting materials and begin building each argument.

## Arguments

In persuasive speaking you not only have reasoning, you have arguments as well. The difference between the two is primarily structural. Arguments are the larger structures of a speech. Each argument is typically a main point with supporting subpoints and

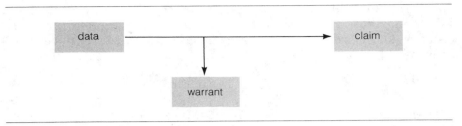

**Figure 16.1** The Toulmin Model

evidence. Thus, a persuasive speech may contain several arguments that make up the body of the speech. An argument can contain one or a number of patterns of reasoning within it. Some arguments may be based primarily on one pattern of reasoning, such as example reasoning. Other arguments may have two or more patterns of reasoning nested in the main point and the subpoints.

The actual structure of an argument can take one of many forms. One of the most common structures for an argument, however, has been illustrated by Steven Toulmin (1958). Toulmin suggests that arguments have three main parts: data, claim, and warrant. Data are evidence such as examples, illustrations, statistics, and so forth. They are proof for the claim, which is the conclusion or the proposition that the speaker wants the listeners to adopt. The warrant is a back-up assertion that justifies the connection between the data and claim. It explains why you should believe in the claim. It is a linking proposition that underlies the main line of the argument. Figure 16.1 illustrates the basic parts of the Toulmin model of arguments.

Sometimes the three-part structure is modified by adding a reservation, which essentially removes some of the definitiveness of the final claim. Figure 16.2 shows a complete argument according to the Toulmin model. In this situation the speaker is trying to convince the audience to retain the 55 mph speed limit (the claim). The speaker supports that claim with data ("Statistics show . . .") and by referring to the warrant ("Slower highway . . .") that explains the connection between the statistics and the conclusion.

Let's try another example. Look at Figure 16.3. In this example, the person is trying to guess who sent in the large donation. The speaker reasons that Frieda did it (the claim), based on Frieda's commitment to the cause (the warrant). But notice also that a reservation is stated, just in case Frieda did not make the donation.

The examples provided in Figures 16.2 and 16.3 are illustrations of Toulmin's basic parts of an argument. They are not fully developed arguments as you would expect to find in a persuasive speech. Because they are not completely developed (they lack

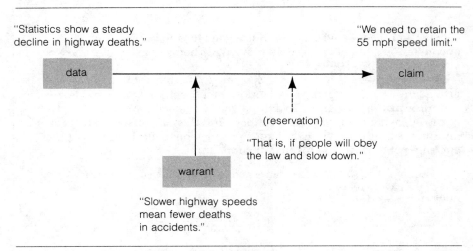

**Figure 16.2** Complete Argument Using the Toulmin Model

enough evidence and explanation), they would not be very persuasive. In your persuasive speeches, you can use Toulmin's pattern of argument, but each part (data, warrant, reservation, and claim) would need to be expanded to make a complete case. How you would do that, of course, depends on your topic, your preparation, and the time limits. Just remember: You cannot build a persuasive speech using the reasoning patterns mentioned earlier and/or Toulmin's model of argument without fully developing the body of the speech. The guidelines for doing that are found in Chapter 13.

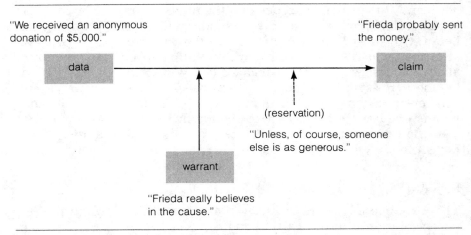

**Figure 16.3** Another Argument Using the Toulmin Model

Inoculation theory suggests that it is a good idea to present your opponents' arguments as well as your own when you give a persuasive speech (McGuire, 1969).

This strategy is best used when you know that your opponent will give a later speech. When you mention the opposition's point of view, you forewarn the listeners. By telling your audience a weakened version of the opposing point of view, you inoculate them against the stronger arguments that they will hear later from the opponent. Mentioning the opposite point of view helps to defuse the impact of that point of view.

W. McGuire, "The Nature of Attitudes and Attitude Change," in *The Handbook of Social Psychology,* vol. 3, ed. G. Lindzey and E. Aronson (Reading, Mass.: Addison-Wesley, 1969).

## Promoting Attitude Change

An effective speech to persuade depends on good organization, thorough research, and valid reasoning. It also depends on specific decisions about strategies. An effective persuasive speaker takes advantage of established principles of persuasion in planning the strategies for his or her speech. The following principles are derived from research on the persuasion process, and they should help you make strategical decisions for your speech.

### CENTRALITY

The centrality principle argues that the more central the belief is to a listener, the more difficulty the persuader will have in changing that belief. Our most important beliefs are the ones we cling to with the strongest grip. Whereas you may be willing to change your mind about the best way to cook pancakes (a low-priority belief), you will be more resistant to changes in your beliefs about your parents (higher-priority beliefs). The more ego-involved people are with their beliefs, the less likely they are to change them. If you are advocating a position that runs counter to the central beliefs of the audience, you have a tough job ahead of you.

### REWARD

The principle of reward suggests that the more rewarding the proposed solution appears to the audience, the more likely they are to be persuaded. For instance, if you offer a child a candy bar for cleaning

When facing a large audience such as this one, it is important to take advantage of the principles of persuasion that promote attitude change. (Photo courtesy of Jeff Albertson/Stock, Boston, Inc.)

up her room, she is more likely to comply with your request than if you offer a less attractive reward. The key to using the reward principle in planning your persuasion is to know, with certainty, just what your audience considers rewarding. What may be rewarding to you may not seem very favorable to your audience. Rewards serve well as motivators, but only when the person being rewarded truly desires the reward.

## THRESHOLD

The threshold principle says that the more difficult the solicited response, the more personal commitment is required from the audience. Thus, it may be easy to convince listeners that we need to support the poor overseas orphans. But it is harder to persuade these same people to volunteer for service overseas to help the poor. Since the response threshold is much higher for volunteer service, only the most committed listeners will step forward. As you plan your persuasive message, consider what you are asking your listeners to do. If they lack enough personal commitment, they may not respond as you want them to. In that case, you may have to change your plans.

## READINESS

This fourth principle is related to the threshold principle. The readiness principle states that if the listeners do not feel any need to respond, they won't. As a persuader, then, you must create a need in the listeners, or take advantage of the listeners' immediate needs. TV commercials often fail because of this principle. Too often the person watching television feels no particular need for the product being advertised. Consequently, the TV viewer heads for the refrigerator during the commercials. Thus, if you can't take advantage of an immediate need of the audience, you had better be good at creating one during your speech. If you fail to create a need, you may end up with polite listeners who choose to do nothing.

## CONSISTENCY

The consistency principle argues that the more consistent an idea is with the listener's beliefs, the more likely the listener is to adopt the idea. Thus, your speech should fit your audience's beliefs. If you advocate something that is too far astray from the listeners' beliefs, your speech will be unheeded. You must consider how closely your position aligns with your listeners' beliefs. The closer to home you hit, in terms of your listeners' beliefs, the more readily they will adopt your recommendations.

## CREDIBILITY

This last principle centers on you as a speaker. More accurately, it centers on your listeners' opinions of you. The principle of credibility suggests that the more credibility you appear to have, the more influential you will be to your listeners. Credibility can be equated with believability. In order to be seen as believable, you must appear to be competent and trustworthy. If your image is such that people don't think you are intelligent and good at your job, or if the people cannot trust you, you cannot have much influence on them. Consequently, you must do all you can to appear both competent and trustworthy.

## Sample Outline

Now that we have considered reasoning, arguments, and the principles of persuasion, let's see how a persuasive speech might be constructed to be as motivating as possible. The following sample content outline should give you some idea of how to put together the persuasive speech.

A Guaranteed Annual Wage

**Goals:** I want my listeners to be persuaded enough to sign the petition.

**Running Theme:** We need to adopt a national guaranteed annual wage.

### Introduction

Last month my neighbor, a father of three children, was laid off from work. For nearly a month, he had no source of income to provide for his family. Fortunately, he was called back to work before he entered financial ruin. He was lucky.

Think what it would have been like if Bill didn't go back to work in time. What would have happened to his family? How would he feed his kids, pay the electric bills, or meet his mortgage? Unless we find a way to assist unemployed families beyond what we are doing now, many American families will be destroyed.

### Body

I. We need to ensure a worker's financial welfare.

    A. Unemployment is up, and that means people stand a greater chance of being laid off.

        1. In the 1950s unemployment was reasonably low.

        2. Today, the unemployment rate varies from 7 to 9 percent.

        3. If the trend continues, we may experience a 10 percent unemployment rate in the next few years.

    B. Individual savings accounts deposits are down.

        1. This means that the average worker has no "nest egg" to fall back on.

        2. Inflation has caused people to pay bills rather than save money.

        3. Many households need two incomes just to pay bills.

    C. Industry suffers when people are broke.

        1. Industry profits drop because buying decreases.

        2. New product development is halted when the public is not buying.

II. A guaranteed annual wage will solve the problem.

    A. This is how it works.

        1. Every worker contributes 5 to 10 cents per work hour into a fund.

        2. During layoffs, this fund is used to keep unemployed workers solvent.

    B. It is a workable plan.

        1. Ford Motor Company has a plan that works like this.

        2. Other companies have similar plans.

        3. When these workers are laid off, they don't contribute to the problem because they have some income to live on.

III. Imagine what it would be like if 10 percent of the American population had to go on welfare or resort to crime because they didn't have a guaranteed annual wage.

    A. It is well known that many crimes are committed by destitute people.

    B. How much better it would be if these people were saved from destitution.

**Conclusion**

I don't know about you, but I don't want to see my neighbor turn to welfare or crime because he can't support his family. I don't want to see a father in jail because he has to steal to feed his family. I'm sure you feel the same. Won't you join me in signing this petition to encourage Congress to pass a guaranteed annual wage bill?

## Summary Propositions

The quality of any persuasive speech is ultimately determined by the listeners. If you have prepared carefully, taking advantage of the information in this chapter, you are on your way to success. But remember this: Your success as a persuasive speaker is a function of you, your speech, the listeners, and the occasion. If all of these parts of the communication model work together harmoniously, you will be an effective, convincing speaker.

1. The main goal of the persuasive speech is attitude change.

2. Reasoning refers to the way you come to conclusions.

3. There are four kinds of reasoning:

   a. Reasoning by example

   b. Reasoning by sign

   c. Reasoning by cause

   d. Reasoning by analogy

4. Arguments are the larger structures of the persuasive speech.

5. Toulmin's structure of arguments includes:

   a. Data

   b. Warrant

   c. Claim

   d. Reservation (optional)

6. You can increase your chances of persuading by adapting your speech according to the following principles of persuasion:

   a. Centrality

   b. Reward

   c. Threshold

   d. Readiness

   e. Consistency

   f. Credibility

## References

**Jensen, K., and Carter, D.** "Self-Persuasion: The Effects of Public Speaking on Speakers." *Southern Speech Communication Journal* 46(1981):163–174.

**McGuire, W.** "The Nature of Attitudes and Attitude Change." In *The Handbook of Social Psychology*, vol. 3, edited by G. Lindzey and E. Aronson. Reading, Mass.: Addison-Wesley, 1969.

**Minnick, W.** *The Art of Persuasion*. Boston: Houghton Mifflin, 1968.

**Toulmin, S.** *The Uses of Argument*. Cambridge, England: Cambridge University Press, 1958.

# APPENDIX

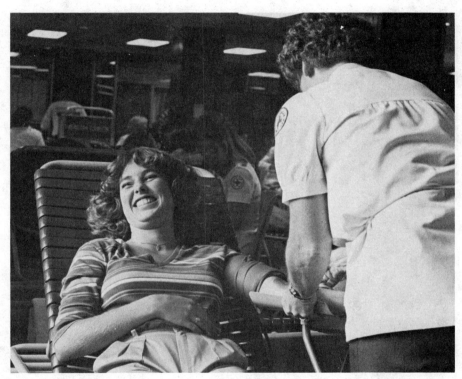

Here's the rest of the picture shown on page 50. (Photo courtesy of Tom Dunning, <u>Oklahoma Daily</u>.)

Here's the rest of the picture shown on page 85. (Photo courtesy of the Norman Transcript.)

# APPENDIX

**Misuses of Probability in Life**

■

**The Speaker and the Ghost: The Speaker Is the Speech**

■

**F**ollowing are two sample speeches for you to review. These speeches are included not to show you how a perfect speech should read, but rather as illustrations. You need not model or imitate these speeches in your planning, building, and presenting of your message. In fact, both of these speeches have shortcomings as well as strengths. So read them for your enjoyment, and consider what you like and dislike about each.

## Misuses of Probability in Life

Three hundred years ago, a gambler asked Blaise Pascal, the French philosopher, how to calculate the odds on certain dice throws. Pascal's answers were the beginning of probability theory as we know it today.

People use probability theory in everyday decision making. But some use it more correctly than others. For instance, physicists carefully calculate the path of a neutron as it passes through matter; geneticists use probability theory to determine the likely characteristics of unborn infants; and business professionals use probability theory to calculate the probable success of a decision. In contrast, lay people, untrained in the specifics of probability theory, often use probability in decision making, but inaccurately. In fact, the lay person's probability theory is really an intuitive one as opposed to a precise mathematical one. Thus, the average person often miscalculates the actual probabilities of many daily decisions.

Because I believe that a better understanding of probability theory can help you make better decisions, and because it is important to know how people misuse probabilities, my goal in this speech is to demonstrate some common misconceptions about the probabilities of everyday affairs. To do this, I will talk about catching an elevator, finding someone with the same birthday as you, and the likelihood that a family with three children will have all girls or all boys.

Have you ever wondered why, when you are waiting for an elevator, the first one to arrive is always going up when you want to go down? Intuitively, most people think that the chances of catching an up-going elevator are the same as those of catching a down-going one. Yet, the actual probabilities depend on the number of elevators operating and on the floor from which you are waiting for an elevator. Let me explain. Suppose you are on the second floor of a 10-story hotel, and you are waiting to go up. Given that most of the elevators are likely to be above you, the first one to stop is likely to be going down. Likewise, if you are on the seventh floor waiting to go down, you will most likely encounter an elevator on the way up before you catch one going down. Unless you are the only one in the building requesting an elevator at the time, you will not always find the first available elevator to be the one you want.

By the way, one implication of this phenomenon is that whenever you check into a hotel and have a choice of floors, you should ask for the lowest one you can get. In this way, you will stand a good chance of catching an elevator when you want to go down to the lobby or to a floor below you. If you end up on the uppermost floors, you may have a nice view but a longer wait for an elevator when you want to go down.

Another misuse of probabilities by lay people is in calculating the likelihood of meeting someone in a group who has the same birthday as you. Intuitively, you probably think it doesn't make sense to expect anyone else at a party to have your birth date. But do you know that it takes only 23 people gathered together to reach a 50-50 chance of two of them having the same day and month for birthdays? Mathematically, when two people meet, their chance for identical birthdays is very remote. In fact, the probability that their birthdays differ is 364/365. Add a third person to the meeting and the probability drops to 363/365, and so on. By the time you assemble 23 people together, the series drops to approximately 50-50. Most people find this hard to believe, but mathematically it is possible.

My final example of faulty thinking about probabilities comes from the ever popular argument over the possibility that a family can produce three or four offspring of the same sex. Many family arguments have been started by aunts and uncles and other relatives trying to guess whether "Susie is going to have another girl this time." Many people believe that the chances of having three children of the same sex are 50-50. Certainly, the probability of having a girl or a boy at any one delivery is 50-50, but the chance for a series of three boys or three girls across three separate deliveries is not 50-50. The correct probability is 1 in 8 if you are predicting three boys or predicting three girls. If you are predicting three children of the same sex (and not specifying either boys or girls), then the actual probability is 1 in 4. Laying out all the alternatives, as shown in my chart, the possible combinations for three-children families are: BBB, BBG, BGG, BGB, GBG, GBB, GGB, GGG. Thus, there are eight possible outcomes, and depending on your prediction, the probability must be based on these eight possibilities.

In this brief speech, I have tried to point out some common errors people make in probabilistic decision making. Obviously, an understanding of the laws of probability calls for a lot of study. And each of us should realize our obligation to know more about these processes since they affect our daily decision making. Whenever you are making an ordinary decision, stop and calculate the probabilities involved in your decision. Don't let intuition rule your decision making. Unless the decision is on a trivial matter, you should think twice before you leap to a conclusion and decide what to do. Many bad decisions can be avoided if you will simply hesitate long enough to know your probabilities before you decide.

## The Speaker and the Ghost

### THE SPEAKER IS THE SPEECH

By Carolyn Lomax-Cooke, *Communications Specialist, Cities Service Company*
*Delivered to the Tulsa Chapter of the International Association of Business Communicators, Tulsa, Oklahoma, October 20, 1981*

First of all, I must confess that I'd like to ask all of the speechwriters in the audience to get up and leave. The number one rule of speechmaking is this: Never speak to your professional peers. It scares you to death! That's why economists are in such demand as speakers. No one understands economics, so economists feel very comfortable talking to everyone. They even feel comfortable talking to each other because they all disagree.

Actually, we are all speechmakers—and we all practice our speeches in our imaginations before we actually deliver them to our husbands, wives and children. My mother was the first speechmaker that I really noticed. Did you ever notice how mothers deliver speeches to their children? I think that they all secretly long for a podium. My mother's first speech was the one about my face. (Mothers have a way of getting personal in their speeches right away.) She would say, "Look at that expression on your face. Do you want your face to freeze into that expression? Go look in the mirror—you're about to step on your lip." Then came the speech about how faces are a reflection of the person's spirit. I'm sure your mothers had speeches, too. And those speeches were delivered with such frequency and conviction that you remember them.

But how many other speeches do you remember? How many other speeches would you actually consider "good"?

Tonight I want to talk candidly about what makes a good speech, a good speaker and a good speechwriter. Please notice that I am emphasizing "good" in each instance. We have all heard unimpressive speeches. But what we want to look at tonight is that special quality that makes a speech memorable.

My message is very simple—for the good speech, the good speaker and the good speechwriter all center around one understanding of the speech occasion. And that understanding is this: the speaker IS the speech. The man IS the message. The woman IS her words. If the speaker and the speechwriter understand this fundamental of a good speech, all will go well. If the partners fail at this point, so will the speech.

But what do I mean—the speaker IS the speech? I mean that the listener cannot separate the content of the message from the character of the speaker. During a speech, the message itself and the vehicle through which it is delivered (the speaker) are so integrated that when the audience evaluates one, it automatically evaluates the other. The speaker and the speech are one and the same.

Communications professors get fancy about theory at this point. They say that speeches appeal on three levels. One level is source credibility, called "ethos." Another is the emotional appeal of the speech, called "pathos." Third is the so-called "logos" level, which relates to the rational, factual appeal of the speech. But when you subtract the Greek from this theory, you will find that professors are saying some very simple things about the human nature involved in listening to a speech. The listener asks three questions as he listens to a speechmaker. He asks: "Is this speaker reliable? Do I like him? Can I trust his facts?" And whether the speaker likes it or not, these questions will be answered through his own personality and character as he delivers the speech—not through statistics, charts, or intricate explanations of technical data.

Since the audience responds to personality and character, the good speaker will take care that the speech truly reveals his character. Personality, life, conviction, excitement or despair—these must shine through the speech as a reflection of the speaker. The audience recognizes such honesty and always responds to personal stories, anecdotes about the speaker's family, or a reference to a book that the speaker has read. Because let's face it, the audience came to hear the speaker—not to watch a human body mouth the words of a written treatise.

When Hannah introduced me, she said that I have written more than 40 speeches during the past three years. What she didn't tell you is that many of those speeches are unimpressive, simply because they fail at this point of integrating the speech and the speaker.

And I can tell you right now that if you are interested in being a speechwriter, you will face this same difficulty. Many corporate speechmakers simply do not want to reveal any hints about themselves as people. They want to strike all references to their outside activities, to their opinions, to their personal experiences. They honestly believe that the audiences want facts—not warm human beings. Also, these guys are just plain modest. They don't want to draw any attention to themselves. And, like all other speakers, they are nervous. I read in the *Wall Street Journal* that Maurice Granville, former chairman of Texaco, complained to his wife about his nervousness when speaking. Her advice for him was wonderful. She said: Look out there and just imagine all those people in their underwear, and that will make you feel better about it. Granville reports he tried it and it worked. But mostly executives just want to deliver the facts and get off the stage.

What is the result of these corporate speeches? When the speaker is *not* the speech—when the content of the speech does *not* reflect the character of the speaker—the audience responds with the same emptiness which the speaker delivered. Mistrust and lack of persuasion result.

Just look at oil industry speaking activities. The American Petroleum Institute has calculated that during 1980 more than 4,000 oil industry speakers addressed more than 18,500 different audiences. If those audiences held an average of 50 people, then oil industry spokesmen talked to almost 1 million people in 1980 alone! And oil industry people have had active speaking programs for years.

Yet what are the results of this activity? Studies show that almost 80 percent of the general American public still believes that oil industry profits are out of line. Only 13 percent of the public is "very confident" of the industry. And half of the public still thinks the oil industry should be broken up into separate producing, transportation, refining, and retail companies.

Somewhere along the line, oil industry speakers have failed to impress their audiences with their thinking—and I am willing to bet that they have failed because they did not recognize the one fundamental which I have stressed: that the man IS his message, and that his personality must shine through the content of his speech in order for him to be believable.

Conversely, every truly impressive speech that you can remember is memorable because of the melding of speech content with the speaker's character and life experiences.

For instance, no one but Aleksandr Solzhenitsyn could have delivered his stirring Harvard commencement address in 1978. No one but this great Russian author—rejected by officials of his nation, imprisoned for his writing, and finally exiled from his country—could speak so convincingly about the important things in life such as honor, courage, strength, and conviction about eternal things. Who but Solzhenitsyn could say this to Harvard graduates, "I could not recommend your society as an ideal for the transformation of ours. Through deep suffering people in our country have now achieved a spiritual development of such intensity that the Western system in its present state of spiritual exhaustion does not look attractive." Only he could say this—out of his own experience.

And who but Barbara Jordan could have delivered her powerful keynote address at the 1976 Democratic Convention? This black Congresswoman, with her forceful voice, said: "A lot of years have passed since 1832 (when the first Democratic Convention met to nominate a Presidential candidate), and during that time it would have been most unusual for any national political party to ask that a Barbara Jordan deliver a keynote address . . . but tonight here I am, and I feel that notwithstanding the past that my presence here is one additional bit of evidence that the American Dream need not forever be deferred."

From that point on, the audience was hers. She was the speech and the message was hers alone. No one else could have delivered it.

If you think that you need a fancy platform or an impressive audience to deliver a great speech, you are mistaken. Peter the fisherman stood on an ordinary street in Jerusalem not too long after the crucifixion of Jesus and delivered one of the most effective speeches of all history. He had no podium, no microphone, no notes, not even an invitation to speak. But he spoke from his heart, with the simple honest words of his own experience when he told his fellow Jews that they had killed the Messiah promised by God and foretold by the prophets. His message: "Repent and be baptized." I characterize this speech as a highly effective action-oriented presentation, because 3,000 people were baptized into the Christian faith that day as a result of his words. Now, we have more than our share of ministers on the Tulsa Main Mall—but not one of them is getting this kind of response!

You can see through these examples that when the speech is good, it is because the speaker is the speech, the woman is her words. But if the speech must reveal the speaker in a personal way in order to be effective—what is the role of the speechwriter?

I said earlier that the speaker and the speechwriter are partners. They are, but the ghost writer is the silent partner. A behind-the-scenes person. In fact, almost an invisible person.

The speechwriter is a server—one who serves the speaker in a variety of ways. Foremost, the speechwriter must keep in mind the fundamental which I have harped on for the past ten minutes—that the speech and the speaker are one. The ghost writer must reach into the man or woman to find the message. The ghost writer must make the message come alive through anecdotes, testimonies, humor from the speaker's point of view. The executive will likely resist efforts to personalize his or her comments. Your job as a speechwriter is to encourage him and persuade him that the audience asked to hear his ideas—not yours.

Then—and only then—should the writer focus on the practical aspects of speechwriting. The speechwriter's first service is to do extensive research. You must become an expert in the speaker's fields of interest. It is your job to keep up with daily developments in those areas. This involves a lot of newspaper and journal reading.

Secondly, the speechwriter serves by writing with the flair and polish that the corporate speaker generally lacks. You must learn to write for the ear, not the eye. You are not a novelist, not a journalist, not an editor of a company newspaper. You are a speechwriter—and speeches require a different cadence, a different vigor than do editorials and news articles. You can learn this skill by reading other good speeches, by writing a lot of bad speeches and getting embarrassed when they fail, and by delivering speeches yourself to see what works.

And now, I want to give you some tips about how to actually create the speech. Write this first tip indelibly upon your hearts and minds—no matter what your boss says, *call* the speaker before researching or writing one word of a speech. Even if you have to do it on the sly (and many of us have done it that way), call the speaker and ask him what he wants to say to this particular audience. Set up a meeting with him so that you can establish a rapport with him, and so that you can help him develop his ideas. I must warn you that he may not have any ideas. It happens—frequently.

Then it is your job to do as much research as time allows. Check newspapers, books, polling services, professional organizations, interview experts in the field—any source which might have material that involves the subject of the speech. Read the material as time allows. Don't spend a lot of time taking notes, because when you actually write the speech your message must be painstakingly simple.

Next, write your outline. You should be able to summarize a good speech in one or two sentences. Then develop the main idea all you want. Use illustrations, quotes, facts to amplify the idea. But do not have five main points and ten subpoints which you want to make. Your audience will never remember past point number one. And your speaker will get lost in the intricacy of his message.

This actually happened to a corporate executive recently. He was speaking to a large group—using a very impersonal, well-written speech with complicated information and lots of slides. When he was through, a woman stood up and asked him what his purpose was in talking to her group. He couldn't answer the question. He couldn't remember why he was there! He even tried to turn the question over to the moderator. He lost all credibility through that exchange.

You've summarized your main points and outlined the speech. Now is the time to put ink on paper. To exercise the creative power of words. This is the time to use all the flair and skill you have as a writer. This is the time to use those personal tidbits you have collected which reveal the speaker. Don't let yourself lapse into that special lingo called "corporate English." We laugh at our office about the guys in the Company who write that they have "jumboized" their tankers. Others are in the process of "prioritizing inputs." I implore you to say what you mean in straightforward English. Audiences shouldn't be called upon to translate speeches as they listen to them.

Many writers worry about length of the speech. Most speeches run about 20 minutes, but audiences have been mesmerized for more than an hour by speakers who really have a message for them—so worry about the message, not length when you are writing the speech.

Finally, you must face the approval process. Here a new series of difficulties begin—internal politics. Send the speech to the speaker and your bosses AT THE SAME TIME. A good speech cannot survive a long approval line. All corrections (except for factual changes) should be made directly between yourself and the speaker. Otherwise, all liveliness and honesty will evaporate from your words.

Does this process sound time-consuming? It is. A reporter once asked Truman Capote why he could not produce a book in two weeks, as another writer claimed he could. Capote retorted: "That's not writing, that's typing!"

Speechwriting takes time, too—it's not a matter of "just typing." The final product is the speechwriter's reward: a speech occasion where the speaker is the speech and the audience responds warmly to the life of the message.

Finally, a word of encouragement. If you do not think you can tolerate ghost writing speeches—become a mother or father instead. Then you can practice and deliver your own speeches to a captive audience! And if you are fortunate, you may even see some good results coming from your performances!

From *Vital Speeches,* Dec. 1, 1981, pp. 125–128. Reprinted by permission of *Vital Speeches of the Day* and Carolyn Lomax-Cooke.

# INDEX